JEFFERSON ON DISPLAY

JEFFERSONIAN AMERICA

*Jan Ellen Lewis, Peter S. Onuf, and
Andrew O'Shaughnessy, Editors*

Jefferson on Display

Attire, Etiquette, and the Art of Presentation

G. S. WILSON

UNIVERSITY OF VIRGINIA PRESS

CHARLOTTESVILLE AND LONDON

University of Virginia Press
© 2018 by G. S. Wilson
Printed in the United States of America on acid-free paper

First published 2018

ISBN 978-0-8139-4129-5 (cloth)
ISBN 978-0-8139-4130-1 (e-book)

9 8 7 6 5 4 3 2 1

Library of Congress Cataloging-in-Publication Data
is available for this title.

Cover art: Thomas Jefferson by James Sharples, c. 1797. Pastel on paper. (Bristol Museum and Art Gallery, UK/Bridgeman Images)

MONTICELLO
Preparation of this volume has been supported
by the Thomas Jefferson Foundation at Monticello.

For Jim

CONTENTS

ILLUSTRATIONS

ACKNOWLEDGMENTS

I did not start out to write a book. After joining the Thomas Jefferson Foundation, I became curious about Jefferson's appearance in his life portraits: What was he wearing, how was he being presented, and why? My previous career as a clothing historian and costume designer for the theatre made me aware of Jefferson's appearance in each portrait and raised the larger question of how his changing image related to the political scene in which he was a principal player. Resulting research and thoughts evolved into a few papers and conference presentations, but my immediate supervisor, Andrew O'Shaughnessy, Director of the International Center for Jefferson Studies (ICJS) at Monticello, first saw this interest could go further and began to refer to these scattered bits and pieces as my "book." Early in the process Peter Onuf, the Thomas Jefferson Foundation professor at the University of Virginia, took interest in my conference papers and encouraged me to expand my research. He has continued to provide advice and support. Frank Cogliano, a frequent visiting scholar at the ICJS, suggested I put this study towards a doctoral degree at the University of Edinburgh, where he directed the program in early American history. I am very fortunate to be able to claim these three historians as mentors and friends. Their support and counseling has made this scattered inquiry on the Jefferson image come together as a book.

Each contact widens the pool of scholars and colleagues who can support effective research and writing. At Edinburgh, Frank recruited Professor Stana Nenadic as my second supervisor, and she offered invaluable guidance in readings in art and material culture. Professor Simon Newman, director of the American history program at the neighboring University of Glasgow, added to the scholarly exchanges between the two universities, and I am especially grateful to Simon for reading and making valuable comments on my dissertation, which fed into this book. Personal friendships from this period at Edinburgh have remained especially important. I value deeply the support from fellow students (and now dear friends) Felicity Donohoe, Johnathan Singerton, and Sonia Baker. Sonia offered interim housing at various times and wonderful road trips during my flying trips to Scotland. Felicity, Jon, and Sonia have contributed to some of my fondest memories during my learning experience at Edinburgh.

As my manuscript pulled together, my three mentors, Drs. O'Shaughnessy, Onuf, and Cogliano, directed me towards the University of Virginia Press and provided an introduction to acquisitions editor Dick Holway. I am grateful to Dick and other members of the press who turned the final stages of creating this book into a smooth and pleasant process. Thank you to copyeditor Leslie Tingle for her careful eye and suggestions for refining my final manuscript.

At the ICJS I have been fortunate in having an excellent group of colleagues and resources that have assisted with this book in so many ways. Next door to my office building stands the Jefferson Library. Headed by foundation librarian Jack Robertson and very ably supported by librarians Endrina Tay and Anna Berkes, this library covers all aspects of Jefferson and the early American republic through print and electronic sources. In addition, the library team has remained forthcoming with their personal expertise and assistance. On the top floor of the library building are the offices of *The Papers of Thomas Jefferson: Retirement Series*. Editor Jeff Looney and managing editor Lisa Francavilla have supplied access to many of those Jeffersonian documents not yet published but needed for my research. This has been a tremendous help, enhanced by frequent exchanges of ideas with Lisa on our personal research projects. A special thank you to Chad Wollerton, Director of Digital Media, for supplying the electronic images needed from the Monticello archives for my book. Then there are my officemates in Kenwood House. These are the work colleagues with whom I share ideas daily. They deserve a big thank you for contributing to a constructive work environment and offering their incredible support: Mary Scott-Fleming, Gayle Jessup White, Whitney Pippin, Niya Bates, and Aurelia Crawford. In addition, I thank three colleagues who have moved on to other positions, but whose past encouragements and conversations are not forgotten: Christa Dierksheide, Kate Macdonald, and, of course, Tasha Stanton. I must also thank past president of the Thomas Jefferson Foundation Dan Jordan for his support and encouragement, which have continued under current president Leslie Green Bowman.

Some returning ICJS fellows have become special friends and advocates.

Sandra Reebok has aided my discussions on Jefferson and science, and I must mention Keith and Linda Thomson. Keith has added much to the field on Jefferson and science, and I have benefited not only from Keith's writing but also from the generosity of Keith and Linda's recurring invitations to stay in their beautiful home during my research trips to Philadelphia, including a month-long fellowship at the American Philosophical Society.

This project has evolved through various papers and presentations that I have given on behalf of Monticello. An early paper was a collaboration with former associate curator Elizabeth V. Chew. A thank you to Elizabeth for her scholarly contribution to my ongoing work. This early research was supported through the assistance of some outstanding ICJS interns. I am grateful to Allison Caldwell Bliss, Mical Tawney, Wayne Dell, Mary Robert Carter, and Derek Jackson for their willingness to compile data and secure images. Tasha Stanton spent her spare moments in the ICJS front office plowing through the historic newspaper database for those mentions of Jefferson. This proved an invaluable resource. A special acknowledgment to Mary Vee Connell for lending her professional expertise in research and her gathering of information on various historic figures such as Margaret Bayard Smith, William Thornton, John Adams, and others who had things to say about Thomas Jefferson. All of this work contributes to what we can offer scholars at ICJS, and my work has benefited as well.

My thanks to those who took on the task as friendly readers of my manuscript: John Ragosta, Michael Kranish, and Joan Wilson (stepdaughter and good friend). Sometimes support comes from groups, and I am appreciative to the staff and fellows at the National Portrait Gallery who allowed me to present a portion of a book chapter at one of their Lunch Bag discussions. Feedback from art historians was especially beneficial for my work on the Jefferson image. I am particularly grateful to NPG curators Ellen Miles and Brandon Fortune for their interest in my project. I not only have benefited from their personal feedback, but their published works are amply cited in my book.

A sometime fellow at the NPG, Leslie Reinhardt, is a dear friend who dates back to my days at the University of Texas, which brings me to a special thank you in memory of her father, the late Paul Reinhardt. He was my graduate supervisor and mentor in the study of clothing history and design at the university. Dr. Reinhardt was influential in starting me down the path to where I am today, and Leslie has added encouragement in more recent years. I must add another good friend and supporter in the study of clothing history, Gweneth West. She was my former college roommate and now heads the costume design program and teaches clothing history for the theatre department at the University of Virginia. Gweneth has listened patiently to reports on the progress of my book.

Long-term friends Robert and Christine McDonald deserve my special thanks for their participation in this book project. Some of my earliest research trips were to the US Military Academy at West Point, where Rob is a professor of American history. Christine and Rob provided room and board and pointed the way to the special collections in the USMA academic library. Rob introduced me to David Reel, Director of the West Point Museum, who also deserves recognition for his very generous help with access to files and paintings in the museum's collection. Rob McDonald was one of my final readers, and I cannot fail to mention that I owe Christine and Rob a special acknowledgment for coming up with the title for my book. Their brainstorming was gladly received when I was totally out of fresh ideas.

Special recognition must go to my husband, Jim, who often put his own projects on hold to accompany me to Edinburgh and on the many research trips. I will always be grateful that he chose to share this experience with me and for his patience during the writing process. A special thanks as well to our good friend Eleanor Winsor, who has been supportive in so many ways, from fetching us at the airport to cooking meals so that I could write. Stephanie Leap and Faye Shifflett made the time away possible by their responsible care of our home and dog. My mother has continued to offer encouragement, and I will always hold special gratitude to my sister Beverly Kennedy for carrying so much of the family responsibility through my process of researching and writing this book. In summation, this book has been possible through the support, advice, and good wishes of many people whom I sincerely acknowledge and hold dear.

JEFFERSON ON DISPLAY

INTRODUCTION

Thomas Jefferson "was playing a game." Or such was the opinion of the British legation secretary, Augustus John Foster. He was outraged by what seemed to be deliberate disregard of appropriate state protocol and at the slovenly dress that so frequently defined President Jefferson. Foster reasoned that as a member of the Virginia gentry, Jefferson was an American aristocrat. He had been a guest at Jefferson's Virginia estate, Monticello, and pronounced the country house "as agreeable a place to stay at as any I know"—though he wished Jefferson had been willing to more fully open his large library to guests. As a young British aristocrat, Foster had spent time in Paris and was familiar with the society in which Jefferson had circulated when he served as minister to France. This led him to conclude that "Mr. Jefferson knew too well what he was about." It was all a "game" to further his political ambitions.[1]

Foster's observations of Jefferson were valid on many counts. Jefferson was from Virginia gentry and owned a large estate. He had designed and built a very fine house, Monticello, that was unique to American architecture at the time of Foster's visit in 1807, and he had acquired an exceptional library. Jefferson's intellectual and cultural experiences were enhanced by five years spent living in Paris. But on his first meeting with the president, Foster reported that Jefferson was dressed in worn, mismatched clothing and yarn stockings, his slippers down at the heel, and looked more like a "tall large-boned farmer" than the first officer of the nation. He regretted the lack of formality and established etiquette that he had heard marked former President Washington's administration.

Foster believed that Jefferson aimed "to show contempt of European usages and forms and to gain popularity by trampling upon them and those who favoured their continuance in the United States." He witnessed Jefferson's influence spreading among other members of the government. Though Foster did not identify the Jeffersonian Republican from a good family who appeared at dinner parties in dirty boots and with disordered hair, he interpreted this man's behavior as a deliberate disregard of fashionable Europe, done in imitation of President Jefferson. These observations and personal encounters led Foster to conclude that Jefferson's "game" was the deliberate manipulation of his public image as a means of winning political popularity and retaining power for himself and his party.

Not everyone shared Foster's views. Architect Benjamin Henry Latrobe met Jefferson during his presidency, when the two worked together on completion of the Washington Capitol and the renovation of the President's House (now the White House). Latrobe makes for a good comparison with Foster, as he too was native to England, and though not of Foster's aristocratic standing, he came from a well-positioned family, was educated, and his travels included the Grand Tour of Europe. He came to admire Jefferson but acknowledged that he was "different." Latrobe wrote, "He is one of the best hearted men that ever came out of the hand of Nature and has one of the best heads also. But he thinks, writes, and acts differently from others; and who ever does that must submit to abuse." However, he could see a purpose to Jefferson's actions that went beyond the game of popularity imagined by Foster. Rather, Latrobe concluded, "As a political character he has not his equal anywhere in patriotism, right intentions, and uniform perserverance in the system he has conceived to be the most beneficial for his country." But still there were the "oddities": "Nothing in fact exists, in his whole character, on which to fasten ridicule and censure but his manner, and a few oddities of appearance and of conduct which are perfectly innocent and probably very right."[2]

Foster and Latrobe illustrate the extremely polarized views of Jefferson at the apex of his political career, when he pushed the limits of his self-fashioning to its most radical point. Foster's criticism was especially pointed, as he seemed aware that had he met Jefferson as an American diplomat in Paris or even when he served as secretary of state, his appearance and self-presentation would have been quite different. He would have met a polished, eighteenth-century gentleman, dressed and groomed in the fashion of the time. Here was the paradox that perplexed both political friend and foe alike—the chameleon Jefferson.

From his first steps onto the virtual stage of national and international politics, Jefferson adeptly created and managed an image that could change as needed to compliment his political goals. In the twenty-first century this might be called "branding," but no such term entered the eighteenth-century gentleman's vocabulary, even though all were quite aware of the importance of maintaining an appropriate public appearance. And certainly Jefferson could not claim to be the first to push the limits of self-fashioning as a tool in the political arena. He was a sincere devotee of the venerable Dr. Franklin, as he always referred to his mentor, and no doubt was familiar with the famous image of Franklin in fur cap and spectacles with hair not dressed (see fig. 5, p. 29). In the late eighteenth century the times were changing rapidly as revolution in France followed revolution in America, reform movements swept England, and unrest troubled much of Europe. The Zeitgeist produced extremes in clothing styles that reflected the more radical political thinking and broke with established eighteenth-century European traditions. These breaks with convention will be discussed in more detail as this book deciphers Jefferson's self-fashioning of his public image and offers a different approach to this controversial yet important figure in the founding of the American republic.

Eighteenth-century society recognized the civilizing influence of the gentleman and identified what should be expected from one who claimed this position. Personal presentation reflected reputation and character. The profile had evolved from Old-World prototypes, and American colonists drew guidance primarily from the mother country and the landed gentry of Britain. The gentlemanly image was composed of many parts. Self-fashioning through clothing, grooming, manners, and decorum was most obvious. Witty and spirited conversation displaying cultural and intellectual accomplishments enlivened this image. These attributes were enhanced by the setting: a performance space such as a stately residence that showcased an elegant dinner table well appointed with china and silver plate and offering sophisticated cuisine and wine. Even mode of travel—a personal coach and fine horses—was a mark of elite standing. In Jefferson's world these outward trappings indicated status, rank, and character. They were a vocabulary in themselves that could be read and understood by a cross-section of eighteenth-century society both in Europe and America.[3]

A well-bred eighteenth-century gentleman would have been attentive to the questions that the Earl of Chesterfield posed to his son. "Do you dress well, and not too well? Do you consider your air and manner of presenting yourself enough, and not too much? Neither negligent nor stiff? All these things deserve a degree of care, a second-rate attention; they give an additional lustre to real merit."[4] The popularity of Lord Chesterfield's letters to his son, first published in 1774, exemplified the importance of defining what constituted the gentleman in the eighteenth century.[5] Chesterfield's work was in Jefferson's library; however, early on, even before Chesterfield's advice reached his bookshelves, Jefferson was attentive to the advantage of adding "lustre" to personal merit and virtue through appearance and demeanor. As Foster noted, he had the advantage of growing up among Virginia's gentry, and even though this may have been a colonial version of civility, he enjoyed some exposure to the influences of art, music, books, and conversation. These were the tools of the gentleman and tools that Jefferson understood. They were his to use—or very deliberately ignore or push against—as he cultivated his art of personal presentation.

Jefferson never commented upon his own self-fashioning, but others did. Descriptions might be written or taken from visual sources. Fortunately, extant life portraits—either painted or sculpted—and prints derived from these portraits provide visual evidence of his appearance as interpreted by contemporary artists, and they form the primary basis for this discussion.[6] As evidenced by Foster and Latrobe, written observations could be both positive and negative and were recorded in private letters, journals, and commercial publications that included the growing number of American newspapers. When taken together, these sources provide a means to determine how Jefferson presented himself and how others perceived him on the political stage. Jefferson's personal presentation must always stand against the backdrop of the political issues that compelled his thoughts and actions. *How* did Jefferson create and manage his public image, and *why* would Jefferson seek to fashion himself as he did on the public stage? This book attempts to answer these questions through a careful analysis of Jefferson's use of the material culture around him to create and then manage his public image to support his political goals.

Foster accused Jefferson of playing a game to win political favor with the general populace, of playing to the people with no regard for the larger issues of statecraft. Many of Jefferson's statements and actions challenge Foster's accusation that his self-presentation was merely about popularity in this game of politics. Certainly, Jefferson worked to secure positions for himself and his Democratic-Republicans, but in many instances he expressed a larger vision. In his retirement years he reviewed his long career in public office, recalled the critical issues in the early days of the republic, and maintained that a very real contest was waged between the monarchical versus republican forms of government. He wrote, "The contests of that day were contests of principle, between the advocates of republican, and those of kingly government." He believed that had he and his political allies not pushed against the "monarchists" (his political opponents, the Federalists), "our government would have been, even at this early day, a very different thing from what the successful issue of those efforts have made it."[7] For Jefferson the fashioning of image and perception was not just a popularity contest but a struggle to determine the direction of the American republic. A lot was at stake. Jefferson recognized that in the larger worldview, Americans had much to do to overcome the stigma as provincials at the edge of the Western world.

At the edge—this was the Old World's view of American colonists. They lived at the edge of Western civilization, and their distance from the metropolises of Europe branded them provincials. For many in Europe this implied that Americans were countrified and rustic, unsophisticated and lacking cosmopolitan vision, and more likely to be undereducated. The perception persisted that the Anglo-American population had sprung from the "lower sorts," some even of the criminal element that had chosen immigration to these outlying regions over incarceration. The stigma persisted throughout the eighteenth century that the level of American civilization fell below that of Europe.[8] But this distance from the center could make New World accomplishments distinct.

In his essay "Provincialism," art historian Kenneth Clark writes specifically of artists and their painting, but his discussion can be applied more broadly. He states that the strength of the provincial is to cut through the "sophistries," to offer originality and a different vision. In Clark's words, the "application of common sense to a situation which has become over-elaborate, has been recognised since classical antiquity as the great provincial achievement."[9] It is interesting to apply this concept to Jefferson, the outlier in the cosmopolitan world. How might he appear the gentleman who was aware of the European intellectual world and its importance to the advancement of civilization without ever losing his identity as the simple American republican? Jefferson sought the balance, especially when living in Europe, and he would forever push against the stigma of provincialism. Yet he recognized that while Americans might criticize the traditions of Europe as "over-elaborate" and pride themselves as the bearers of "common sense," translating this into their often-used boast of "republican simplicity," they could never completely ignore Europe's opinion. Jefferson and other early American leaders fully realized that they had to counter the caste of provincialism without totally giving up their New World identity.[10]

The contrasting opinions of Foster and Latrobe are only two of many that will be explored in this book, as *Jefferson on Display* follows Jefferson from the moment of his arrival in Paris in 1784 as US minister plenipotentiary at the court of Versailles through his years in national offices to his retirement at Monticello and his death there in 1826. In Paris he was bound to the protocol and dress code of the French court but was conscientious of not denying his position as representative of a republican nation. His return to the United States threw him into the controversies and political contests that erupted as the country moved from revolution to the complex problems of nation building. The new constitution was in place by the time Jefferson assumed his duties as secretary of state, but many questions remained, and he was soon in conflict with Secretary of Treasury Alexander Hamilton. After a brief hiatus at Monticello, he returned in 1797 to the seat of national government, then in Philadelphia, to serve four years as vice president before being elected to the presidency in 1801. He was the first president inaugurated in the nation's new capital at Washington, and he served two terms before handing over the presidency to his close friend James Madison in 1809. The final chapters look at Jefferson in retirement at Monticello. Here the Sage stood on the periphery of politics, but he greeted his many visitors in homespun clothing in support of American home manufacturing and expressed his concern for the future of the American republic. He was equally concerned with how the history of the founding would be retold and what was to be his own place in that history.

This book focuses on how Jefferson created his public image and directed his self-fashioning to support his political vision for the early American republic. He worked to form a nation that incorporated the credo of Western civilization, one that could eventually hold a place equal to that of Europe. But this had to be accomplished within a democratic system of government that represented a majority of its citizens and was open to their participation. Launching any new polity is never easy, and the size of and distances covered by this new republic made the efforts especially complex—as complex as Jefferson himself. Merrill Peterson, in his highly regarded work *The Jefferson Image in the American Mind*, describes Jefferson as "highly complex, never uniform and never stationary." He points out his contradictions: "philosopher and politician, aristocrat and democrat, cosmopolitan and American."[11] Jefferson baffled many of his contemporaries. Augustus John Foster was aware, however, that as much as Jefferson might pose as the democratic-republican, he began as an American aristocrat; he was a member of Virginia's landed gentry. These were his beginnings ...

Jefferson came from well-established Virginia families. His mother was a member of the prestigious Randolph family. His father, Peter Jefferson, was of the lesser gentry, but he became a prosperous and extensive landholder, held public offices, and earned the prominence to style himself "Gent" on court documents even before marrying Jane Randolph. Jefferson wrote only briefly of his parents in his autobiography. He was forthright that his father had little formal education but was obviously proud of his accomplishments, especially as a surveyor and mapmaker. Peter Jefferson had worked alongside surveyor Joshua Fry, a former mathematics professor at the College of William and Mary, to finalize a survey of the boundary between the colonies of Virginia and North Carolina and produce what was, for the time, a definitive map of Virginia. Jefferson pointed to this accomplishment as proof that his father had improved himself intellectually without benefit of formal education.[12]

Jefferson was less generous with his mother's family in his autobiography and was disapproving of what he perceived as their aristocratic pretensions. He wrote, "They trace their pedigree far back in England & Scotland, to which let every one ascribe the faith & merit he chooses."[13] He may have felt a personal sting from the Randolphs' aristocratic posturing. Thomas was only two years old when Peter Jefferson moved his entire family to the late William Randolph's plantation, Tuckahoe, to manage the estate following the death of his close friend and relative by marriage. (Jane Randolph Jefferson was William's cousin.) In his role of executor of the estate and guardian of William's children, he managed Tuckahoe for approximately five years before returning to his own plantation, Shadwell. Jefferson's great-granddaughter wrote of the family's move to Tuckahoe and noted that "some of Randolph's descendants, with more arrogance than gratitude, speak of Colonel Jefferson as being a paid agent of their ancestor."[14] This was a demeaning allegation for a gentleman. Assuming it was a part of the Randolph family tradition, it helps explain Jefferson's reserve towards the Randolphs and his aversion towards the inequalities generated by defined class hierarchies.

Peter Jefferson's principal farm, Shadwell, lay much further inland than the early-established Tidewater plantations and those founded just above the fall line of the James River, such as Tuckahoe. Shadwell was located in Virginia's central piedmont region at the foot of the Blue Ridge Mountains, a part of the Appalachian chain. At the time of Jefferson's birth there in April 1743, the plantation lay at the edge of Anglo-American settlement.[15] In confronting the stigma of being the outlier, whether within his own family sphere or on the broader stage of cosmopolitan politics, Jefferson appeared ready to incorporate the tools that best suited him, from personal self-presentation to intellectual achievement.

As a young man he began engaging the ideas of Enlightenment civilization and pursued the classical education that Peter Jefferson never received but wished for his son. He studied with local tutors before entering the College of William and Mary in Williamsburg at age seventeen. Here he met a young professor fresh from Scotland named William Small, whose influence he credits as "what probably fixed the destinies of my life." Small offered Jefferson his "first views of the expansion of science & the system of things in which we are placed." Small also introduced Jefferson to one of Virginia's ablest jurists, George Wythe, and through these two men he was included in small dinners hosted by the acting governor of Virginia, Francis Fauquier, and frequently became the fourth member of what he termed a "partie quaree" at the governor's palace. This speaks to the teenage Jefferson's precociousness; in addition, he was a good listener and later wrote that "to the habitual conversation on these occasions I owed much instruction."[16] Jefferson was fortunate in his early experience of genuine intellectual company, as Fauquier was a member of the Royal Society in London, and Small would become a founding member of the Lunar Society of Birmingham, England, following his return to Britain in 1764.

These foursomes gave Jefferson his first real experience with conversation interspersed with Enlightenment ideas and no doubt introduced him to the pleasures of a table graced by well-prepared food and superior wine. Then there was music. Governor Fauquier held musical evenings, and the talented young Jefferson contributed his abilities on the violin (and perhaps cello). He was complimentary of Fauquier and wrote, "The Governor was musical also & a good performer and associated me with 2. or 3. other amateurs in his weekly concerts."[17] Along with the pleasure of music, the governor's evenings offered early lessons in how a fine dinner with its accompanying conversation could influence and direct thought. This lesson would serve Jefferson well throughout his political career, as acting the cosmopolitan host became an important part of his image. Early in Jefferson's first term as president, prominent Washington architect Benjamin Latrobe recognized that "there is a degree of ease in Mr. Jefferson's company that everybody seems to feel and enjoy."[18] Many who did not agree with Jefferson politically enjoyed the pleasure of his table. The Virginia Governor's Palace gave this young provincial his first glimpse into a more cosmopolitan world. These evenings may have fostered a dichotomy in Jefferson, for even when he began to pose as the simple American republican, he never lost his appreciation for the finer things inspired by the Old World.

After many pleasant evenings in the Governor's Palace, twenty-three-year-old Jefferson was reaching the end of his formal education. His two years at the College of William and Mary were followed by training in the law under George Wythe. But prior to taking his bar exams, he took a tour. From May to July 1766, he traveled from Williamsburg through Annapolis and Philadelphia to New York, then returned to Virginia by water. This was the closest he would come to the young gentleman's Grand Tour. When he reached Annapolis, the Maryland assembly was in session, and he disdainfully commented on the appearance of the speaker of the lower house. "The first object which struck me after my entrance was the figure of a little old man dressed but indifferently, with a yellow queue wig on, and mounted in the judge's chair." He was equally dismissive of the other assembly members, to whom he referred as the "mob (for such was their appearance)."[19]

Thirty-five years later, the situation had turned. As president of the United States, Jefferson would be receiving rather than directing critical comments about appearance. The political opposition labeled him slovenly and negligent in his clothing and accused him of deliberately ignoring decency and propriety. This was when British attaché Foster came to his conclusion that this was calculated and that Jefferson knew better. Certainly as a young Virginia "aristocrat" on his tour of the Atlantic coast, he accepted the dictate that clothing and appearance should serve as signs of rank and position. The speaker of the Maryland assembly should not be dressed "indifferently," and his wig should be white—freshly powdered—and not yellow. Even in the provinces, appearance indicated social order and was entitled to respect. But in those thirty-five years between Jefferson's first visit to Annapolis and his first year as US president in 1801, much would change.

The first major change in his adult life was a pleasant one. At age twenty-nine he married a young widow named Martha Wayles Skelton on January 1, 1772. By all accounts the marriage was a very happy one, though it ended just ten years later with her death. Jefferson was devastated and kept her memory very private. In his autobiography he added only a few sentences to say that the affection was "unabated on both sides" and that he had enjoyed "ten years in unchequered happiness."[20] This marriage changed his financial standing considerably. Just a little over a year into their marriage, Martha's father, John Wayles, died, and estimates of her portion of the estate included 11,000 acres of land and 135 slaves. Jefferson's inheritance from his father had allowed him the position of a gentleman with over 5,000 acres of land and 20 slaves, which by 1774 had increased to 41. His inherited wealth allowed him to live in comfort, but his wife's patrimony added considerable prestige, although it was accompanied by sizable debt. All became complicated by the American Revolution and the devaluation of the currency received from land sales that were meant to pay the debts.[21] Despite encumbrances, however, Jefferson image as a propertied gentleman was enhanced, even though the inherited debts were never totally resolved. When he arrived in Philadelphia to join the Continental Congress, it was as a member of the Virginia gentry.

Jefferson traveled to Philadelphia to serve as a member of the Continental Congress first in 1775 and again in 1776. His *Memorandum Books* show expenses and purchases that profile a gentleman of the period. He hired a servant in Williamsburg in June 1775 named Richard who served him on his first trip to Philadelphia. In route he outfitted Richard with boots and a "postillion whip." He purchased a horse along the way fine enough that he recorded the horse's lineage, and for his stay in Philadelphia his boarding fees were for "four horses." On the way to Philadelphia he had to have his phaeton repaired, but he must have arrived in his own carriage pulled by fine Virginia horses and appropriately attended by Richard as postilion.

A small accessory item purchased as he traveled through Fredericksburg, Virginia, also points to a formal, gentlemanly appearance. This was a "hair-bag," which was likely a black silk bag designed to cover the hair when pulled back into the queue. This formal dress accessory was required for British court dress, and its use spilled over into expectations for the colonies on such occasions as the king's birthday celebrations and when a more formal appearance was expected. During both visits to Philadelphia he made many payments to "Byrne the barber" for "shaving & dressing," which insured he remained well groomed. Another purchase during his first stay in Philadelphia that related to the dress of a gentleman was a sword-chain, used to attach a dress sword to a sword belt. He recorded payments to a Philadelphia tailor; purchased gloves, handkerchiefs, shoes, and boots; and bought many women's items, obviously for his wife and possibly his sisters. On his second trip to Philadelphia he took Bob, who was most likely Monticello slave Robert Hemings, and bought him shoes and stockings on different occasions.

In brief, his accounting records imply that he appeared in Philadelphia very much the gentleman, well-groomed, appropriately accessorized, and attended by Richard in 1775 and Robert Hemings in 1776.[22] He arrived in a private carriage, even if a modest phaeton, with well-bred horses, a dress sword, and a servant, which suggests his image was one of a gentleman who could afford to live comfortably according to American standards.

Martha's household accounts supplement Jefferson's own records with occasional inventories of the family's clothing. The list of September 1777 was the most complete, and it shows that Jefferson owned ample numbers of coats, waistcoats, and breeches. These three pieces, whether worn as a matching suit or in a combination of contrasting fabrics, had been the staple items in the Western male wardrobe since the 1660s.[23] Rich and poor owned these pieces, so the visual status was achieved through the quality of the fabric, the expertise of the cut and fit, and the richness of trim and buttons. Martha's inventory enumerated the garments and identified some fabrics and colors but supplied no further detail. However, her list profiles the wardrobe of a country gentleman who owned clothing in textiles suitable for outdoor wear but also possessed finer "cloth" coats, waistcoats, and breeches for dress occasions. She noted "2 brown holland coats," which designated unbleached linen suitable for warm, humid summers in Virginia. She also listed a coat of "Virginia cloth," which would have been a homespun or locally made fabric, possibly a blend of wool and linen or wool and cotton. Around the time of the American Revolution, homespun, or Virginia cloth, became more popular as fabrics that usually came from Britain were neither available nor desirable.[24] However, the eleven cloth coats listed were quite likely of wool broadcloth and the textiles possibly from Britain. Martha lists twenty-three waistcoats ranging in fabrics from cotton dimity to wool broadcloth to damask. Breeches were made of utilitarian fabrics, such as cord and jeans, and finer wool. Stockings also show a range from white silk to brown cotton. Jefferson had twenty-seven shirts, ruffled and plain, along with neck stocks, handkerchiefs, and nightcaps. His wardrobe would have accommodated seasonal changes and included pieces suitable for wear at Monticello, in the Virginia capital of Richmond, and in Philadelphia. A damask waistcoat, a ruffled shirt, white silk stockings, and a dress sword would have offered visual status even if the coat were not heavily trimmed.[25]

Weather played a role in Virginia clothing and required it be lightweight for summer wear. Following his return to England, William Small offered advice on clothing appropriate for life in Williamsburg. He advised Stephen Hawtrey, whose brother Edward was contemplating a position at the College of William and Mary, to have clothing as thin and light as possible for the Virginia summers. The heat would be beyond his conception. He might be able to wear a wool coat without lining through May, but for the summer months many men turned to brown holland coats. Waistcoats should be large and loose or they might "stick to your hide when you perspire." Calico shirts would absorb moisture better for summer, though Irish linen would be comfortable in winter. He would need a linen stock as a neckpiece, and he would have to have one silk suit to wear on the celebration of the king's birthday at the Governor's Palace. Gentlemen were expected to appear in full dress that one day of the year, but this was the only occasion on which fine clothing was necessary. Thread stockings were worn more frequently than silk, and shoes were quite expensive. Life was much more casual in Virginia.[26]

The eighteenth-century revolution in thought, governance, and social order extended to fashion. True to the Zeitgeist, changes in appearance kept pace to suit the need and look of the new order of things. Men's clothing moved from decorative splendor early in the eighteenth century—with brilliant colors, rich surface textures, and trims that added sheen and glitter to the man when formally dressed—towards a simpler, straighter silhouette composed of subdued, natural colors and plain woven textures as the century advanced. This reflected the larger shift in Enlightenment thinking that embraced empirical knowledge and the concept of natural law, making the colors of nature appealing for male attire. A 1781 painting of Sir Brooke Boothby by Joseph Wright of Darby illustrates this shift (fig. 1). Boothby reclines in nature, almost blending with his surroundings in a suit of light taupe that appears well fitted with a narrow cut. He wears a frock coat with its signature utilitarian turndown collar and a broad-brimmed, round hat. Both styles were inspired by the practical garments of the working classes, and by the latter part of the eighteenth century they began to be incorporated by the country gentleman into his own wardrobe (fig. 2). Eventually these country-inspired clothes became acceptable for the city and even made their way from Britain to France. But Boothby does not forego the

FIGURE 1. Sir Brooke Boothby by Joseph Wright of Derby (1734–1797), 1781.

Sir Brooke Boothby exemplifies men's daywear in the 1780s and fashion's relationship to Enlightenment thought. As he reclines in nature, Boothby displays a volume by Jean-Jacques Rousseau. The neutral color and simplified lines of his unadorned three-piece suit blend with his natural surroundings.

subtle signals that he is a gentleman and displays his status in the exacting cut of his suit, the finely fitted leather gloves, spotless white stockings, and hair dressed in side curls. The volume of Rousseau that he holds with his forefinger casually pointing to the title further suggests position and learning.[27]

Both the formal coat and the daytime coat changed silhouette as the century progressed. The original fullness in the skirt continued to diminish until it evolved into the nineteenth-century tailcoat. Large cuffs became smaller and fit closer to a longer, tapered sleeve. The formal coat retained the standing collar, while the frock coat, which became the dominant daytime coat, had its characteristic turndown collar (fig. 3). Both collars grew in height as the body of the coat grew slimmer, creating an elongated silhouette by the end of the eighteenth century. Splendor persisted at European courts, and men's coats and waistcoats did not let go the richness and

FIGURE 2. Detail from *Lord Grosvenor's Arabian with a Groom* by George Stubbs, c. 1765. Oil on canvas, 39⅛ in. × 32⅞ in.

Lord Grosvenor's groom wears the working-man's frock coat and round hat that inspired the fashionable suit worn by Sir Brooke Boothby.

glitter in fabric and trim for formal occasions. But the elites and aristocrats wearing such finery were being challenged. When Jefferson was in Paris he noticed the change, but he noted as well that the royal courts, the very highest rungs of society, would be the last to let go symbols of status. Beyond court society, change rippled throughout the Western world. Government officials, merchants, manufacturers, and other professional men had to appear ready to work, while none wanted to compromise status by appearing in less than the proper mode.[28] American provincials had fewer changes to make. Their neutral-hued frock coats, adopted partly by choice and partly due to lack of availability of European fabrics, positioned them, rather paradoxically, at the leading edge of fashion.

By the end of the summer of 1776, Jefferson was impatient to return to Virginia. He knew from correspondence with family members that Martha

FIGURE 3. John Musters by Sir Joshua Reynolds, 1777–c. 1780.

Reynolds shows Musters in a brown frock coat with no trim beyond the decorative buttons. The turn-down collar was retained from the working-man's coat, a detail that distinguished it from the dress coat with its standing collar. Waistcoats might still feature more elegant fabrics. The walking stick took the place of the gentleman's dress sword.

had not been well, and he was extremely concerned for her health. He knew also that the Virginia legislature was beginning work on a new state constitution. At this point the politics in his home state of Virginia were as important to him as the momentous events in Philadelphia, and he wanted to be a part of the decision making. He missed the major work on the state constitution, but in the autumn of 1776 he was placed at the head of the committee charged with revising colonial laws to make them appropriate for the new state.

Reviewing and enacting the revisions of the laws as proposed by Jefferson and his committee would continue in the Virginia legislature over the next decade. He was already living in Paris, engaged in a very different life, when James Madison secured passage of the Statute for Religious Freedom in 1786. Jefferson felt this bill was extremely important, and it was one in which he felt some pride, even though he would later admit that during the contest for the presidency and even afterwards, it had caused him the greatest abuse. Many Americans misunderstood the bill's purpose, which was not to abolish the church but rather to make public worship open to any belief or domination. Of special concern to Jefferson was the Bill for the More General Diffusion of Knowledge, which the legislature did not pass. Ultimately his frustrations over the lack of adequate public education in his state prompted him to found the University of Virginia.[29] But many eventful years would pass before he undertook this last major project.

Martha was with him through the revolution and through his difficulties as war-time governor and the British invasion of Virginia. Her health was failing during this trying period, and she never recovered from the birth of their sixth child in May 1782. She died the following September.[30] Of their six children, two daughters lived into adulthood. Maria (Mary) died at age twenty-five in 1804, and only Martha, the eldest, survived her father. Jefferson never remarried, and oral tradition holds that this stemmed from a promise he gave his dying wife. Martha Randolph's mother had died soon after her birth, and she had been raised by stepmothers. Did she not want this for her own daughters?[31] Possibly, but a more compelling question — one that has been given considerable deliberation — asks whether Jefferson later began a second family with his slave Sarah (Sally) Hemings. Much evidence, both scientific and circumstantial, supports this theory, and a strong oral tradition suggests that Sally Hemings was Martha Jefferson's half-sister, the daughter of John Wayles and his slave Betty Hemings. This involved and ongoing story extends beyond the scope of this study and has been admirably treated by other writers, especially Lucia Stanton and Annette Gordon-Reed.[32] Whether one accepts Jefferson's paternity of Heming's children or not, the rumor that he kept a slave concubine was attached to his image when he was president.

From all the Old World had to offer, Jefferson developed a special appreciation for things French, whether art, furniture, wine, or food. This partiality extended to many of his long-term friendships. His earliest French acquaintances were among the officers who fought with the American forces during the revolution. As governor, he corresponded with the marquis de Lafayette on military matters during the British invasion of Virginia. Following the surrender of the British command to the allied American and French forces at Yorktown, the marquis de Chastellux paid a four-day visit to Monticello that led to a friendship that remained extremely cordial until Chastellux's death in 1788.

Chastellux left his impressions of revolutionary North America and many of its people in his journal, first published in France in 1786 and the following year in London as *Travels in North America*. Aware that the key founders of the colony of Virginia were Englishmen distinguished by rank or birth, Chastellux believed he saw "prejudices of nobility" still at work in the state and predicted that "the government may become democratic, as it is at the present moment; but the national character, the spirit of the government itself, will always be aristocratic."[33] These views paralleled Foster's label of Jefferson as a Virginia aristocrat and struck at one of Jefferson's primal political fears: that the American republic would slide from a democratic government into some form of monarchy or aristocracy, perhaps a constitutional monarchy as practiced by Britain.

Upon their first meeting, Chastellux found Jefferson "serious, nay even cold," but this initial impression quickly changed. He continued, "But before I had been two hours with him we were as intimate as if we had passed our whole lives together; walking, books, but above all, a conversation always varied and interesting." Ultimately, he pronounced him "an American, who without ever having quitted his own country, is at once a musician, skilled in drawing: a geometrician, an astronomer, a natural philosopher, legislator, and statesman." He respected the sensibility and research reflected in Jefferson's design of his house and stated, "Mr. Jefferson is the first American who has consulted the fine arts to know how he should shelter himself from the weather." He added further that Jefferson had placed his mind, just as his house, on an elevated height. These achievements were evaluated within the context of the revolution, and Chastellux noted that "all the while, Mr. Jefferson . . . played a principal character on the theatre of the new world."[34]

This high esteem becomes more unique when viewed alongside Chastellux's opinion of other Virginians, which was not so positive. He wrote, "I was desirous of celebrating the virtues peculiar to the Virginians, and in spite of my wishes, I am obliged to limit myself to their magnificence and hospitality." He explained, "It is not in my power to add generosity; for they are strongly attached to their interests; and their great riches, joined to their pretensions, gives more deformity to this vice."[35] Chastellux was invoking the notion of public virtue that called on citizens to place personal interests in subservience to the needs of the greater public good. The pursuit of private interests over those of the public led to corruption.[36]

Chastellux seemed aware that Jefferson had maintained his obligations to his civic duties while building a fine house and planning improvements to his estate. He served in the "famous Congress," referring to the Continental Congress, and was governor of Virginia during the difficult period of the British invasion—a public service that Jefferson might wish forgotten, as he was held to blame for Virginia's initial humiliation. In addition, Chastellux seemed satisfied that Jefferson was proficient in the highest level of gentlemanly conversation, the philosophical dialogue. Jefferson held in his library the writings of the 3rd Earl of Shaftsbury, who advocated the belief that the gentlemanly art of enlightened conversation was the chief contribution to the mode of politeness and sociability needed for civilized society.[37] Conversational arts comprised a part of his image that Jefferson refined and learned to use well. His many attributes as identified by Chastellux would be referenced again and again during Jefferson's long public career, sometimes positively and at other times negatively, usually depending on the political affiliations of the observer. His fondness for the French, as exemplified by his instant friendship with Chastellux, was never lost, but it would cause political tension in the early years of the republic.

In the autumn of 1782 Jefferson took on a new role as a minister plenipotentiary to the court of France from the now sovereign United States. This was not Jefferson's first appointment. In September 1776 the Continental Congress elected him a member of the original peace commission. He was to accompany Benjamin Franklin and Silas Deane to treat with the British in Paris in seeking an end to the American War of Independence. He declined this appointment due to his wife's failing health; she could not make the voyage and he would not leave her. He declined again in 1781, as Martha's health had not improved. Following her death in September 1782, the grieving Jefferson accepted the renewed appointment and welcomed the prospect of a change of scene.[38] Meanwhile, the Treaty of Paris (1783) ended the conflict, so he did not leave for his new post until the summer of 1784.[39] He was a forty-one-year-old widower before he actually arrived in Europe. He was not naïve of the culture offered there or unaware of Enlightenment society. After declining the first appointment as envoy in 1776, he wrote Franklin that he regretted he could not join him in Paris at "a polite court" among "literati of the first order."[40]

When Jefferson accepted the appointment to France in November 1782, he hurried north, hoping to sail with Chastellux and General Rochambeau, the head of the French forces in North America. In his letter to Chastellux he explained his acceptance of a ministerial position in France following the death of his wife. He proposed that should they sail together and continue their dialogue on the natural sciences, they might consider "chess too a matter of science."[41] Delays prevented his sailing with Chastellux and Rochambeau, and with the peace treaty concluded his appointment was rescinded. Over a year would pass before he was voted a new appointment as minister plenipotentiary to negotiate treaties of amity and commerce, and by July 1784 Jefferson was ready to depart for France, where he would join Franklin and Adams. He sailed from Boston Harbor accompanied by his eldest daughter, Martha, and a young Monticello slave, James Hemings, whom he planned to have trained as a chef while in Paris. After a smooth, nineteen-day crossing, they landed in Cowes, on the Isle of Wight, then sailed on to Havre de Grace, where they disembarked for Paris.

He had read the books, occasionally heard the music performed, viewed works of art, and listened to those who had been there. Some notions of European culture and the advances in science grew in his imagination, but it was not until August 6, 1784, that Thomas Jefferson arrived in Paris to begin his real-life experience of Europe. He would learn, evaluate, and formulate his own opinions of the Old World.

I

The European Experience

In what country on earth would you rather live? — Certainly in my own, where are all my friends, my relations, and the earliest & sweetest affections and recollections of my life. — Which would be your second choice? — France.
— Thomas Jefferson, draft autobiography, 1821

1

AT THE FRENCH COURT AND
AMONG THE LITERATI

"Behold me at length on the vaunted scene of Europe!" Jefferson exclaimed. He followed this bold statement by speculating, "But you are perhaps curious to know how this new scene has struck a savage of the mountains of America."[1] He went on to express conflicted feelings towards this world he was experiencing for the first time. He found "the general fate of humanity here deplorable" and invoked Voltaire's observation that "every man here must be either the hammer or the anvil." The disparity among classes of people would be a fault he would level against Europe throughout his lifetime, but he would do so without ever resolving the institution of chattel slavery in the United States. He even criticized the European family structure and asserted that it did not afford the stability found in America. Then he suddenly changed tone—the savage had to admit to his awe of the "vaunted scene."

Jefferson could not conceal his excitement in finally experiencing the intellectual and cultural atmosphere of Europe. He freely admitted that in science the literati led America by half a dozen years. And then there were the books. He tried taking the position that America was lucky to have the lag time from publisher to bookseller to allow the "swarm of nonsense" to fall away, but fifteen crates of books followed him to America upon his return.[2] Even the polite manners and the "pleasures of the table" were commendable and something to be emulated in the Unites States. He concluded his summary by enthusing, "Were I to proceed to tell you how much I enjoy their architecture, sculpture, painting, music, I should want words."[3]

Jefferson entered this letter into his epistolary journal as "My View of Europe." It was written at the end of his first year abroad to a friend in Virginia. Interestingly enough, this "view" changed little during his five years in France (1784–89). What he observed and experienced in Europe, of both the culture and the people, would have a lasting influence on his self-fashioning and image management for the political stage. Meanwhile, he had to function as a minister plenipotentiary representing a newly formed republican nation. A lingering curiosity surrounded these colonials who had managed to gain their sovereignty from the powerful British Empire. But curiosity aside, after just four months at his post Jefferson had to admit that "we are the lowest and most obscure of the whole diplomatic tribe."[4] His job was not going to be easy. He might pose facetiously as a "savage" from the wilds of America in epistolary exchanges, but to perform his role effectively, he had to comply with the expectations of French court society. Even to realize his ambition of acceptance into the circles of the literati and their intellectual salons, he would need to temper his provincial appearance with the polish of Europe's elites while not visually denying his position as a representative of a new republic. He must find a balance to succeed in *Ancien Régime* France, where rank was asserted through social display.

At the French court Jefferson entered a world that placed extraordinary emphasis on appearance. The courtiers surrounding the monarch under-stood the importance of self-presentation. They must be graceful in their gestures and movement, accomplished in their manner of speaking and conversation. Self-discipline extended to facial expressions that mastered passion and strong emotions. Dress and grooming deserved particular attention and could never be neglected. Even the houses (the hôtels) in which the courtiers lived must provide the correct setting. Stepping outside the bounds of court etiquette meant a loss of prestige and power.[5] John Adams was intrigued with the "Easy Air, the graceful bow, and the conscious Dignity" of the court nobility; how "every Muscle, Nerve and Fibre of both [men and women] seemed perfectly disciplined to perform its functions." He recognized "the Perfection of the French Air" and questioned if another court could rival this outward grace and composure. Even the peers of the English court, which he largely preferred, were "decent and graceful enough," but he had to admit that they could not compare with the grace and elegance of the French.[6]

This formation of court society came together during the reign of the autocratic Louis XIV and continued under Louis XV. When Louis XVI came to the throne in 1774, the same courtly protocol was still very much in place, even though the aristocracy was feeling the strain of the gradual but ongoing loss of wealth and the pressures this exerted. Financial resources were shifting to the bourgeois financiers and merchants. Still, prerevolutionary France remained an absolutist society where the king alone ruled, and titles were the king's reward. A display of rank persisted as a necessity for elites. As sociologist Norbert Elias explains, "A duke who does not live as a duke has to live, who can no longer properly fulfil the social duties of a duke, is hardly a duke any longer."[7]

Social demands placed on the French nobility extended to the diplomatic corps. Franklin, Adams, and Jefferson all expressed concerns over the costs associated with attendance at the French court during their tenures. Even Franklin, who famously created his own rustic, less formal style, could not completely escape the sartorial demands of court. "As the Article of clothes for ourselves here is necessarily much higher than if we were not in public Service," he complained to Adams, "I submit it to your Consideration whether that Article ought not to be rekoned among Expenses for the Public. I know I had clothes enough at home to have lasted me my Lifetime in a Country where I was under small Necessity of following new Fashions."[8] His complaint summarizes succinctly the differing emphasis placed on the richness of appearance demanded of elites in the Old World and the leaders of the New World.

The imperative to look French annoyed Adams, who grumbled that "the first Thing to be done, in Paris, is always to send for a Taylor, Peruke maker and Shoemaker." He suspected a conspiracy on the part of the French court. "For this nation has established such a domination over the Fashion, that neither Cloaths, Wig nor Shoes made in any other Place will do in Paris. This is one of the Ways in which France taxes all Europe, and will tax America," he predicted. "It is a great Branch of the Policy of the Court, to Preserve and increase this national Influence over the Mode, because it occasions an immense Commerce between France and all the other Parts of Europe."[9] Adams was not wrong. Since the reign of the powerful Louis XIV, France had dominated the fashion industry. French textiles and the styles produced by French tailors were widely imitated and sought throughout European courts.[10] Even the rival British court adopted the style of French formal wear for men (fig. 4).[11]

Abigail Adams shared her husband's opinions on the influence of French dress. She wrote her sister in New England, "Fashion is the Deity everyone worships in this country and from the highest to the lowest you must submit." Their daughter Abigail, known in the family as "Nabby," wrote in her

FIGURE 4. *Gallerie des Mode et Costumes Français, 28e Suite d'Habillemens à la mode en 1781. 1er Cahier pour le 3e Volume. mm. 209, Duc et Paire décoré des Ordres du Roi occupant une des premieres places à la Cour: Ilest vetu d' un habit d'été brodé,* Nicholas Dupin after Pierre-Thomas LeClerc, 1781. Hand colored engraving, 10¾ in. × 7 in.

This French fashion plate illustrates the *habit habillé,* also called the *habit françois.* With a dress sword and a *chapeau bras* tucked under the left arm, the figure provides an example of the appearance expected at the French court or on other formal occasions.

journal, "There is no such thing here as preserving our taste in any thing; we must all sacrifice to custom and fashion." Nabby saw proof of this in her own father. Even with his "firmness and resolution," he adhered to the French fashion and was "a perfect convert to the mode in everything, at least of dress and appearance." Jefferson's daughter Martha had a similar experience upon their arrival in Paris and wrote to close family friend Elizabeth House Trist, "I wish you could have been with us when we arrived. I am sure you would have laughed, for we were obliged to send immediately for the stay maker, the mantumaker [mantua-maker or dressmaker], the milliner and even a shoe maker, before I could go out."[12] Jefferson's accounting records confirm that procuring appropriate clothing for Martha began immediately upon their arrival in the French capital.

Jefferson joined the transformation from American provincial to a gentleman in the mode of fashionable Paris. His accounts show that on their first day in the French capital, as Martha began her fashion conversion, he purchased a pair of lace ruffles, the following day a hat, and three days later a dress sword and belt. Lace and sword signified a gentleman and were integral parts of court dress. His records give no indication of the type of hat purchased, but if it was the *chapeau bras,* then he had acquired an important accessory required for appearance at the French court.[13] Before his first month in Paris ended, Jefferson had paid a sizeable amount for what he listed simply as "clothes" for both himself and for Martha. His itemized expenses included having a dozen shirts made, along with ruffles for shirt fronts and wrists in both lace and cambric. A comparison of one set of lace ruffles for court attire at 120f and six pair of cambric ruffles for daywear at 27f gives some idea of the expense attached to properly appearing at Versailles. Other items purchased were shoes, stockings, gloves, buckles and handkerchiefs.[14] Thus began the "sacrifice to custom and fashion" in the French style that Nabby Adams had observed in her own family.

Jefferson experienced the sartorial demands of court protocol within the first month of his arrival in Paris. A period of mourning was declared for a young Germanic prince, eight years of age, whose family was allied with the French throne. The *Journal de Paris* of September 3, 1784, provided the specifics. The mourning would be observed for eleven days, from the 2nd through the 12th, and the dress required of the men was *l'Habit noir complet.* This meant that Jefferson quickly obtained a black suit to assume his duties at court.[15]

Abigail Adams confirmed Jefferson's compliance with these directives. She wrote to relatives in New England, "Mr. Jefferson had to hie away for a Tailor to get a whole black silk suit made up in two days, and at the end of Eleven days [the designated mourning period] should an other death happen, he will be obliged to have a new Suit of mourning of Cloth, because that is the Season when Silk must be cast of [*sic*].We may groan and scold but these are expences which cannot be avoided."[16] She chose to avoid this expense, however, by not going out into company for the eleven days. She had black clothing but not in the silk required for the current season. Since the period of mourning concluded September 12, if Abigail's calculations were correct the season for silk ended mid-September and the appropriate fabric following that date would be wool broadcloth.

The practical Abigail Adams complained that this mourning had "put these Gentlemen to 50 Guineys expence in order to appear at court to day where they are obliged to go every Tuesday." The real irony, as it turned out, was that Adams had just learned court was to be cancelled that day. When Jefferson and legation secretary David Humphreys arrived that morning at the Adams's residence in Auteuil in route to Versailles, Abigail teased them over breakfast that their new black suits must be laid aside, as most likely the next period of mourning would be past the season for silk. She observed: "Mr. Jefferson . . . is really a man who abhors this shew and parade full as much as Mr. Adams, yet he has not been long enough enured to it, to Submit with patience, or bear it without fretting."[17] Jefferson may have expressed some irritation at his tailor's bill of over 766 livres for a suit that must be put aside so quickly while he was still negotiating the expenses of establishing his household in Paris.[18]

Jefferson's visit to Versailles was postponed until the following week. On September 15 the American commissioners met with the French minister of foreign affairs, the Count de Vergennes, to present a copy of their commission from the United States Congress authorizing them to negotiate commercial treaties with France. On his first official visit Jefferson made no comment on the grandeur, the art, or the architecture of Versailles. He only noted that he paid to see the gardens.[19]

Diplomatic assignments shifted in the spring and summer of 1785. Franklin had been in France since 1776 and petitioned Congress to return to the United States. When his request was granted, Jefferson was unanimously voted to take his place as minister plenipotentiary to France. John Adams was reassigned to the British Court of St. James as the first American minister. He was both excited by the prospect and uneasy as to the reception he might receive in London as a former colonist representing a now-independent nation. He expressed his apprehensions to a family member in New England and also remarked that "I shall part with Mr. Jefferson, with great Regret."[20] His wife echoed these sentiments and was reluctant "to leave behind me the only person with whom my Companion could associate with perfect freedom, and unreserved."[21] Adams had a reputation as irascible but while in Paris, Jefferson became close with him and his family. His devotion to Franklin never wavered. As he prepared to present his new credentials to Louis XVI on May 17, 1785, the Adams family was packing for their move to London, and Franklin was planning his voyage home.

Franklin would not be easy to follow. He had created a sensation upon his arrival in Paris in 1776 with his rustic appearance; additionally, his reputation as a man of science and a statesman had preceded him. His *Experiment and Observations on Electricity* had been translated and published in France in 1752, and on his visits there in 1767 and 1769 he was presented to Louis XV.[22] Following his arrival in Paris late in 1776, the artist Elisabeth Vigée-Lebrun wrote that "no-one was more fashionable, more sought after in Paris than Doctor Franklin: the crowd chased after him in parks and public places; hats, canes and snuffboxes were designed in the Franklin style, and people thought themselves very lucky if they were invited to the same dinner party as this famous man." The first time she saw him "he was dressed in grey and his unpowdered braided hair fell upon his shoulders; if it had not been for the nobility of his face, I would have taken him for a stocky farmer, such was the contrast he made with the other diplomats who were all powdered and dressed in their finest clothes, bedecked with gold and coloured sashes."[23] This comparison to other "diplomats" suggests that Franklin appeared at court dressed as the rustic without giving offence to the king. His reputation as the American who stood at the forefront of experimentation with electricity insured his international fame and granted his dispensation in regard to court dress.[24]

Franklin must have relished his notoriety. He described himself with some glee as "very plainly dressed, wearing my thin, grey straight hair that peeps out under my only *coiffure,* a fine fur cap, which comes down my forehead almost to my spectacles. Think how this must appear among the powdered heads of Paris"![25] Franklin in his fur cap and spectacles as sketched by the artist Charles Nicolas Cochin and engraved by Augustin de Saint-Aubin caught Europe's attention (fig. 5). Historian Charles Sellers explains that even though it was a good likeness, the Cochin/Saint-Aubin print was never intended as a step towards a formal portrait: rather, it was for publicity and commercial purposes. The print, as advertised in the *Journal de Paris* of June 1777, announced Franklin's arrival in his "sensational"

FIGURE 5. Benjamin Franklin by Augustin de Saint-Aubin, 1777. Engraving, 7½ in. × 5⁷⁄₁₆ in.

This image of Franklin in his fur cap and spectacles became popular and widespread. Such a signature look was not one that the younger, relatively unknown Jefferson could adopt.

costume, which worked exceptionally well to create a strikingly memorable image.[26]

Jefferson did not share Franklin's reputation as an international statesman and man of science. A presentation style so far removed from what was expected at the French court was not an option for the younger, unknown Jefferson. "The succession to Dr. Franklin, at the court of France," he acknowledged, "was an excellent school of humility." To the question, "It is you, Sir, who replace Doctor Franklin?," Jefferson famously replied, "No one can replace him, Sir: I am only his successor."[27] But how much inspiration was absorbed from this man that Jefferson so genuinely admired, both as a man of science and for his iconoclastic self-fashioning?

Along with this shuffling of positions, Jefferson took a different residence in Paris, which stood to bolster his image. He moved from the Cul de sac Taitbout to the more spacious and elegant Hôtel de Langeac at the corner of the Champs-Élysées and Rue de Berri, adjoining the Gille de Chaillot.[28] The French *Encylcopedie* explained the differences in dwellings: *la maison* was for the bourgeois, *l'hôtel* housed nobles, and the *palais* was reserved for the prince or king.[29] Jefferson's new residence, which also served as the American legation, illustrates his awareness that place was vital to his image and that of his country. He admitted to Abigail Adams that the rental fee was "dearer" than his first residence but rationalized, "It has a clever garden to it."[30]

Jefferson supplied little detail of his audience with the king in his report to US Foreign Secretary John Jay. He wrote only that "on the 17th delivered my letter of credence to the king at a private audience and went through the other ceremonies usual on such occasions."[31] The etiquette surrounding the presentation of a diplomat during the *Ancien Regime* was described in the memoirs of the comte de Cheverny. The ambassador (or minister plenipotentiary) and his legation secretary were presented in the king's private bedchamber in the presence of the king and his couturiers. The presentation was brief: the ambassador executed three low bows as he approached the king, then gave his address and received the king's response. After presenting his secretary and staff, the ambassador retreated from the room, again performing the three low bows. This performance was repeated in the queen's chamber and before other members of the royal family. Following the presentations, the ambassador would join others of the diplomatic corps for the grand dinner provided each Tuesday.[32]

The legation secretary, David Humphreys, participated in this initial presentation to the king but added no further information on the presentation itself. He did provide, however, some observations on the typical diplomats' day at court. He wrote, "My public character puts it in my option to be present at the King's Levee every tuesday, & after the Levee to dine with the whole Diplomatique Corps at the Cte de Vergennes." He observed, "It is curious to see forty or fifty Ambassadors, Ministers or other strangers of the first fashion from all the nations of Europe assembling in the most amicable manner & conversing in the same language."[33] His choice of words, that these men were of the "first fashion," indicates the attention to personal appearance required of all who attended the French court, as they conversed in French and partook of the dinner provided by the foreign minister. Jefferson said of his own abilities, "I write the French very indifferently; I understand it however well enough to receive any commands in French."[34]

The perfunctory descriptions given by Jefferson and Humphreys were augmented by the observations of a wealthy young American on his Grand Tour of Europe. Thomas Lee Shippen of Philadelphia was presented at the French court in February 1788 under Jefferson's patronage. In a lengthy letter to his father, William Shippen, he described his presentation and the diplomatic protocol observed during those Tuesdays spent at court.[35] He was fascinated with court etiquette but was somewhat taken aback that his presentation could not be made at Minister Jefferson's discretion. As the United States offered no hereditary distinctions, those received at court and presented to the king had to establish some affiliation with an office of honor. In compliance, Jefferson introduced Shippen as the nephew of the former president of Congress (Richard Henry Lee). The day was long, and Shippen admitted to some tedium but was nevertheless awed by "so much of Oriental splendour and magnificence." He was impressed by the palace, the gardens, the food served, the large-as-life portraits of the royal family—but the high point of the day was his audience with the king.

The presentation took place in Louis's private apartments towards the conclusion of the morning's ceremonial dressing of the king. Shippen wrote that as they entered the king's chamber, "he was just pulling on his coat, a servant was tying his hair in which there was no powder, while one of his attendants was arranging his sword belt."[36] The ritual of dressing, the *lever,* and undressing, the *coucher,* of the king had long played a significant role at the French court. Phillip Mansel states, "The King of France was an anointed monarch. Dressing him had a semi-religious aspect, like the robing and un-robing of priests before and after a service." This custom existed early in French history but reached a new level of formality under Louis XIV. Dress indicated status and wealth among the nobility and sent an important visual message to the public that reinforced rigid class distinctions. This message and the rituals attached would continue until the revolution and deposition of Louis XVI.[37]

The *lever* was structured so that different groups entered in turn, the *entrées*. The Gentlemen of the Bedchamber monitored the door and determined who had the right to pass inside. Those in closest attendance to the king, the *entrée familière*, entered first, followed by the *grand entrée* of the nobles. The ministers and ambassadors came in with the third group, *entrée de la chambre*. The actual dressing began during the *grand entrée*, as the nightshirt was exchanged for the day shirt. From Shippen's remark that the king was being assisted with his coat and sword, the process was nearing completion. By this point the room would be full of men hoping for a word from the king and exchanging information among themselves, thus this rigorous performance of etiquette became a time to do business as well.[38]

Shippen seemed somewhat disappointed at the actual presentation. In his words, the king "hobbled from one side of the room to the other, spoke 3 words to a few of the ambassadors and 2 to a German Prince who was presented with me, and left the room." Shippen and Jefferson received no words from the king—but then Shippen was not a prince, and Jefferson was a second-rank minister plenipotentiary, not a full ambassador. Shippen learned that "the king is bound up by etiquette to distribute his monosyllables among those of *Ambassadorial* rank [Shippen's italics]." But this did not seem to disturb Jefferson, as the business he needed to conduct was with the foreign minister, comte de Montmorin. He counseled with Montmorin while Shippen strolled the gardens and found other amusements.[39]

In recounting his day at Versailles, Shippen briefly referenced Jefferson's personal appearance. He noted that all the ambassadors, ministers, and envoys were in "full dress," which would be the *habit habillé*. He continued, "I observed that although Mr. Jefferson was the plainest man in the room, and the most destitute of ribbands crosses and other insignia of rank that he was most courted and most attended to (even by the Courtiers themselves) of the whole Diplomatic corps."[40] Shippen may have been biased in his observation that Jefferson was the most courted, and his description of Jefferson as "the plainest man in the room" raises questions as to what he meant by "plain." No doubt Jefferson appeared in the required full dress that Shippen

FIGURE 6. Comte de Vaudreuil by Elisabeth Vigée-Lebrun, 1784. Oil on canvas, 52 in. × 38⅞ in.

The comte de Vaudreuil is identified as a Chevalier of the Ordre du Saint-Esprit by the cross emblazoned on his coat and the diagonal sash across his chest, the *cordon bleu*. The badge suspended from the buttonhole of his coat shows his membership in the military order of Saint Louis.

observed on the other courtiers, and both Americans had to meet the approval of the Gentlemen of the Bed Chamber to be admitted for their audience with the king. But Shippen makes one point clear—Jefferson was not wearing a sash or medals or any other indications of rank.

A portrait of the comte de Vaudreuil painted by Elisabeth Vigée-Lebrun illustrates the insignias that Shippen noted on the French noblemen during his day at Versailles (fig. 6). The portrait, painted in 1784 and thus contemporary with Jefferson's arrival in Paris, presents an example of formal dress. Vigée-Lebrun painted Vaudreuil wearing a matching coat and waistcoat of rich brown trimmed with gold braid. His *chapeau bras* is appropriately tucked under his arm, and one hand loosely holds his dress sword. Very fine lace adorns his shirt front and encircles his wrists, and hair dressed and powdered completes the requirements of a formally attired gentleman. His dress is modest compared to some French court attire; nevertheless, his display of knightly orders identifies him as elite. The cross embroidered on the coat and the blue moiré ribbon (the *cordon bleu*) worn diagonally across the chest signify that Vaudreuil held the Ordre du Saint-Esprit, the highest knightly order of France. The cross of the military order of St. Louis hangs from a buttonhole, suspended by a red ribbon. On her trips to Versailles Nabby Adams learned to recognize the *cordon bleu* and observed fellow dinner guests who "by their ribbons, I suppose were great folks." On another visit, she could identify the aristocracy "by their having the Cross of *St. Louis*." She concluded, "I supposed they were noblemen."[41]

Jefferson viewed such knightly orders with suspicion and was uneasy with the prospect of a similar organization in the American republic. He opposed the Society of the Cincinnati, organized by officers of the Continental army following the war. As membership in the society passed to the eldest son, Jefferson feared that this elite military organization could be the beginnings of an American nobility. The Cincinnati's emblem of an eagle suspended by a blue-and-white ribbon could come to represent "privilege and prerogative," just as Nabby Adams recognized the "great folk" by their sashes and ribbons.[42] Jefferson and others who opposed the Cincinnati were equally disturbed to learn that chapters were planned for each state, creating a network that could spread nationwide.[43] He began forming these opinions before his assignment to Europe, and while at Versailles his fears were reinforced as he observed the influence and interworkings of the knightly orders. He became even more convinced that the Cincinnati, with its fostering of hereditary aristocracy, would change the young American government for the worse.[44] True, he had not served in the Continental army and thus was not eligible for the Cincinnati's diamond eagle, but his opposition was grounded not in personal exclusion but in his fear of aristocracy.

Jefferson made no specific reference to France's order of the Saint-Esprit, but Adams had observed an induction ceremony in June 1778 and found it intriguing. The king was on his throne; the queen, dazzling with diamonds, sat opposite in her gallery, and according to Adams, "Her Dress was every Thing that Art and Wealth could make it." What affected Adams most, however, was the sight of the knights kneeling on the marble floor of Versailles's chapel for two hours: "The distinction of the blue ribbon, was very dearly purchased at the price of enduring this painful Operation, four times in a year."[45] Vergennes confessed to him that "he was almost dead, with the pain of it."

Following the induction of the knights, Adams attended the *Grand Couvert*, at which the royal family ate a meal before the court. As Nabby Adams described when she attended, the ceremony was designed "to give all the world the opportunity to see them [the king and queen] eat and drink."[46] The royal supper began at nine o'clock in the evening. John Adams noted the arrangement of the seats on both sides of the hall that struck him "like

Seats in a Theatre." The king carved the beef and took generous portions of food; however, the spectators saw "the magnificent Spectacle of a great Queen swallowing her Royal Supper in a single Spoonful, all at once." One spoonful of soup was all that she ate, but Adams added the detail of how "this was all performed like perfect Clockwork, not a feature of her face, nor a Motion of any part of her Person, especially her Arm and her hand could be criticized as out of order." During this episode when the royal family was displayed before the court, Adams felt on display himself. He believed his seat assignment was quite deliberate and that he was being treated as a curiosity. The "raw American" was escorted towards the front among the ladies of the court, while the courtly figures gazed at him. He obviously felt self-conscious but defended his dress and wrote, "My Dress was a decent French Dress, becoming the Station I held, but not to be compared with [the] Gold and Diamonds about me" (fig. 7).[47]

The New Year's Day celebration was one of those special days when

FIGURE 7. John Adams by John Singleton Copley, 1783. Oil on canvas, 93¾ in. × 57⅞ in.

Copley's artistic skill makes Adams's suit appear to be velvet. The standing collar shows the coat's formal cut, but it is devoid of extravagant trim— perhaps not unlike the "descent French dress" that Adams wore at the *Grand Couvert.*

attention to dress went beyond that of the usual Tuesday assemblies. Nabby Adams was taken with the splendor of the clothing and confirmed in her journal, "Upon these occasions it is customary for the court and the ambassadors to dress more than usual."[48] New Year's Day 1785 would have been Jefferson's first opportunity to attend this special celebration, but he had not been well and his records do not indicate that he attended. However, for the next four years, from 1786 through 1789, he paid the *étrennes,* the monetary gifts traditionally given to the court staff on New Year's Day, so presumably he attended the ceremonies.[49] Over this four-year period he had the opportunity to observe the induction ceremony for the knightly order of Saint-Esprit and to attend the long-established ritual of the monarchs dining before their court in the *Grand Couvert.* As a member of the diplomatic corps he had a place among those attending this exclusive day at the royal palace and must have collected impressions and formed opinions of these elite celebrations. Years later, as US president, he would plan national celebrations that were far more inclusive.

The Americans were finding their way among these extravagant displays at the French court. They struggled with expenditures and questioned how elaborately they should present themselves as representatives of a republic. John Adams defended his appearance at the *Grand Couvert* when given the role of "the raw American." On more than one occasion Jefferson defensively claimed that he was "savage enough to prefer the woods, the wilds, and the independence of Monticello," but this image was not one he could indulge among the French aristocrats.[50] The American emissaries accepted their roles as provincial curiosities, and Franklin even managed to use this image to his advantage. Yet fashion was changing and, ironically, drawing much closer to what suited the Americans' simpler, more sedate style. Jefferson arrived in Paris on the cusp of a new era that was enveloping the Old World. While fashion and decorum remained rigid at court, in the city of Paris new styles along with new thinking were being tested.

Jefferson was aware of changing fashion and its relationship to politics. In 1787 he wrote, "In Society the *habit habillé* is almost banished and they begin to go even to great supper in frock." But this was in Parisian society, not at court. He observed that "the court and diplomatic corps however must always be excepted. They are too high to be reached by any improvement." He grasped the significance of this fashion change and continued, "They are the last refuge from which etiquette, formality and folly will be driven. Take away these and they would be on a level with other people."[51]

The "frock" was taking the place of the traditional formal dress suit, the *habit habillé,* and in Jefferson's estimation this was an improvement, as he recognized dressing down as emblematic of a leveling of society.[52]

The frock (or *frac,* in the French spelling) was a man's coat that defied the traditional currents of fashion. The "trickle-down theory" held that clothing styles moved from the elites to the middling and lower levels of society. Through the years the term "frock" had been applied to a variety of men's outer garments, but by the beginning of the eighteenth century a "frock" generally referred to the coat worn by men of England's working classes. Country gentlemen began adapting it for their wardrobes for informal wear and especially for sporting occasions. To a contemporary eye it was distinguishable from the formal dress coat by the loose cut of the body, its lack of trim, and the use of utilitarian fabrics. The most recognizable feature was the turndown collar, which served the practical function of protecting the throat against the weather. As the frock coat gained popularity and acceptability among the gentry, the fit became more exact, requiring finer wool adaptable for tailoring, but the coat retained its turndown collar. By the 1780s the collar had increased in height to match that of the standing collar of the formal dress coat, but it retained the turndown shape. The sleeves of the frock coat followed the fashionable trend of a slimmer cut with narrow cuffs or a vertical opening at the wrist (see figs. 1, 2, and 3, pp. 13–15).[53]

The frock coat not only had moved from the bottom rungs of society upwards, but it also challenged France's hegemony on fashion as it moved from England to France. It is not surprising, perhaps, that the frock coat became sartorially associated with a shift towards democratic leveling within fashionable society. While this style of coat came to represent the English way of life, it also encompassed social and political thought. An English traveler wrote in 1752 that while visiting Paris and dressed in the formal French style, "I frequently sighed for my little loose Frock, which I look upon as an Emblem of our happy Constitution; for it lays a Man under no uneasy Restraint, but leaves it in his Power to do as he pleases."[54] However, by the end of the century the loss of the American colonies and the revolution against the monarchy in France led some British aristocrats to view the growing informality in dress represented by the frock with skepticism. Lord Glenbervie wrote in his journal of 1794 that "for these last three or four years, if a man has been to Court he cannot go ... to dine out or to an assembly without putting on a frock." He then speculated how this had removed barriers and contributed to "levelling and equalizing notions."[55]

The frock coat was introduced into France by fashion-conscious young men and reflected a more general vogue for things English, from the constitution to the customs of country life. Looking back from 1816 on the pre-revolutionary years, the comte de Ségur reflected in his *memoirs* that "the laws of England were studied and envied by men of a mature age; English horses and jockeys, boots and coats after the English fashion, could alone suit the fancy of young men." It became obvious to Nabby Adams while she still lived in France that "the beaux in this country aim very much at the English dress."[56]

Jefferson wears a frock coat in the one formal portrait that he commissioned of himself while in Europe. The portrait was not considered his best likeness by contemporaries who knew him well, but it remains important in suggesting how Jefferson may have made the transition from provincial gentleman to one suitably fashioned for European society. The portrait, by American artist Mather Brown, was begun in London in the spring of 1786 (fig. 8).[57] Adams had requested that Jefferson join him in the British capital when he believed there was a favorable opportunity for negotiating a commercial treaty with Great Britain and for meeting with emissaries from Portugal and Tripoli as well. Jefferson arrived in early March and stayed through mid-April. Unfortunately, the diplomatic negotiations proved less than successful, yet Jefferson seized the opportunity to explore London's shops and theatres and to join Adams on a brief excursion into the countryside for a study of English country houses and their gardens.[58] He spent approximately six weeks absorbing London and its culture.

When the Adams family arrived in London in late May 1785, Mather Brown, a native of Boston, was establishing himself in the London art market. Nabby Adams referenced the family's portraits being taken during their first summer in London in a letter to her brother, John Quincy. She wrote, "What a rage for Painting has taken Possession of the Whole family. One of our rooms has been occupied by a Gentleman of this profession, for near a forghtnight, and we have the extreme felicity of looking at ourselves upon Canvass." She identified Brown by quoting an excerpt from the London newspaper: "The paper yesterday had this paragraph, 'Sir J. Reynolds is employd in takeing a portrait of Lady Dungannon. Copely and Brown are exerting their skill upon their illustrious Country Man Mr. Adams the American Ambassador.'" Nabby goes on to speculate, "I expect it will be next that Mr. Brown is painter to the American Ambassadors family. He has been

FIGURE 8. Thomas Jefferson by Mather Brown, 1786.

The original of this portrait was commissioned by Jefferson when he served as American minister to France. Jefferson's hair and clothing show him appropriately attired for European society,
although the coat's turndown collar defines it as a daytime frock and not what he would have
worn to court.

very solicitous to have a likeness of Pappa, thinking it would be an advantage to him, and Pappa Consented."[59] This indicated some public curiosity surrounding this new minister arrived in London to represent what had been British colonies, even though Sir Joshua Reynolds, the more highly acclaimed artist, was busy with a portrait of Lady Dungannon, and it was the transplanted American artists who were seeking Adams's patronage.

By the time of Jefferson's visit, Brown had painted John Adams, Abigail, and Nabby, and thus it is likely that Jefferson was introduced to Brown through the Adams family. It turned into a dual commission for the young artist. In addition to his own portrait, Jefferson commissioned an original of Adams, and Adams in turn requested copies of both portraits.[60] The extant portrait of Jefferson held by the National Portrait Gallery in Washington is the one that was owned by the Adams family, while the whereabouts of Jefferson's version is unknown. It never made his list of portraits that hung at Monticello, whereas his portrait of Adams hung first in the Hôtel de Langeac then took a respectful place in Jefferson's collection following his return to the United States.

Brown depicts Jefferson as elegant, exhibiting a definite European flare in clothing and grooming while surrounded with objects that placed him within a context of republican ideology. The coat in Brown's portrait appears likely to be a French version of the frock. A former curator of the Musée de la Mode et du Costume in Paris, Madeleine Delpierre, identified the French *frac* as a "[man's] coat in the English style, informal, loose-fitting, and without buttons or pockets."[61] Pockets are not visible on Jefferson's seated figure, and while the coat does have buttons, they are quite inconspicuous, as they are small and of the same color as the coat. Common to the English version of the frock in the 1780s were flat, decorative metal buttons reaching below the waist and positioned at the sleeve, either in a vertical row or edging the top of a small cuff, as in Brown's companion portrait of John Adams, completed in 1788 (fig. 9).[62] The strongest evidence that Jefferson preferred the French *frac* appears in his own accounting records. His entries indicate that he continued to purchase his coats only from Parisian tailors, while he began adding other garments tailored in London to his wardrobe.

Shortly after his arrival in the British capital he sat up an account with London tailor Robert Cannon. Extant invoices from Cannon show purchases of waistcoats and breeches. In fact, it is possible that the elegant white-and-gold-striped waistcoat Jefferson wears in the Brown portrait was made by Cannon, as his invoice of March 14, 1786, three days after

FIGURE 9. John Adams by Mather Brown, 1788.

Brown's portraits of Adams and Jefferson exemplify the differences in British versus French men's fashion. Adams's portrait compliments Jefferson with its display of *Notes on the State of Virginia* as a part of the setting.

Jefferson's arrival in London, included a charge for "making a waistcoat Silk Strip'd Compleat" along with two pair of breeches. The choice of stripes demonstrated fashion awareness, whether on the part of Jefferson or his London tailor, as the curvilinear shapes of the rococo were giving way to the straight lines of the neoclassic. Jefferson continued to order waistcoats and breeches from Cannon during the remainder of his stay in London and even after his return to Paris, but the orders never included coats.[63]

Brown depicts Jefferson's hair dressed and heavily powdered in a style that reflects the formality of French court society. Jefferson's accounts show no evidence that he purchased wigs, even though he was not fond of the process involved in attaining the appropriate hair dressing for court and social appearances. His annoyance was repeated by Abigail Adams to a relative in New England, as she wrote, "His Hair too is an other affliction which he is tempted to cut off. He expects not to live above a Dozen years and he shall lose one of those in hair dressing."[64] Despite his inclinations, it would be many years before Jefferson would indeed crop his hair. While in France he abided by protocol, and even though his accounts show no purchases of wigs, they do show regular reimbursements to his *valet de chambre* for "apparatus for shaving & combing" and the "papers" and "pomatum" that were needed for dressing the hair and grooming.[65] These expenditures begin appearing in his accounting records shortly after his arrival and continue through his years in Paris.

During his stay in London, hair dressing and shaving duties must have fallen to the French servant traveling with him, Adrien Petit. There are no entries for shaving and hairdressing in Jefferson's accounts while in the city, but when he and Adams were on their tour of the English countryside and gardens, he paid a hairdresser. Perhaps Petit remained in London. If indeed Petit was acting as personal servant, it could account for Brown picturing Jefferson's hair more in keeping with the French style. The artist shows the hair dressed higher and more heavily powdered than that of Adams's in the companion portrait.

The Jefferson in Brown's portrait appears quite European in dress and grooming, and it is left to other elements to suggest republican ideals. The figure holds a lengthy parchment on which Brown indicated writing, although other than the artist's signature and date, it was not intended to be legible. Such a prop was often used to signify someone learned or involved in statecraft. This was appropriate to Jefferson's current position as international envoy engaged in diplomatic affairs. A more overtly republican symbol is the statue of the Goddess of Liberty that stands behind Jefferson's left shoulder, identifiable by her classical dress and the staff supporting the *pileus,* or liberty cap.

This symbol of *libertas* dates from the classical world and became a popular icon in Europe and the American colonies after Johann Joachim Winckelmann published his archaeological findings in *Versuch einer Allegorie* (1766). Winckelmann describes Roman rituals freeing slaves from bondage in which the slave would be touched by the staff and then given the cap, a symbol of freedom. By the mid-eighteenth century, images of the goddess with staff and cap or just the cap and staff alone began to appear on both sides of the Atlantic. When Franklin, Adams, and Jefferson were tasked with designing the Great Seal of the United States in July 1776, the Goddess of Liberty with staff and cap was included in all their proposals. Although their designs were not adopted, the goddess was incorporated into the Great Seal of Virginia.[66]

In Mather Brown's dual portraits, Adams, like Jefferson, is shown with a sheaf of papers and is seated in front of a deep red drape, although the Goddess of Liberty is replaced with books. The title on the spine of one volume clearly reads *Jefferson's / Hist. Of / Virginia*. When the Adams family left France for their new post in London, Jefferson had presented them with a copy of his recently published *Notes on the State of Virginia*. Adams predicted that *Notes* would bring honor to both the author and his country. The obvious reference to the work in the Adams portrait was a testimonial to viewers of Jefferson's contribution to Enlightenment literature. As Jefferson's initial sitting for Mather Brown took place the year before Adams began publication of his lengthy work *A Defence of the Constitutions of Government of the United States of America*, he could be excused for not reciprocating the gesture.

Jefferson had to wait two years to receive his own portrait and the portrait of Adams from Brown. As the Adams family prepared to return to the United States, Jefferson's correspondence with Adams's son-in-law, William Stephens Smith, became more anxious. "Remember Mr. Adam's [*sic*] picture," Jefferson wrote Smith. "When they shall be ready, I would wish to receive them with my own which Mr. Brown has." Shortly thereafter Jefferson wrote again: "I must remind you also of Mr. Adams's picture, as I should be much mortified should I not get it done before he leaves Europe."

In March 1788 Jefferson no doubt was pleased to hear from Smith that Brown had begun the Adams portrait: "Brown is busy about the pictures." But he would not have appreciated the rest of the message: "Mr. Adams is like. Yours I do not think so well of." Jefferson's secretary William Short agreed with Smith's opinion that the "picture by Brown of Mr. Adams is an excellent likeness; that of Mr. Jefferson is supposed by everybody here to be an étude." In September 1788 Jefferson wrote that "the pictures are received in good condition" but made no further comment.[67]

Brown's portrait of Adams may have been hurriedly done, but it was considered a good likeness by those who knew him well. Adams's matching coat and waistcoat, subdued in color and displaying large metal buttons, reflect English fashion preferences. The high collar of the frock coat and the slim sleeve with a vertical vent in the narrow cuff portray Adams in keeping with the trend. The ruffle attached to the front of Adams's shirt is far less elaborate than the double-fluted ruffle shown in Jefferson's portrait, but judging from the ruffle circling his wrist, it was of very fine, lightweight linen. The wrist-ruffle is edged with narrow lace, which adds to the appearance of quality. His hairdressing (or wig) is formal, but in being dressed closer to the head and powdered only to a grey tone, it appears more conservative than Jefferson's. In fact, these companion portraits allow a comparison of the subtleties in men's clothing, accessories, and hairdressing that distinguished the French style from the English.

Jefferson was building a collection of portraits, and Brown's portrait of Adams was an essential addition. Jefferson was clear in his intent for this portrait, stating, "I wish to add it to those of other principal American characters which I have or shall have."[68] He would later refer to this collection as his "American Worthies."[69] It would consist of images of men notable for their contributions to the formation of the American republic from settlement to nationhood. Jefferson's enjoyment of art was balanced with a didactic purpose, for the collection he was building not only would present the face of American history, it would also serve political purposes.

He was following a well-established European tradition that traced back to the classical world. "Pantheons of Worthies"—collections of sculpted bust portraits of heroes, rulers, and military leadership—were displayed, generally in public spaces. With the advent of Renaissance humanism, sculpted busts were often joined by portraits on canvas, but such paintings retained the responsibility of depicting virtue and character. The growth and spread of Enlightenment thought enlarged the influence of men of science and letters, and so they began to take their places in the pantheon as well. An eighteenth-century "worthy" should display a sense of civic virtue, placing the public interest above his own. The painted and sculpted portraits were commemorative, yet they also incorporated a belief in the positive influence such depictions might exercise upon the future. In this respect they became a form of persuasion, even propaganda, when exposed to a broader audience.[70]

In his early eighteenth-century work *Essay on the Theory of Painting*, Jonathan Richardson observes that "to sit for one's picture, is to have an abstract of one's life written, and published, and ourselves thus consigned over to honour or infamy." He muses, "I know not what influence this has, or may have, but methinks 'tis rational to believe that pictures of this kind are subservient to virtue: that men are excited to imitate the good actions, and persuaded to shun the vices of those whose examples are thus set before them." Portrait artists thus faced greater expectations, as Richardson maintained that achieving a likeness was not enough. "A portrait painter must understand mankind, and enter into their characters, and express their minds as well as their faces."[71] Therefore, following Richardson's thinking, portraits could join the more prestigious history paintings as a genre capable of public persuasion.

Jefferson began his collection as he was preparing to leave the United States for Europe with a hurriedly commissioned portrait of George

FIGURE 10. George Washington by Joseph Wright and John Trumbull, 1784–86.

Jefferson commissioned this portrait of Washington shortly before leaving for Europe and carried it unfinished to Paris, where it was later completed by John Trumbull. This was a key portrait in his collection of "American Worthies" at the Hôtel de Langeac and was displayed in the dining room.

FIGURE 11. Benjamin Franklin, copy attributed to Jean Valade after original by Joseph-Siffred Duplessis, c. 1786.

Jefferson thought he was purchasing an original of Franklin by Jean-Baptiste Greuze, but this work is one of the many copies made of Duplessis's famous fur-collar portrait. Duplessis's portrait was first exhibited in the Paris salon of 1779 and became a lasting image of Franklin. Jefferson's copy joined his collection of worthies in Paris and later occupied a position in the top tier of paintings in Monticello's parlor.

Washington from American artist Joseph Wright, who was working in Philadelphia (fig. 10). Wright had time to complete the head only and to indicate drapery before Jefferson sailed for Paris. The background and Washington's uniform were completed two years later by another American artist, John Trumbull, during a visit with Jefferson in Paris.[72] Soon after his arrival in Paris, Jefferson obtained a fine copy of the well-known portrait of Benjamin Franklin by Joseph-Siffred Duplessis, which he purchased from French painter and art dealer Jean Valade (fig. 11).[73]

His collection began to extend beyond just American revolutionary heroes to include those who had in some way affected the history of the New World. From the Uffizi in Florence he acquired copies of painted portraits of the early explorers who had made first contact with the New World. These acquisitions were negotiated by his former Virginia neighbor Philip Mazzei, who had since returned to his native Italy. Jefferson was satisfied with the works he received and wrote, "I was much gratified to receive yesterday [January 11, 1789] from Italy the portraits of Columbus, Americus Vespuciu[s], Cortez, and Magellan." He continued, "Observing by the list of the pictures in the gallery of the Grand duke at Florence that these were there, I sent to have them copied. They appear to be well done."[74] On his tour of the English countryside with John Adams in 1786, he saw a portrait of the early colonizer of Virginia, Sir Walter Raleigh, in Birmingham. Jefferson used Adams's son-in-law, William Stephens Smith, to act as his agent in securing a copy.[75] These portraits told more of the American story, and he believed it important that the history be visually preserved. Several years after the commission of these portraits, he explained that "I considered it as even of some public concern that our country should not be without the portraits of its first discoverers."[76]

He expanded his collection by adding the Enlightenment thinkers that he admired most. Jefferson was adamant that he could not leave Europe without portraits of "the three greatest men that have ever lived, without any exception": Francis Bacon, John Locke, and Isaac Newton. He commissioned copies of the portraits of them that hung in London's Royal Society. John Trumbull served as his agent in London and saw the commissions executed.[77]

To these canvases Jefferson added a series of very fine sculpted bust portraits. He became acquainted with the acclaimed French sculptor Jean-Antoine Houdon when charged by the Virginia legislature to arrange for a full-length statue of Washington and a bust of Lafayette for the state capitol. Soon after his arrival in Paris, he determined that Houdon was deemed by many as "the first statuary in the world."[78] He met with the artist and convinced him to make the Atlantic crossing to take Washington's portrait from life. Franklin supported the choice, and the two men sailed on the same ship to the United States in July 1785, where Houdon hoped to be engaged for an equestrian monument of Washington in addition to the life-sized sculpture for Virginia.[79] His willingness to make the ocean crossing

FIGURE 12. Turgot (*left*) and Voltaire (*right*), modern copies after Jean-Antoine Houdon. Plaster, originals 1775 (Turgot) and 1778 (Voltaire).

Jefferson admired these two giants of the French Enlightenment: Voltaire, philosopher and writer; and Turgot, economist, writer, and French finance minister. He added these bust portraits by Houdon to his Paris collection, and a floorplan of Monticello created years later by his granddaughter Cornelia Jefferson Randolph showed them in prominent positions, standing on either side of the doorway into Monticello's entrance hall, where these modern plaster copies stand today.

speaks to a continued interest in American revolutionaries and indicates in particular Washington's reputation in the Western world.

Houdon fulfilled his Virginia commission for the full-sized statue of Washington and the bust of Lafayette. He sculpted other American revolutionary figures as well, including John Paul Jones and Franklin, and he completed a bust of Washington. Jefferson acquired plaster copies of these for himself along with a copy of the Lafayette. To these revolutionary figures Jefferson added copies of Houdon's busts of important French enlightenment thinkers Turgot and Voltaire (fig. 12).

His own portrait was taken by Houdon early in 1789 before he left Paris to return to America (fig. 13). The resulting bust portrait was exhibited at the Paris salon that opened on August 25, 1789, almost a month exactly before Jefferson's departure from Paris on September 26. This allowed

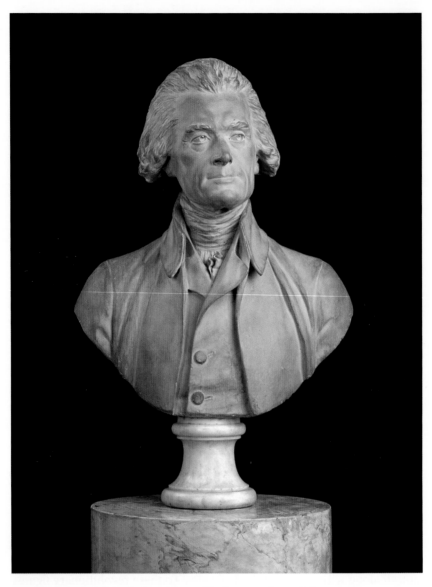

FIGURE 13. *Thomas Jefferson* by Jean-Antoine Houdon, 1789. Original plaster.

Thomas Jefferson at age forty-three, while serving as American minister plenipotentiary to France. This bust by the French sculptor Jean-Antoine Houdon has proved a lasting prototype for the Jefferson image.

Jefferson an opportunity to view his sculpted image on display and read the salon review that congratulated Houdon on an excellent likeness; it stated, "M. Houdon . . . distinguished himself in the portrait of M. Jefferson, expressing his lively and witty character."[80] Jefferson was not usually described as "lively and witty," although Houdon was noted for capturing expression. He gives Jefferson a faint smile and lifts his gaze above the viewer and off into the distance. From a remark made by Jefferson many years later, we can assume that Houdon made a life mask, as he so often did for his portraits. This would support the observations by contemporaries that it was a very good likeness.[81] With Houdon's bust considered the definitive portrait of Jefferson, it is not difficult to see why Jefferson's London friends did not feel that Mather Brown had totally succeeded in capturing the Virginia statesman. In Brown's portrait the forehead and cheeks are not as well defined as in the Houdon, and Brown misses the nuance of expression. However, the two artists agree on the clothing, and both portray him in the French-style frock coat.

At least one Houdon bust of Jefferson and possibly more accompanied his shipment of personal belongings from Paris to Philadelphia after his return to the United States. This bust portrait would become an important image of Jefferson in the early republic and would serve as the prototype for presidential medals. In the twentieth century the Houdon bust was used for the Jefferson profile on American coinage and has proved a lasting image.[82] The fate of Jefferson's Mather Brown portrait of himself remains a mystery. His portrait of John Adams would eventually hang in the parlor at Monticello and was listed in Jefferson's catalog of paintings, along with others that he began collecting in Paris, but there is no mention of his own portrait from Brown.

Jefferson's assemblage of painted and sculpted portraits of worthies told the American story. These likenesses gave faces to the victors in the break with Britain. They were joined by the thinkers and explorers who had laid the foundation for what would become the United States. These were the American heroes whose images served as patriotic propaganda to support and legitimize the American cause. By late summer of 1789 a visitor to the American legation at the Hôtel d'Langeac would have seen much of Jefferson's collection in place, which could have included his own image with his self-commissioned portrait by Mather Brown and a sculpted bust by Houdon.

His collection of art and its celebration of American worthies also served a more personal purpose. It identified him as a man of taste and cosmopolitan culture, a man who could claim to be an enlightened thinker. These characteristics would continue to play a role in his public image and identity as a connoisseur. Jefferson styled himself in correspondence as the "savage from America," but the portraits by Mather Brown and Houdon show this savage with a decided European flare in dress and grooming. The work of another young American artist would record Jefferson looking very much the American patriot. On his trip to London in March 1786, Jefferson met John Trumbull.

2

REMEMBERING THE REVOLUTION

Before Jefferson was a diplomat, he was a revolutionary—a radical thinker and writer. He might have been willing to temper his personal image to suit the needs of his courtly duties and to gain entry into intellectual circles, but he never compromised his belief in the importance of the American Revolution and the republican system of governance it produced. He maintained, "I have no fear that the result of our experiment will be that men may be trusted to govern themselves without a master." In the summer of 1789 he became excited by the events that were sweeping Paris—the storming of the Bastille and the calling of the Estates-General to address France's worsening financial crisis. The old order in France was being challenged to change. Jefferson was encouraged by what he saw happening and believed that the revolution in America could prove a model and inspiration for others to follow. He always upheld his belief that "the inquiry which has been excited among the mass of mankind by our revolution & its consequences will ameliorate the condition of man over a great portion of the globe."[1]

It was essential to keep alive the accomplishments of 1776 if the American Revolution was to be upheld as the model for change. Jefferson must have recognized an excellent opportunity for a visual memorial to the revolution when he met the American artist John Trumbull in London in March 1786. Trumbull was engaged in a series of history paintings based on scenes from the colonies' struggle with Britain. Jefferson was supportive of Trumbull's work, and an exchange began between Jefferson the statesman and Trumbull the artist that both men hoped would persuade the world of the importance of the American struggle for independence. If successful, these works of art might serve as well to remind their viewers of Jefferson's and Trumbull's own participation in that struggle and so contribute to their personal legacy.

"The Declaration of Independence I always considered as a theatrical show. Jefferson ran away with all the stage effect of that . . . and all the glory of it."[2] This was John Adams's memory of the events of 1776, as he reflected on "the theatrical exhibitions of politics." But he wrote from the vantage of the early nineteenth century as he ruminated on what he believed was a public oversight of his own contribution. In 1776 and for the years immediately following, the starring role in this piece of political theatre, to use Adams's metaphor, was still vague. Jefferson was not recognized with the title of "author" of the Declaration of Independence, as would later be inscribed on his gravestone. Yet from July 4, 1776, some years would pass before Jefferson began to gain credit as the primary author of the document that is often cited as the manifesto of the American Revolution.

Jefferson's colleagues did acknowledge his contribution. Benjamin Franklin commiserated with him while his draft was edited by Congress by telling him the story of a hatter who designed an elaborate sign for his hat shop outlining his talents and services only to have it finally reduced by well-meaning critics to his name and the picture of a hat.[3] Jefferson sent his rough draft along with the final copy as passed by Congress to fellow Virginians so that they might decide if "it is better or worse for the Critics." Richard Henry Lee wished that "the Manuscript had not been mangled as it is." He assured Jefferson, "However the *Thing* is in its nature so good, that no Cookery can spoil the Dish for the palates of Freemen." Edmund Pendleton also believed it was "altered much for the worse."[4] Jefferson winced at the editing and rewording of his draft but never let go his belief in the cause it represented—or the desire to have his name attached to the final document.

One of the earliest public references linking Jefferson and the declaration came from a 1783 sermon by Ezra Stiles, a leading Congregationalist minister and the president of Yale College. His address before Connecticut governor Jonathan Trumbull (father of the artist) and the general assembly convened in Hartford reminded Americans of the gratitude they owed to the many defenders of their rights and liberties during their struggle for independence. Stiles listed many names that he identified as the "great characters in the Patriotic Assemblies and Congress," including "Jefferson, who poured the soul of the continent into the monumental act of independence."[5] In this short sentence Stiles links the name "Jefferson" with the critical accomplishment of uniting the "continent" into a cohesive whole through the Declaration of Independence. This sermon was published the year it was given and so reached a broader audience than just the governing body of Connecticut. Stiles sent Jefferson a presentation copy inscribed to "His Excellency Thomas Jefferson American Ambassador and Minister Plenipotentiary of the United States." This important citation of Jefferson's contribution as penman of the declaration reached the American reading public thanks to the printed edition of Stiles's sermon. Jefferson's copy would remain in his library until it joined the other books and printed works he sold to Congress in 1815.[6]

On July 4, 1789, Jefferson was still in Paris, and he hosted a dinner at the American legation attended by a group of resident Americans. He was honored with a speech prepared for the occasion that was directed to the man "who sustained so conspicuous a part in the immortal transactions of that day—whose dignity energy and elegance of thought and expression added a peculiar luster to that declaratory act which announced to the world the existence of an empire."[7] This stopped short of granting him the title as sole author of the declaration, but his participation was "conspicuous." Gradually Jefferson's name was becoming attached to the document and to an event that was gaining iconic stature.

Jefferson was gifted as a writer but not as an orator. John Adams recalled of Jefferson that "during the whole Time I sat with him in Congress, I never heard him utter three sentences together," but he agreed that "Mr. Jefferson had the Reputation of a masterly Pen."[8] Edmund Randolph's *History of Virginia* describes a similar Jefferson: "Without being an overwhelming orator, he was an impressive speaker, who fixed the attention." But, Randolph adds, "his style in writing was more impassioned."[9] Throughout his public life Jefferson was described by both supporters and detractors as soft-spoken and usually reticent in a large group. In the Continental Congress it was John Adams whom Jefferson pronounced "our Colossus on the floor," who possessed "a power of thought & expression, that moved us from our seats."[10] Jefferson's power of thought was put into writing, as his image developed as the literary or "philosophical-statesman."

The radical ideas he put forward in "A Summary View of the Rights of British America," written for Virginia's revolutionary burgesses in 1774, had made their way into print and preceded him to Philadelphia. By the time he arrived at the first Continental Congress, many members were aware of this young Virginian with the fiery rhetoric who reminded King George that he was "no more than the chief officer of the people, appointed by the laws." The king's duty was to work the great machine of government that ultimately was for the people. What the colonists requested were not favors but their rights.[11]

Rhode Island delegate Samuel Ward referenced both Jefferson and his pamphlet, commenting that the newly arrived young Virginian seemed "a very sensible spirited fine Fellow & by the Pamphlet which he wrote last Summer he certainly is one."[12] This was where Jefferson made his mark. His contribution, and hence his future legacy, rested largely in his abilities with the written word, not in debate or public speech. His fame and his place among the Argonauts of the American Revolution were attached to the most notable document coming from the Continental Congress, the Declaration of Independence.

Fame — not necessarily a negative aspiration for a gentleman and a statesman so long as it was countered with moderation and not heavily weighted with an ambition that could be tainted by corruption. Francis Bacon, whom Jefferson named as one of the world's greatest men, wrote in his essay on "Honor and Reputation" that in considering the degrees of honor, the first belongs to the founders of states and commonwealths.[13] The second position belongs to *legislatores,* or lawgivers, as they too are founders and their ordinances remain after them. Jefferson qualified in both categories through his work in the Continental Congress and his subsequent work in revising the laws for his native state of Virginia. But Bacon further suggested that one must never "affect" honor. It must spring from true virtue, and even the appearance of virtue must be tempered. Bacon cautioned that "some, contrariwise, darken their virtue in the show of it, so that they be undervalued in opinion." The Enlightenment man of honor and virtue must walk a very narrow line and establish an exemplary public image, and as Bacon advised, he must also take much care in its promotion. Jefferson would not disregard the advice of a figure that he so openly admired. He respectfully held Bacon's writings in his own library while recommending them to others, and Jefferson attended his advice that ambition must be "bridled." But when he met the artist John Trumbull, he must have recognized an opportunity to memorialize an event important to him personally, an event that could serve as a means to persuade the world of the historic importance of the Declaration of Independence.

John Adams possibly introduced Jefferson to John Trumbull during Jefferson's diplomatic visit to London in the spring of 1786. Trumbull was an aspiring young American artist from Connecticut who was studying painting with the successful Anglo-American artist Benjamin West.[14] Despite a thirteen-year age difference, Trumbull and Jefferson quickly established a friendship. Their mutual interest in the fine arts linked Jefferson the collector and gentleman architect with Trumbull the aspiring professional painter. What seems to have caught Jefferson's attention was Trumbull's enthusiasm for his current undertaking, a series of history paintings based on scenes from the recent Revolutionary War. He recognized Trumbull's talent, certainly, but his dedication to visually memorializing and explaining the events of the revolution especially would have appealed to Jefferson.

Under Benjamin West's tutelage, Trumbull had launched an ambitious project of recording "the History of our country" but in his own "language," that of the brush.[15] He wished to build his reputation as the "patriot-artist" and was well positioned to record these historic scenes, considering that he had participated in the early period of conflict in New England.[16] He borrowed Enlightenment terms to explain his ambitions to Jefferson. Rather than creating art that was "frivolous, little useful to Society," he intended his work "to diffuse the knowledge and preserve the Memory of the noblest series of Actions which have ever dignified the History of Man." Jefferson warmed to Trumbull's enthusiasm. Before leaving London, he extended an invitation to the artist to visit Paris and stay in his home. Ultimately, this shared experience of revolution and a belief in the importance of the American experience would provide a lasting connection between these men.

As a New Englander, Trumbull had observed the Battle of Bunker Hill through a field glass, and, in his own words, he "caught the growing enthusiasm," joined the Continental army, and was soon made an aide-de-camp to General Washington. He became frustrated when Congress was slow to authorize (and then misdated) his field appointment to the rank of colonel. He resigned abruptly and returned to the study of painting; however, he retained his title of colonel.[17] This impatience and quickness to feel that his honor had been slighted would reappear from time to time and would ultimately color his relationship with Jefferson.

Trumbull noted in his journal his impressions of Jefferson. "He had a taste for the fine arts, and highly approved my intention of preparing myself for the accomplishment of a national work. He encouraged me to persevere in this pursuit, and kindly invited me to come to Paris, to see and study the fine works there, and to make his house my home, during my stay."[18] When he met Jefferson, Trumbull was finishing his first two paintings of the series he would call his "national enterprise": *The Death of General Warren at the Battle of Bunker's Hill* and *The Death of General Montgomery at the Battle of Quebec.* He had begun work on a third scene of battle, *The Death of General Mercer at the Battle of Princeton,* before he visited Jefferson in Paris in the summer of 1786.[19]

This choice of subject aimed Trumbull towards the highest tier of painters, those who depicted heroic episodes from history. Trumbull's mentor Benjamin West was among the artists who made this grand style of painting more accessible for contemporary viewers by avoiding classical subject matter and choosing scenes that were still a part of living memory. West had enjoyed acclaim with *The Death of General Wolfe,* which drew from the not-so-distant French and Indian War and the capture of Quebec by the British in 1759. The scene became even more immediate when he dressed his figures in contemporary uniforms while still maintaining a sense of the heroic.[20] Trumbull had chosen the right studio in which to study and develop his talent. He expressed to his brother Jonathan his wish to move beyond the necessity of portrait painting as a means of financial support. He believed that success as a history painter offered freedom from "all the trumpery & caprice & nonsense of mere coping faces—& places me the servant not of Vanity but Virtue."[21] Still, heroic scenes required faces, and he would devote much time and attention to collecting accurate likenesses, clothing details, and suggestions of individual character.

Trumbull took full advantage of Jefferson's invitation to Paris. It came at a time when he was looking for an engraver capable of creating prints from his two completed paintings. Benjamin West had encouraged him to pursue this direction and had put him in contact with an agent, who felt, however, that London did not offer at that time an engraver with the skills necessary to undertake such a high-level project and who suggested that he look abroad. By midsummer 1786 Trumbull was on his way to Paris with his scenes of war.[22]

Jefferson was enthusiastic of Trumbull's talents and the ambitious undertaking of his American Revolution series. He wrote to a friend in Philadelphia, "Our countryman Trumbull is here, a young painter of the most promising talents. He brought with him his Battle of Bunker's hill & Death of Montgomery to have them engraved here, & we may add, to have them sold; for like Dr. Ramsay's history, they are too true to suit the English palate." This comparison to Ramsay's *History of South Carolina* (1785) was a compliment to Trumbull and an indication that Jefferson took seriously his endeavor of recording history with a brush. He encouraged Trumbull to remain a while in Paris then to travel on to Rome for further study, but meanwhile Jefferson opened his house for members of Paris's art circles to view Trumbull's work.[23]

Jefferson appeared genuinely supportive of Trumbull's mission. If successful, his paintings could become a means of preserving key scenes of the revolution and contribute to persuading the world of the importance of these events. Before Jefferson met Trumbull, he had encouraged a French historian, Hilliard d'Auberteuil, to write the history of the American Revolution. Jefferson predicted, "The memory of the American revolution will be immortal and will immortalize those who record it."[24] He may have encouraged Trumbull with this same thought.

Upon returning to London that November, Trumbull directed his energy towards a new composition for a painting he would title *The Declaration of Independence*. The young Trumbull acknowledged Jefferson's contribution to the concept for this painting: "During my visit, I began the composition of the Declaration of Independence, with the assistance of his information and advice." Jefferson drew a diagram from memory of the hall in which the Congress had met while debating the issue of separation from Great Britain. On the extant pen-and-ink drawing, Trumbull noted, "Done by Mr. Jefferson—Paris 1786: to convey an Idea of the Room in which congress sat, at the Declaration of Independence on the ground floor of the old state house in Philadelphia." Trumbull added a preliminary pencil sketch that he labeled "first idea of Declaration of Independence, Paris, Sept. 1786."[25] Many years later, in 1817, he acknowledged again Jefferson's participation: "You recollect the Composition, which you kindly assisted me to sketch at Chaillot [Jefferson's Paris address]."[26]

With Jefferson's encouragement, Trumbull moved from depicting battles scenes to considering an important moment in statecraft. The subject of the presentation of the Declaration of Independence was quite a change from the physical action of battles, and it challenged the artist to express a quieter drama, yet nevertheless one filled with intense emotions and impact of outcome. In his preeminent eighteenth-century work *The Theory of Painting*, Jonathan Richardson advises that a "historical picture" must be "a representation of one single point of time."[27] The moment Trumbull chose to depict was that of the declaration committee standing before the president of the Continental Congress, ready to submit their draft. The title he gave

FIGURE 14. Study for *The Declaration of Independence, July 4, 1776*, John Trumbull, 1787–1820.

This became Trumbull's most notable painting from his Revolutionary War series. He credited Jefferson as assisting with this initial study in 1787 and wrote that it was begun in the library of Jefferson's Paris residence.

the painting, *The Declaration of Independence, July 4, 1776* (fig. 14), contradicts the moment he chose. The draft was presented to Congress on Friday, June 28; the debates began the following week, and the final draft was ratified on the 4th.[28] Still, if this had been a real stage piece (as in the analogy used by Adams), it would have been the turning point in the play towards the climax and dramatic resolution, as Congress moved through the debates and to the vote that bound the colonies into a single unit that would strive for independence from Great Britain. The moment offered drama to the painting, and in Trumbull's composition Jefferson held center stage.

Back in London, Trumbull began work on the configuration of this new painting. His journal recorded that he "arranged carefully the composition for the Declaration of Independence, and prepared it for receiving the portraits, as I might meet with the distinguished men, who were present at that illustrious scene." His first opportunity came as the Adams family prepared to return to the United States. He wrote, "In the course of the summer of 1787, Mr. Adams took leave of the court of St. James, and preparatory to the voyage to America, had the powder combed out of his hair. Its color and natural curl were beautiful, and I took that opportunity to paint his portrait in the small Declaration of Independence."[29]

Jefferson's portrait was painted directly into the study during Trumbull's second visit to Paris in the autumn of that year. Unfortunately, he made no comment on Jefferson's appearance as he had Adams's, but he did depict him with his red hair neither powdered nor formally dressed.[30] Trumbull's Jefferson and Adams look considerably different from their images in the Mather Brown portraits; most importantly, they no longer appear as diplomats prepared for a European court. In Trumbull's final study Franklin stands at Jefferson's left, and his hair is worn in what had become his trademark style, loose and falling to his shoulders. Adams stands to Jefferson's right, and Roger Sherman and Robert Livingston stand slightly behind the three lead figures and complete the group. Their fellow congressmen, soberly dressed in neutral-hued suits not inappropriate in style for 1776, watch the presentation. Many of them appear to have their hair modestly dressed and powdered, which affords a degree of difference with the figures in the central group. Trumbull does not comment on this difference, but as he was so taken with the effect of Adams hair on the eve of the statesman's return to America, he must have been aware that the manner in which the hair was portrayed made a statement, even if subtle.

Trumbull gives these three figures prominent positions within his composition, but Jefferson stands at the center of the focal group. He is the tallest figure, and Trumbull casts him in the key role of handing the document to the president of the Congress, John Hancock. To further insure that this important gesture of presenting the document is not overlooked, Trumbull dresses Jefferson in a red waistcoat and breeches, while the other figures—even Adams and Franklin—are in neutral or dark tones. Color palette, positioning the figure, and gesture all work to draw the eye to the image of Thomas Jefferson.

Trumbull adds focus to this central group by having most of the other figures gaze in their direction. An interesting exception, however, shows a group of three men in the back plane of the picture. They appear to be engaged in discussion with a man in a broad-brimmed Quaker hat. The identity of this man in the hat and his relationship to the drama taking place have remained a mystery, although a possible candidate is John Dickinson of Pennsylvania, as noted by Trumbull biographer Irma Jaffe.[31] Dickinson was a member of the Quaker sect and was remembered for his refusal to sign the declaration. Just as the theme of the painting itself seems a seed planted by Jefferson, could this small subplot have been a suggestion as well? Jefferson harbored some resentment at Dickinson's stand on reconciliation with the mother country and believed that Dickinson had managed to postpone independence for at least a year. In his autobiography, begun in 1821, he wrote that some patriots had "stopped at the half-way house of John Dickinson who admitted that England had a right to regulate our commerce, and to lay duties on it for the purposes of regulation, but not of raising revenue."[32]

Jefferson eventually made his peace with Dickinson, but the Quaker sect as a whole he held suspect. He reviewed his thoughts on Quakers in an 1817 letter and maintained that they were "foreign to the land they live in . . . implicitly devoted to the will of their Superior and forgetting all duties to their country." His suspicions revolved around the location of the "mother-society" of the sect, which was in England. This made him question where they might actually place their allegiance in times of conflict. But he concluded that, all in all, "they are . . . silent, passive, and give no other trouble." He would later enjoy friendships with individual Quakers, and he and Dickinson eventually engaged in cordial correspondence.[33] These suspicions would have been far fresher when Trumbull visited him in Paris in 1786 as they planned the painting in the library of Jefferson's Paris home.

A subject for a second painting was apparently discussed in Jefferson's Paris library. Trumbull returned to his London studio with yet another idea for his series. As he worked at completing his composition for the *Declaration,* he began a study for the *Surrender of Cornwallis at Yorktown* (fig. 15). No journal entry indicates how he decided on this theme. Jefferson could hardly have offered the same level of counseling as he provided for the *Declaration,* since he was not present at the British surrender on the Yorktown battlefield on October 19, 1781. Nevertheless, the scene would have held special interest for Jefferson. It visually upheld the importance of the American-French alliance, and it related directly to the lowest and most humiliating point of his public career, his position as Virginia's wartime governor during the invasion of the state by the British forces in the spring of 1781.[34]

A consequence of the invasion was the scrambled retreat of the Virginia legislature from the capital at Richmond, first to Charlottesville and then into the Blue Ridge Mountains. Governor Jefferson was accused of incompetence, and some critics labeled him a coward. In the flight from

FIGURE 15. Study for *The Surrender of Lord Cornwallis at Yorktown, October 19, 1781,* John Trumbull, 1787–c. 1826.

Jefferson could not offer Trumbull firsthand advice on this scene, but he did have an emotional investment. The British invasion of Virginia marked the low point of his tenure as governor and continued to haunt him throughout his life. The surrender at Yorktown ended the British occupation and restored some credibility to the former governor. Trumbull considered the individual studies of the French officers made for this series during his second visit to Jefferson in Paris as among his best small portraits.

Charlottesville towards the mountains, Jefferson did not join the retreating legislators. He considered that his term as governor had ended, so he gave precedence to conducting his family to safety at his holdings in southern Virginia.

He received the news from good friend Archibald Cary of Staunton, Virginia, where the rump legislature was in session, that there was to be an inquiry into his conduct as governor over the past year. Cary was sure that Jefferson would acquit himself well and that "it will give you no Pain." Cary was very wrong on this count. The proposed reprimand stung the sensitive Jefferson deeply and followed him the rest of his life. With the success of the American and French forces at Yorktown and safety restored to Virginia, the remonstrance against Jefferson subsided quickly. The charges were dropped and rather Jefferson was voted an official "Resolution of Thanks."[35]

Even though he was publically vindicated, Jefferson's fleeing Monticello before the British dragoons, coupled with the implications of cowardice and irresponsibility, provided a story that was continually referenced by his political opponents. During the presidential election of 1800, a critic questioned how his firmness could be trusted "when we recollect him flying through Virginia, before an handful of British horse."[36] The other line of criticism was that Jefferson had not acted fast enough in calling up the Virginia militia. Whether warranted or not, it became a part of his public image. Late in life he still worried about how this episode might threaten his honor and legacy.[37]

Trumbull's *Surrender of Cornwallis* illustrates that this Continental victory had not been accomplished with the Virginia militia alone, which as governor was all Jefferson could call upon, and he was restricted even in that. The artist included the most prestigious French and American officers, shown on horseback in facing lines; the French appear to the viewer's left, the Americans to the right, as they define the space for the surrender. Behind the officers Trumbull shows a line of British troops stretching back to the horizon. This invading army was not just a band of British horse, as some critics claimed, that could have been easily contained with prompt action on the part of the governor.[38] It had taken a large and well-armed military force under superior leadership to thwart the British invasion of Virginia. Jefferson would have favored as well the visual reminder of the support the French provided in the American cause for independence. He did not want this alliance forgotten. The victory at Yorktown moved forward negotiations for peace and hastened the conclusion of the War of Independence. The action that began with the Declaration of Independence culminated at Yorktown with the surrender of Cornwallis. They were appropriate companion paintings, and Jefferson's reputation connected in conflicting ways to each scene.

The objective of Trumbull's second trip to Paris was to begin collecting the images of the French officers who were present at Yorktown and to add Jefferson's portrait to his study for the *Declaration*. He wrote Jefferson, asking him "to inform me at what season I shall most probably meet the principal Officers who serv'd in America, at Paris. I shall soon be ready to paint my picture of the surrender of York Town, and must then come to paris. I suppose the winter is the most certain time of meeting them." Jefferson had extended more than one invitation for Trumbull's visit and fully expected him in August for the prestigious biannual Paris art salon. Earlier in the year he had promised, "Your apartment will expect you, and that you become a part of our family again." As the salon opened, he tempted Trumbull with a list of the artwork and the opinion that "the best thing is the Death of Socrates by David."[39] However, Trumbull did not arrive in Paris until December, when he was better assured of meeting with the French officers who had been at Yorktown. He immediately began collecting portraits and recorded the results in his journal: "I regard these as the best of my small portraits; they were painted from the life, in Mr. Jefferson's house."[40] In gratitude for his interest and support, Trumbull promised Jefferson an oil study of the Yorktown scene, though he would not be able to fulfill his offer until after both men had returned to the United States.[41]

Yorktown saved Virginia from a prolonged occupation by the British army and brought to closure the invasion that caused Jefferson humiliation as wartime governor. The surrender illustrated in a fine painting offered an exorcism of Jefferson's lowest moment and a balm for the most lasting damage to his public image of any single episode. Eventually Trumbull's oil study would be given a place among the paintings in Monticello's parlor.

From the portrait of Jefferson that stood central in his *Declaration of Independence,* Trumbull created a series of miniatures that placed Jefferson's image among European friends and with his own family. Trumbull called his small studies "miniatures," although generally they measured approximately 3 × 4 inches and were painted in oil on wood panels. The miniatures popular in this era were more often smaller and could be worn on the person; the favored medium was watercolor on ivory. But the intent was the same. These small portraits were personal, intimate, and not intended for public display (fig. 16).[42] Thus, Trumbull's miniatures of Jefferson would not have contributed to his public image, although they were available to a select but prestigious audience in Britain, and they underscore a distinction in the differences in style between European elites and Americans, even well-dressed Americans.

These miniatures were created as gifts for two women in Trumbull and Jefferson's mutual circle of friends, and the third was presented to Jefferson's eldest daughter, Martha. Trumbull introduced Jefferson to Maria Cosway and Angelica Schuyler Church, who were themselves close friends. Trumbull had met artist Maria and her husband, Richard Cosway (also an artist), while in Paris in the summer of 1786 and had in turn introduced Jefferson

FIGURE 16. Miniature portraits of Thomas Jefferson by John Trumbull, for Maria Cosway (*top left*), Angelica Schuyler Church (*top right*), and Martha Jefferson (*bottom*), 1788. Oil on wood, 4 in. × 3¼ in.

Trumbull painted these three small portraits for women close to Jefferson. Maria Cosway and Angelica Schuyler Church both lived in London, and Trumbull gave them each a Jefferson appropriate for a European audience. The third portrait, for daughter Martha, makes an interesting contrast, as Jefferson looks more American with his hair casually dressed and unpowdered.

to the couple. An instant attraction sparked between Maria Cosway and Jefferson. The nature of their relationship has remained a mystery, but they maintained a correspondence throughout their lives.[43] She kept Trumbull's miniature of Jefferson, and it accompanied her to her last home in Lodi, Italy.[44] Angelica Church was an American by birth who was living in London with her British husband, John Barker Church, whom Trumbull first met during the revolution. Trumbull had escorted Mrs. Church to Paris, where her daughter Katherine entered the exclusive boarding school attended by Jefferson's daughters. The circle of friends widened to the next generation as the daughters became good friends and continued a correspondence for many years. These relationships would be complicated by the political animosity that developed in the 1790s, when Jefferson and Alexander Hamilton, Angelica Church's brother-in-law, became political adversaries, but in the late autumn of 1787 all this lay ahead.

Trumbull must have shown his study for the *Declaration of Independence* to Maria Cosway, as she wrote Jefferson, "Will you give Mr. Trumbull leave to make a Coppy of a certain portrait he painted at Paris?" Impatient, she wrote again the following month: "I cannot announce the portrait of a friend of mine in my Study yet, Trumbull puts me out of all patience."[45] Her study was on the upper floor of the Cosway's house in London, where she displayed to either side of the fireplace small paintings and drawings of her most intimate friends.[46] The sharing of portraits with close friends or acquaintances was a practice that distinguished the intimate portrait from the formal portrait. The audience might be limited, but Cosway's circle was a very mixed group that included the socially elite of London, who could form an opinion of the American diplomat by what they saw in Trumbull's painting.

Perhaps it was with this group in mind that Trumbull created a Jefferson groomed quite differently from the figure standing at the center of the study for the *Declaration of Independence*. Cosway's portrait shows Jefferson in a dark frock coat that resembles the English style with its large metal buttons; it is worn over a buff-colored waistcoat. The most notable difference is in the formal styling of his hair, which appears heavily powdered, quite similar to that in the Mather Brown portrait.

Angelica Church admitted, "Mr. Trumbull has given us each a picture of you. Mrs. Cosway's is a better likeness than mine, but then, I have a better elsewhere and so I console myself."[47] She may have retained a vivid mental image of Jefferson in heart and mind, but if we compare the small paintings that Trumbull presented to each woman, it is obvious that Cosway's bears a stronger resemblance to the sketch taken from life. The set of the mouth, the shape of the chin, and the averted yet focused gaze more closely replicate the likeness captured by Trumbull in his initial study. But the fashionable cut of the coat and the formally dressed and powdered hair are notably similar in the small paintings for Cosway and Church.

The portrait that Trumbull created for Jefferson's daughter depicts a different Jefferson. Trumbull must have given thought to the probability that at some point Martha Jefferson's portrait of her father would return to the United States, where viewers would be evaluating the image quite differently. Trumbull paints him in a dark frock coat, again in the English style but here double-breasted with large brass buttons; beneath it is a buff waistcoat worn over an underwaistcoat of light blue. The clothing is very stylish; however, the hair is not formally dressed, and given its definite red cast, it was obviously not heavily powdered. Although it appears it may be pulled back into the traditional queue, the sides are loose rather than formed into tight curls, while the crown is left low and smooth. The facial features are not as well developed as those of the Cosway-Church miniatures, as the nose is defined with a linear shadow and the mouth is not as detailed, especially compared to that of Cosway's portrait. The brushwork is sketchy, as though the work was executed quickly, but this gives the likeness a spontaneity absent in the other two. A feeling of openness is conveyed by the frontal positioning of the body—only the head is turned in a three-quarter profile.[48] It is interesting that the pose is very close to that of the Mather Brown portrait, as though Trumbull were suggesting that he could have done better, especially in likeness.

This could have been prompted by Jefferson's hesitation in commissioning a formal, life-sized portrait from Trumbull. When Brown had not yet begun Adams's portrait and the date for the family's departure was drawing closer, Jefferson's anxiety was met with the suggestion from mutual acquaintances in London that perhaps Trumbull should take the portrait. Jefferson wrote immediately, "With respect to Mr. Adams's picture, I must again press it to be done by Brown, because Trumbul does not paint of the size of the life, and could not be asked to hazard himself on it."[49] Jefferson's reservations are curious, as he seemed confident of Trumbull's abilities. He commented in a letter to Ezra Stiles, "Mr. Trumbull has paid us a visit here, and brought with him two pictures which are the admiration of the Connoisseurs. His natural talents for this art seem almost unparalleled."[50] The two pictures he referenced would have been the depictions of the Battle of Bunker Hill and the death of Montgomery at Quebec, but these were studies. To this point all Jefferson had seen of Trumbull's work were his small portraits, nothing the size of life. He particularly wanted a formal portrait of Adams and may have been aware that due to a vision loss in one eye, Trumbull was handicapped when working on a large scale.[51]

FIGURE 17. Thomas Paine by John Trumbull, 1788. Oil on wood, 4 in. × 3½ in.

When Mather Brown did not produce the commissioned portrait of Paine, Trumbull favored Jefferson with this small portrait, where he depicted Paine looking the appropriate English gentleman and not the radical writer.

Jefferson had wished to join his portrait of Adams with one of Thomas Paine. Mather Brown had accepted the commission, but he never produced the portrait. Jefferson received a letter from Trumbull advising him to expect a little case containing two pictures, one for him and another a gift for Martha.[52] The portrait of Paine was identical in size to Martha's portrait of her father, and both were painted in oil on wood panels (fig. 17). It is probable that Trumbull took Paine's image from life, as it does not closely resemble portraits of Paine known to have been available in London at the time and so is not likely to be a copy.[53] This could account for the features appearing more strongly modeled and finished as opposed to the sketchy quality of Martha's miniature. Trumbull hinted that these may have been intended as studies until he could complete more finished portraits, commenting that "it is all I can do untill I have the happiness to see you again."[54]

Jefferson's commission placed with Brown for Paine's portrait had been very explicit as to size: "I would wish it of the size of the one he drew of myself." Mather Brown's portrait of Jefferson measured 36 × 28 inches, the size known in England as a "kit-kat."[55] Slightly larger than a bust portrait, which showed head only, the kit-kat allowed for a hand (and therefore a gesture) and, in the cases of Brown's portraits of Jefferson and Adams, props as well.[56] Nevertheless, when Jefferson received Trumbull's gift of the small painting of Paine, he responded promptly: "I am to thank you a thousand times for the portrait of Mr. Paine." He added that it was a perfect likeness but made no comment about the size.[57]

Jefferson's response that Trumbull had achieved a "perfect likeness" was not disingenuous, as the portrait compares well to other extant works of Paine.[58] The figure is conservatively dressed in a dark blue-grey frock coat. The hair disappears into an uneven shadow, and what might at first appear unkempt is in fact a conservatively dressed hair or wig with side curls and a moderate dusting of powder. The figure who stares back at the viewer could have been any comfortably established British or American gentleman.

This is perhaps the most interesting aspect of the Paine portrait—there is nothing in the clothing or demeanor of the figure as set down by Trumbull that would suggest his reputation as a writer of radical literature that stirred revolutionary fervor. But at the time the portrait was taken, Paine had put aside his writing and was busy with his design for a single-span metal bridge. He moved easily among the network of Americans living in Paris and London. It would have been hard to predict what was to come within just a very few years. Paine would again be writing incendiary works that became extremely controversial, and Jefferson would find himself embroiled in the debates surrounding Paine. This small portrait would signal to some his support of this notorious figure, but Jefferson never removed Trumbull's portrait of Paine from his collection.

Jefferson's first charge while in Europe was to represent the United States diplomatically, focusing on matters of trade and commerce. Then there was personal ambition. He aspired to be accepted among the enlightened men of science, whom he recognized as "literati of the first order." An Enlightenment *philosophe* was not just a moral philosopher but one engaged in pursuits of science, politics, literature, the arts—endeavors useful in advancing civilization and improving the human condition.[59] Paris presented Jefferson the opportunity to broaden his image and reputation among cosmopolitan Enlightenment thinkers and perhaps in doing so bring greater credibility to the intellectual circles of the United States.

He had the privilege of Franklin's influence, and Jefferson continued to strengthen friendships begun in the United States, such as those with Chastellux, Lafayette, and the French consul of New York, St. John de Crèvecoeur. As Jefferson was preparing for France, Crèvecoeur advised, "I beg you'd put Mr. Franklin in Mind of Introducing you To the Good duke of La rochefoucaud." According to Crèvecoeur, the duc de La Rochefoucauld was a chemist and his house was a meeting place for "Men of Genius and abilities." He added, "You have therefore a Right To Share his Friendship." Crèvecoeur was confident that Jefferson would fit well with the literati who gathered at the Hôtel de la Rochefoucauld, and he offered to write a letter of introduction.[60] Jefferson's Italian acquaintance, Philip Mazzei, forwarded a memorandum of persons he should meet in Paris, and the duc de La Rochefoucauld and his mother, the duchesse d'Anville, topped the list. He pronounced the duchesse as one of the "most singular geniouses of the age."[61] Jefferson followed this advice and added both the duc and the duchesse to the enlightened minds with whom he associated.

Following his first invitation, which came in June 1785, Jefferson circulated in several of the salons hosted by accomplished Frenchwomen. In a rare and honest moment, he allowed his personal excitement and pleasure to show through in a letter to Abigail Adams. "I took a trip yesterday to Sannois and commenced an acquaintance with the old Countess d'Hocquetout. I received much pleasure from it and hope it has opened a door of admission for me to the circle of literati with which she is environed." This was not his last trip to Sannois, and at the salon of Madame Helvétius, widow of the famous *philosophe* and a very close and particular friend of Franklin's, Jefferson met and established lasting relationships with scholars and writers such as the comte de Volney, Destutt de Tracy, and Pierre-Georges Cabanis.[62] Another long and close friendship was with the comtesse de Tessé, the aunt of Lafayette. Although she held a position at court as *dame d'honneur de la reine,* she shared many of Jefferson's republican views, as well as their greatest mutual interest—horticulture and gardening. Tessé would lament his return to the United States: "It will never be possible for me to give up the hope of seeing you before I die." She wondered if he still blushed, "because I do not believe that you have altogether lost the habit of doing so."[63] He also came to know and respect the writer Madame de Staël. The two corresponded after his return to the United States, and in reply to one of his letters she wrote, "I will not be exaggerating my feelings toward you when I tell you that the letter you were so kind as to send me . . . is put away in an iron box with my father's will." Here it would be held safe for rereading.[64]

The initial invitation from the "old Countess," the comtesse d'Houdetot, coincided closely with Jefferson's presentation to Louis XVI as Franklin's successor. Franklin had been a favorite with the comtesse and must have recommended Jefferson, or possibly she was curious to meet the new American minister plenipotentiary. At about this same time Jefferson's first (and only) book, *Notes on the State of Virginia,* was published in a limited edition of two hundred copies. Jefferson presented these to acquaintances in Paris and sent some to friends in the United States. This was the book the Adams family read on their move to London and that John Adams included in his portrait by Brown. The publication of this book may have given the old countess further motivation to meet this American writer.

From its beginnings in 1781, this work evolved over several years into a comprehensive natural history that covered the state of Virginia and included data on the westward trans-Appalachian regions. But Jefferson's *Notes* was not just about collecting and recording data. A major objective was to refute theories on the New World put forward by leading French naturalists, primarily the renowned Georges-Louis Leclerc, comte de Buffon. In his *Histoire naturelle* Buffon maintained that the animals of North America were degenerate and inferior to those of Europe due to the continent's warm and humid climate.[65] This renowned naturalist had stopped short of asserting that the climate caused degeneration in the human inhabitants, both aboriginal and the transplanted Euro-Americans, but another French naturalist, the Abbé Raynal, had made such a claim. Neither man had ever visited North America and could not have been writing from empirical evidence, which improved Jefferson's argument for a study of the data and further scientific research.[66] By the 1780s this theory of degeneracy in North America was being questioned, yet the authoritative voices of Buffon and Raynal could not be ignored. Such allegations could discourage immigration and economic investment in North America and produce a negative impact on the future development of the United States.[67]

One of the first presentation copies went to Chastellux along with the request that a second copy provided be forwarded to the comte de Buffon.[68] This led to a dinner invitation from Buffon, and Jefferson accompanied Chastellux to an evening at the Jardin du Roi. This acquaintance with the acclaimed naturalist allowed some name-dropping on Jefferson's part to his fellow members at the American Philosophical Society in Philadelphia. He requested certain items be sent to Monsieur de Buffon in Paris, such as specimens of American birds not present in the king's natural history collection, and Buffon had mentioned some scientific literature available only in Philadelphia that he would like to have.[69] Jefferson must have been gratified to fulfill a request for this world-renowned naturalist whom he had known only by name and reputation for so many years—even if he had disagreed with his assumptions on North America. As a published author of a book on natural history who was personally known to Monsieur de Buffon, Jefferson could circulate with more credibility among the European literati.

Jefferson authorized a French-language edition of his book, which was published in 1787, although he was never happy with this version.[70] He then arranged for another English-language edition, which was published in London in 1787 by John Stockdale.[71] Soon after this publication, Jefferson's name appeared regularly in London newspapers advertising *Notes*. By midyear 1787 he received comments from a friend in the United States confirming the growing recognition of his work there. Joel Barlow wrote, "Your Notes on Virginia are getting into the Gazetts in different States," and he added that he was pleased with Jefferson's refutation of the French naturalists. "We are flattered with the idea of seeing ourselves vindicated from those despicable aspersions which have long been thrown upon us and echoed from one ignorant Scribbler to another in all the languages in Europe."[72] Jefferson's *Notes* offered an alternative view of North America that was gaining credibility.

As circulation of his *Notes on the State of Virginia* grew, Jefferson was pleased as well that the Statute for Religious Freedom for the State of Virginia was being published in Europe in several languages. He reported to James Madison in a December 1786 letter: "The Virginia act for religious freedom has been received with infinite approbation in Europe and propagated with enthusiasm. . . . It has been translated into French and Italian. . . . It is inserted in the new Encyclopedie, and is appearing in most of the publications respecting America." He felt it an honor that the Virginia legislature had stepped forward to declare to the world that "the reason of man may be trusted with the formation of his own opinions."[73] This legislation did not bear his name, but as it emanated from Virginia, it prompted some association with the author of *Notes on the State of Virginia*. Jefferson was adding to his reputation as enlightened thinker. His image as a man of science would follow him back to America. Gouverneur Morris overlapped Jefferson in Paris before Morris assumed his ministerial post. Jefferson and Morris did not always agree politically, but while in Paris, Morris honestly observed, "Mr. Jefferson has in general excited favorable ideas of his intellectual faculties."[74]

Working with Trumbull on the composition for the *Declaration of Independence* must have recalled for Jefferson the place, the people, and the events of that summer in 1776. Before leaving Paris, he would experience the stimulus of observing and participating in the birth of another revolution. On May 5, 1789, the Estates-General were called for the first time since 1614 to debate France's growing financial crisis. Jefferson recorded his presence at the opening day's events and continued to go daily from Paris to Versailles to attend the debates.[75] But then he found himself more personally involved.

He knew many men taking part in the assembly, and some sought his opinion. He reasoned that "being from a country which had successfully passed thro' a similar reformation, they were disposed to my acquaintance, and had some confidence in me." As early as January 1789, prior to the opening of the Estates-General in May, Jefferson alerted Madison that "every body here is trying their hands at forming declarations of rights," but it was their close associate, Lafayette, who called on Jefferson for his input. Historians have presumed that Jefferson offered counsel, but his name was never publically connected with Lafayette's Declaration of the Rights of Man. Rather, it was a dinner that Lafayette organized at the American legation that caused Jefferson some anxiety.[76]

A note came from Lafayette on August 25 with the request, "I Beg for liberty's sake You will Breack Every Engagement to Give us a dinner to Morrow Wenesday." Lafayette planned to bring eight men who were engaged in the current debates on the political future of France and concluded, "I depend on you to receive us." Jefferson played the host and in his memoirs maintained that he only listened quietly; nevertheless, the next morning, he realized that he should quickly call on Foreign Secretary Montmorin. In his account he offered that "I knew too well the duties I owed to the king, to the nation, and to my own country to take any part in councils concerning their internal government." Montmorin knew already of the dinner but was conciliatory. Jefferson was fortunate in the foreign minister's response, as certainly he had overstepped diplomatic protocol. There was little chance for a recurrence, as within a month he was preparing to escort his daughters back to Virginia, where he would take care of business affairs. He was leaving "this interesting scene of action," but he would carry the excitement with him. He took pride in his belief that "the American Revolution seems first to have awakened the thinking part of the French nation in general from the sleep of despotism."[77] In the coming years, as the French Revolution turned into the Terror and so many of his friends and acquaintances were executed, he would remain reluctant to give up this notion.

Jefferson had been waiting several months for permission to leave his post to make a brief trip to the United States. Finally, it came. Foreign Secretary John Jay's letter arrived in Paris on August 23, 1789, which allowed Jefferson to actively prepare for a return voyage. John Trumbull also planned to return to the United States and was of great assistance in booking Jefferson's voyage from Cowes on the Isle of Wright directly to Norfolk, Virginia. Jefferson and Trumbull sailed at approximately the same time but on different ships, one bound for Virginia the other for New York.

During his five years in Europe, Jefferson made impressions and took away impressions. He never reached the celebrity status enjoyed by Franklin, but peers did compliment his presence and abilities as an American diplomat. George Washington received more than one report from Lafayette praising Jefferson. He wrote first in 1786: "Words Cannot Sufficiently Express to You How much I am pleased with Mr Jefferson's public Conduct— He Unites every Ability that Can Recommend Him With the Ministers, and at the time possesses Accomplishements of the mind and the Heart which Cannot But Give Him Many friends." Two years later his respect had grown and he wrote, "I am More and More pleased with Mr jefferson. . . . He enjoys Universal Regard, and does the Affairs of America to perfection."[78] Sir John Sinclair met Jefferson in Paris at a dinner hosted by Lafayette and was impressed. He later wrote, "Mr. Jefferson was undoubtedly one of the ablest men that America has produced."[79] Gouverneur Morris observed, "He commands very much respect in this country, which is merited by good sense and good intentions." He hints of Jefferson's personal style when he comments, "Mr. Jefferson lives well, keeps a good table and excellent wines, which he distributes freely." The elegance of French dining was an experience that enhanced the social skills Jefferson had learned so early at the table of Governor Fauquier. This cultivated taste would serve him well as an important facet of his self-image, and the quality of French dining was one of the positive impressions that he took away.

Jefferson's impressions of monarchy did not improve on his closer examination, however. His opinions remained negative, and he wrote, "I am astonished at some people's considering a kingly government as a refuge. . . . Send them to Europe to see something of the trappings of monarchy, and I will undertake that every man shall go back thoroughly cured."[80] His countryman and close colleague John Adams carried away a more moderate view. He accepted that "these Ceremonies and Shows may be condemned." Nevertheless, Adams believed that "something of the kind every Government and every Religion has and must have: and the Business and Duty of Lawgivers and Philosophers is to endeavor to prevent them from being carried too far."[81] For Adams the monarchical trappings, or something like them, were inevitable, even necessary. For Jefferson they could be dangerous representations of tyranny from church and state. Both Jefferson and Adams saw themselves as good republicans, but they held contrary opinions as to what could be safely retained from the old monarchical prototype. Their differing attitudes would become more pronounced in the political trials that lay ahead. Meanwhile Jefferson prepared for his return to the United States and was a little nervous as to what he might find. He knew things had changed in the five years that he had been away. He might encounter a very different America.

II

The Politics of the 1790s

Men who have been intimate all their lives cross the streets to avoid meeting, and turn their heads another way, lest they should be obliged to touch their hat.
—Thomas Jefferson to Edward Rutledge, June 24, 1797

3

RETURNING TO A NEW AMERICA

"I know only the Americans of the year 1784. They tell me this is to be much a stranger to those of 1789."[1] So Jefferson mused on what he might find as he prepared for a return trip to the United States. The constitution was in place, Washington was elected president, and the newly structured federal government was taking shape. He would be a stranger to these changes that had occurred in his absence. But then he was not staying long. He meant only to resituate his daughters among relatives in Virginia, take care of business affairs, and return to Paris with the favorable spring winds to complete the two years remaining on his diplomatic appointment.[2] This was his intent at least, when he left France.

Jefferson arrived in Virginia's port city of Norfolk on November 23, 1789, accompanied by his daughters Martha and Maria and the two Monticello slaves who had attended them in Paris, James Hemings and his sister Sally.[3] Jefferson was puzzled by announcements in the newspapers naming him as the newly appointed secretary of state. He was in route to Monticello when he received the official letter from President Washington requesting that he head the newly formed Department of State, which would now include domestic affairs along with the office of foreign affairs. Jefferson was not excited by this proposition and preferred to return to his ministerial duties in Europe. He felt that was where he was best suited and predicted that should he undertake the position as secretary of state, "I cannot but foresee the possibility that this may end disagreeably."[4]

Jefferson feared he would be returning to his country as a stranger, but in President Washington's estimation, he returned with a cosmopolitan profile that made him an appropriate choice for the new position as secretary of state. Washington's goal was to establish strong executive offices, and he pushed Jefferson to contribute his international experience and cosmopolitan image in shaping the new government. In his second letter to the reluctant Jefferson, Washington professed that "I know of no person, who, in my judgement, could better execute the Duties of it than yourself."[5] He added further, "So far as I have been able to obtain information from all quarters, your late appointment has given very extensive and very great satisfaction to the Public." Jefferson heard similarly from Madison: "All that I am able to say on the subject is that a universal anxiety is expressed for your acceptance."[6] Washington and Madison presented strong arguments of support in pressing Jefferson to fill the office. The skills he had developed as America's envoy to France could serve him well as secretary of state.

Jefferson was not attuned to the immediate concerns driving Washington and Madison. They had been leaders of the constitutional convention, where Washington presided and Madison was a key organizer. They were far more aware than Jefferson of the many decisions and agreements still needed to implement the new Constitution. Madison admitted, "We are in a wilderness without a single footstep to guide us."[7] In Washington's proposal to Jefferson, he made a statement that would bear on his future actions. He wrote, "I consider the successful Administration of the general Government as an object of almost infinite consequence to the present and future happiness of the Citizens of the United States."[8] Both men were sincere in their commitment to the grand experiment of this new American republic, but Washington and Jefferson would not always agree on the role of the federal government and what would best support the well-being and happiness of the citizens.

Months before Jefferson left Paris, Madison had questioned him about a change of position, to which Jefferson answered negatively; he preferred to remain at his diplomatic post. He was consistent in his response to Washington and offered as support his familiarity with ministerial duties, being careful to couch his one reference to the revolution in France in terms of commerce, not personal interest: "The change of government, too, taking place in the country . . . seems to open a possibility of procuring from the new rulers some new advantages in commerce which may be agreeable to our countrymen." Jefferson would never proclaim, as did Thomas Paine, that "a Share in two revolutions is living to some purpose," but he later acknowledged feeling "fervor" for the revolution commencing in France and maintained his confidence that "the American Revolution seems first to have awakened the thinking part of the French nation in general from the sleep of despotism."[9] He believed that the upheaval in France would be short-lived and that by his return in the spring, the scene would again be quiet.[10]

Jefferson's response to Washington is revealing. His main rebuttal was aimed at the nature of the position itself with its component of "domestic administration" that would leave him exposed to potential public criticism. He replied, "I should enter on it with gloomy forebodings from the criticisms and censures of a public[,] just indeed in their intentions, but sometimes misinformed and misled, and always too respectable to be neglected."[11] This reads as a flashback to his position as wartime governor during the British invasion of Virginia and the public censure he had received, misguided perhaps, but very real and very hurtful. These memories could have contributed to a statement he made while still in Paris: "To glide unnoticed thro' a silent execution of duty, is the only ambition which becomes me, and it is the sincere desire of my heart."[12] The role of minister plenipotentiary suited. He contributed in public service but remained out of the direct gaze of his constituents.

Upon receiving a second letter from Washington urging his acceptance, Jefferson felt he had to comply. He expressed his anxiety to Madison: "I write him [Washington] by this occasion my acceptance, and shall endeavour to subdue the reluctance I have to that office which has increased so as to oppress me extremely."[13] With these reservations, Jefferson left Monticello on March 1, 1790, following the marriage of his eldest daughter, Martha, to her cousin, Thomas Mann Randolph Jr. of Tuckahoe plantation, to join the national government at its temporary residence in the city of New York.[14] His prediction would prove correct—it would end disagreeably.

The newspapers reported the return of Minister Jefferson to his native Virginia and then charted the progress of the new secretary of state as he journeyed to New York to join the federal government. In Alexandria, Virginia, Jefferson was feted with a dinner followed by toasts and an address by Mayor Will Hunter. The mayor referenced Jefferson's recent contributions as United States minister plenipotentiary at the court of France, then quickly recalled his revolutionary participation. The citizens of Alexandria had not forgotten "the whole tenor of your conduct, when we were struggling in the sacred cause of freedom." Now the mayor believed the new nation faced another crisis. What to expect with this new Constitution?

Again the United States needed Jefferson to "fulfill the high expectations of a free and republican people." The citizens of Alexandria saw Jefferson's participation as extremely important at a time when they counted on Jefferson's "virtue and talents" to once more make a difference in the problems facing the nation.[15]

In his response to the mayor's speech, Jefferson made his feelings clear: "The republican is the only form of government which is not eternally at open or secret war with the rights of mankind." He believed the "rights of mankind" were spreading, and he was obviously thinking of France when he claimed, "We are pointing out the way to struggling nations."[16] American leadership in the spread of enlightened, republican government would be a step towards overcoming a provincial profile and would underscore the nation's contributions to progressive ideology. Jefferson would have been extremely disturbed to believe this prospect in danger, and he must have felt heartened by the reception in Alexandria.

Abigail Adams warmly announced Jefferson's arrival in New York in April 1790: "Mr. Jefferson is here, and adds much to the social circle."[17] Jefferson wrote similarly of his reception: "The President received me cordially, and my Colleagues & the circle of principal citizens, apparently, with welcome. The courtesies of dinner parties given me as a stranger newly arrived among them, placed me at once in their familiar society."[18] Rather than being the "stranger," Jefferson had expanded his profile and reputation from gentleman of Virginia to include the luster and experience of Europe. Unfortunately, there are no extant likenesses of Jefferson as secretary of state other than a single portrait by Charles Willson Peale taken in Philadelphia in 1791; however, one senator left notes of his impression of the new secretary of state as the government organized in New York.

The most detailed description of Jefferson during his months in New York came from Senator William Maclay of western Pennsylvania. Maclay had begun keeping a journal of the daily debates in the Senate. These discussions were not open to the public as were most debates in the House of Representatives, which made him feel it even more important to document what transpired and make a record of his personal participation, especially as he often clashed with the president of the Senate, Vice President Adams. His journal entries began to extend outside the Senate chamber and to record his impressions of people and events comprising the new national government. His observations have remained a valuable resource, even though they were often tinged with a cynical edge.[19]

Jefferson and Maclay met for the first time on May 24, 1790. Jefferson was in the early stage of what he called a "periodical" headache. His headaches, possibly a type of migraine, were not a new experience, but they were especially persistent throughout his time in New York. This could help explain Maclay's unflattering observation that Jefferson had "a rambling, vacant look, and nothing of that firm, collected deportment which I expected would dignify the presence of a secretary or minister." Rambling, perhaps, yet Maclay does allow that "he Scattered information wherever he went, and some even brilliant sentiments sparkled from him." He added a brief description of Jefferson's physical appearance, writing, "Jefferson is a slender Man. Has rather the Air of Stiffness in his Manner. His cloaths seem too small for him. He sits in a lounging Manner on one hip, commonly, and with one of his shoulders elevated much above the other. His face has a scrany Aspect. His whole figure has a loose shackling Air. . . . He had been long enough abroad to catch the tone of European folly."[20]

This description contains some contradiction. Jefferson has an "Air of Stiffness in his Manner," but "his whole figure has a loose shackling Air." At a dinner a month later, when Maclay met the three executive secretaries, he repeated his opinion that "Jefferson transgresses on the extreme of stiff gentility or lofty gravity." He said of the secretary of the treasury, "Hamilton has a very boyish, giddy manner"; but he approved of the secretary of war: "Knox is the easiest man, and has the most dignity of presence."[21] Apparently Maclay found Jefferson reserved and formed a different opinion from the citizens of Alexandria who had honored him at the dinner on his way to New York. They had met a man of "amiable manners and engaging conversation."[22] But in that situation Jefferson was speaking to fellow Virginians and did not have a migraine headache.

Maclay's comment that Jefferson's clothes appeared too small would suggest that Jefferson was still wearing the slender coats cut in the French style. This could also suggest that Maclay, formerly a Philadelphia lawyer who was now a landholder in the outlying regions of western Pennsylvania, may not have kept up with the very latest in fashion, which inevitably came to America from Europe or Britain. Throughout the eighteenth century, the cut of men's coats, whether a dress coat or the more informal frock, had continued towards a slimmer shape. By the beginning of the 1790s, the back of the fashionable coat was being cut very narrow, as the midline of the front curved towards the back creating a much narrower skirt. Even the sleeves fit closer to the arm, and if a cuff were attached, it was not over three to four inches wide. The rising height of the collar added to the slender appearance.[23]

Jefferson began assembling a new wardrobe in New York, but for his first few months in the city, he may have largely depended on the clothing that had traveled with him from France. (Clothing left in Paris would be shipped later with his household goods.) He had purchased one American coat upon landing in Norfolk that according to his accounting records was blue broadcloth costing $17.33.[24] Quite possibly it was a simple traveling coat and could have had been cut after the European coats in his wardrobe. Soon after his arrival in New York he began to purchase shirts, gloves, and shoes; however, his first payment to a New York tailor, Christian Baehr, was not made until July 1790.[25] For his meeting with Maclay in May, it is quite likely that he still wore a dress coat brought with him from Paris.

Maclay believed that Jefferson "had been long enough abroad to catch the tone of European folly," and his clothing could have contributed to this assessment without Maclay's awareness. Then, too, Jefferson may have retained mannerisms acquired while in Paris. Very late in his life one visitor to Monticello remarked of his gestures and body language that "they are artificial[;] he shrugs his shoulders when talking, has much of the Frenchman."[26] Something of the Francophile must have remained throughout his life and would have been even more visible when he was freshly returned from Europe.

Jefferson's French-cut coats possibly filled a purpose beyond convenience. It concerned him that Americans remained dependent on British goods. He speculated that curtailing trade with England might prove a very powerful sumptuary law and acquaint Americans with goods of a rival market. France still directed much of Europe's fashion, and restricting trade with Britain could possibly bring French merchandise into greater vogue with American buyers.[27] Jefferson never deliberately took a role as a fashion leader, but by appearing in the French style he offered his personal support of France and French trade, especially over that of England.

The "Frenchness" of Jefferson's appearance may have depended on the eye of the beholder. A mutual friend of Jefferson's and Maclay's, Dr. Benjamin Rush of Philadelphia, did not seem bothered by Jefferson's "European folly" as reported by Maclay. In fact, in Rush's estimation Jefferson appeared unchanged. "It was the first time I saw him since his return from France. He was plain in his dress and unchanged in his manners."[28] Quite possibly Rush saw Jefferson in simple traveling clothes on his way through Philadelphia in route to New York—perhaps the blue broadcloth coat tailored in Newport or the cloak he purchased on his way north.[29] Obviously, Rush was seeing what he wanted to see and added with some relief that Jefferson was still strong in his belief in republican forms of government. Rush and Maclay saw two different Jeffersons, but notably both men showed interest in how much of Europe Jefferson had absorbed and both looked to his clothing and mannerisms as evidence. Political independence may have been won, but the cultural influence of Europe and Britain remained strong.[30]

Jefferson brought much back with him from his five years' experience in Europe. This included an even stronger aversion to monarchy and its impact on the people governed under such a system. Before leaving France he was excited to see the beginnings of what he thought would be positive revolt against the centuries-old monarchy. On his way to New York he was heartened by his reception in Alexandria, whose citizens showed him that their own memories of the revolution were very positive. However, upon his arrival in New York he was disturbed by what he thought he was hearing among the members of the new government. He was admittedly taken aback by the dinner-table conversations. He wrote, "I cannot describe the wonder and mortification with which the table conversations filled me. Politics were the chief topic, and a preference of kingly, over republican, government, was evidently the favorite sentiment."

He validated his own observations with accounts from others and entered into his notes a description of a dinner attended by Thomas Lee Shippen, the young man he had introduced at the French court, and his father, William Shippen. The story he heard was that after dinner the conversation turned to politics, and "Hamilton declared openly, that 'there was no stability, no security in any kind of government but a monarchy.'"[31] The "Hamilton" referenced was Secretary of the Treasury Alexander Hamilton. His name began to appear in Jefferson's notes as a voice in favor of a stronger executive office with monarchical leanings. Tensions between the secretary of the treasury and the secretary of state began to mount and to become more public.

Jefferson expressed shock at what he interpreted as a nascent aristocracy forming in what was to be this exceptional American republic. He expressed concerns that "we were educated in royalism; no wonder if some of us retain that idolatry still."[32] Yet before leaving France, he had heard through Madison accounts of one of the first debates in Congress, the dispute over titles. Jefferson was still in Paris when Madison posted to him the details of one of the first debates before Congress—how to address the president and vice president. With the distance of time, this might seem a trivial deliberation, but Madison was concerned and stated, "The question became a serious one between the two houses." He laid the "cause of titles" to Vice President John Adams. The proposed title for Washington was "His Highness the President of the U.S. and protector of their liberties." Madison did not take the matter lightly and believed it would have "given a deep wound to our infant government" had it passed. He was relieved when the deliberations concluded that the title of the president should remain in its "naked dignity."[33]

Other congressmen also saw danger in this issue. Representative Thomas Tudor Tucker of South Carolina questioned whether titles would alarm the citizens, as they seemed contrived "to lead them on by degrees to that kind of government which they have thrown off with abhorrence." He asked, "Does this look like a democracy, when one of the first acts of the two branches of the Legislature is to confer titles? Surely not."[34] Most of the representatives agreed with Tucker, and it was James Madison who calmed the debate in the House. He was able to conclude his report to Jefferson with the observation that "*Titles* to both the President and vice President were formally and unanimously condemned by a vote of the House of Representatives. This I hope will shew to the friends of Republicanism that our new Government was not meant to substitute either Monarchy or Aristocracy, and that the genius of the people is as yet adverse to both."[35]

Tucker raised the question of how a democracy should look, feeling sure that it did not include titles traditionally reserved for royalty. But how did a democracy—or, more accurately, a newly formed republic—look and behave in matters of ceremony, etiquette, and appearance? Madison's complaint that they were in a wilderness without a guiding footstep applied even to issues of state protocol. Opinions divided between those who viewed an elevated position for the presidential office as appropriate, even necessary for stability, and those such as Jefferson who feared that too much pomp, ceremony and obeisance could lead back into the familiar constitutional monarchy.

Ceremony as nonverbal communication serves as very effective visual propaganda. Historically it had been used to produce distance between the ruler and those they ruled by creating feelings of subservience and homage.[36] John Adams witnessed the persuasive power of visual communication when he was in the presence of the French queen, dazzling with diamonds, on her throne at Versailles. Even as an outsider, he had to admit his awe at the power and wealth communicated by this spectacle.[37] The new federal government of the United States had neither the wealth nor the resources to create a comparable spectacle, but in this provincial society even the requirements of formal dress for a state dinner or social event could form a barrier for many citizens. The question became: How much elevated ceremony and appearance should surround the executive offices to give a show of stability, and at what point did a display of state belie the concept of equal opportunity for all voting citizens?

The "cause of titles" and the aristocratic posturing among some members of the Senate appeared in William Maclay's daily journal. Before he set down his description of Jefferson, he had been keeping a careful record of debates within the Senate chamber. In his estimation the new government was far from being a "powerful machine" and in this start-up phase "need[ed] help and props on all sides."[38] He shared Adams's and Jefferson's apprehensions that this new experiment in republicanism could gradually slide towards the more familiar monarchical model, and he suspected there were many who "cared for nothing else but a translation of the diadem and sceptre from London to Boston, New York, or Philadelphia; or, in other words, the creation of a new monarchy in America, and to form niches for themselves in the temple of royalty." He confided to his journal, "I entertain no doubt but that many people are aiming with all their force to establish a splendid court with all the pomp of majesty."[39] Nevertheless, Maclay joined his congressional colleagues in attending President Washington's levees.

Washington's decision to receive visitation only on Tuesdays and Fridays created discussion among congressmen. Senator Maclay could understand that the president would be overrun with visitors without some form of limitation, yet the idea that he could be seen only at his own levee on Tuesdays and then at Mrs. Washington's drawing rooms on Fridays struck him as too courtly a practice. But Maclay's respect for Washington was totally sincere. He recognized that Washington's presence and dignity smoothed many of the rankling issues surrounding the new government. He had no hesitation in referring to him as "the greatest man in the world," and felt honored by a brief conversation with the president, as Washington made his way around the room addressing those attending his levee.[40]

Maryland representative Michael Stone was one of those who believed the formal receptions and drawing rooms set a needed tone for the new government. Years later he recalled that they were attended only by those who held an official position or had earned an invitation through merit or character, and all attendees were expected to appear in full dress.[41] He added that this was before "democratic rudeness" intruded into governmental circles, thus ensuring that good manners could be counted on and no tolerance allowed for the rabble.

From Stone's description of the list of appropriate guests, Secretary of State Jefferson would have been granted a standing invitation due to his position; however, Jefferson made no reference to his own attendance. Abigail Adams commented that he had added to New York's social circle upon his arrival, and perhaps this did initially include the president's Tuesday gatherings. But just a few months later French consul St. John de Crèvecoeur informed William Short, now chargé d'affaires in Paris, that Jefferson did not approve of the "Stiff Style and Etiquette of New York" and rather devoted his time to establishing the new Department of State and organizing his own household.[42] Later, when the federal government had relocated to Philadelphia, Jefferson excused himself from attending a "birthnight" celebration for Washington, which he strongly opposed due to its kingly precedent, and he gave his excuses "to Mrs. Washington [for] not attending her evenings, to Mrs. Adams the same."[43] These could hardly have been as formal as the European counterparts he attended for five years in Paris, but even a provincial version was not what he envisioned for the American republic.

The new government groped forward with a general consensus that the Constitution was to be respected and the basic form of government was to be democratic-republican, but its outward trappings were controversial. Some were hesitant to follow too closely the models of Europe, while others, not as Anglophobic as Jefferson, saw benefits in a closer relationship with Great Britain and believed the former mother country was not an unfit role model. Jefferson was uneasy as he began to cultivate his image as secretary of state in Washington's administration.

In Paris, Jefferson displayed his awareness that public image extended beyond just personal appearance. Residence, household staff, entertaining all became a part of public image, but as he began to establish himself in New York he found his choices of residence limited. He was disappointed by the shortage of suitable housing and was not able to procure a place close to the government's offices "in the Broadway." He found a small, "indifferent" house at 57 Maiden Lane, as he reported to his daughter Martha, that would do until he could find something more suitable before his furniture arrived from France.[44] But before his household goods could be packed in Paris and cross the Atlantic, the national government was on the move again, relocating to Philadelphia.

Jefferson could look forward to reestablishing himself in this more familiar city. William Temple Franklin, grandson of Benjamin Franklin, acted as Jefferson's agent in securing a new house being constructed in a good area on Market Street. Architect Jefferson was soon involved in the project and negotiating additions and changes. First, he must have a book gallery that he proposed run across the back of the house, as he had added to the small Maiden Lane house in the brief time he was there. Next in importance, judging from his comments, was the dining room. The emphasis that Jefferson placed on the dining room was conveyed by his request for a slightly longer room, 26 feet, rather than the 20 feet 9 inches specified in the building plan, although the original width of 14 feet 3 inches would do. As the placement of fireplaces made walls difficult to move, he was warned he might have to accept the original interior configurations.

Then a stable was needed. Jefferson requested space for five horses with three carriage bays. His phaeton and a chariot had returned with him from Paris in the fall of 1789. The phaeton was then shipped to New York for his use there; the chariot must have remained with his daughters, as the driver's seat had been left in Paris, and in later correspondence he directed that the seat be included with household goods intended for Virginia. However, a second chariot and a smaller, two-wheeled cabriolet were arriving with the bulk of his goods coming from Paris to Philadelphia. He gave special packing instructions for "my chariot and new cabriolet."[45] No description indicates whether Jefferson's chariot approached the elegance of Washington's, which the British attaché pronounced "kingly." Mrs. Adams was impressed that Washington demonstrated the state required of his position and never rode out but with "six Horses to his Carriage, four Servants, & two Gentlemen before him."[46]

Jefferson's equipage was not as grand as Washington's—still, a personal carriage that required four-in-hand afforded a degree of status that not all congressmen enjoyed. This was illustrated in an episode again related by Abigail Adams. Following Washington's first address to Congress, it was proposed that the congressmen call at the President's House to deliver their response. Some members felt this followed too much the monarchical model, but ultimately they went. It had been raining, and Abigail was pleased to report that all the senators rode, led by her husband, even though it required renting hackney carriages for some: "How should they look on foot with a rabble after them splashing through the mud[?]"[47] A proper vehicle, even the smaller cabriolet or phaeton, assured being above the rabble, remaining dry in inclement weather, and usually arriving much faster at your destination. Secretary of State Jefferson had only to walk across the street from his residence to reach the State Department's offices; nevertheless, there must have been occasions when Philadelphians would have seen the secretary in one of his vehicles.[48]

For household staff, Jefferson requested that William Short, his former secretary now handling his affairs in Paris, negotiate with his Parisian *maître d'hôtel*, Adrien Petit, to make the trans-Atlantic move. He wrote, "Petit must be prevailed on to come at all events.... I find I cannot do without him here. I shall not attempt to commence housekeeping till he arrives with my furniture."[49] The furniture arrived in fall 1790; Petit arrived the following July. Eighty crates of books, furniture, art, household goods, even wine and foodstuff, plus the two carriages were delivered to Jefferson in Philadelphia. Six crates were forwarded on to Monticello.[50] These began to fill the house on Market Street, room by room, as the house was finished. This house filled with French furniture, mirrors, and art under the care of a French *maître d'hôtel* would provide a very cosmopolitan backdrop for the secretary of state.

Jefferson's Philadelphia staff generally numbered around three locally hired men plus Petit and slave James Hemings as chef. This was only slightly smaller than the staff he generally maintained in Paris. After his move to Philadelphia, he was having difficulty retaining a satisfactory valet, and in January 1791 he advertised for "A Genteel Servant, who can shave and dress well, attend a gentleman on horseback, wait at table, and be well recommended." This position was finally filled by Joseph, described only as "a small French boy."[51]

That Jefferson required a valet suggested that he still wished to appear very much the gentleman. He sought someone who could "shave and dress [him] well," and his accounting records show regular purchases of pomatum and hair powder and occasional charges for ribbon. This indicates that he continued to follow the dictates of eighteenth-century hairdressing and grooming. The hair would be dressed, possibly with side curls, and the longer hair pulled back into a queue and tied with a ribbon. The style was held in place with pomatum and then powdered. It does appear, however, that he began supplanting his French-tailored coats with American-made garments, first from New York tailor Christian Baehr, and then, following his move to Philadelphia, from tailor Thomas Billington. But how did he look? Only one formal portrait was taken of Jefferson while he served in Philadelphia as secretary of state.

Charles Willson Peale collected portraits, and these were portraits of his own making. His collection dated to the revolution, when, like Trumbull, he had served in the military and began to use his painting skills to record the American story. Unlike Trumbull, however, he chose to tell this story with individual's portraits rather than including them in a larger history painting. He began taking portraits of American and French military officers and soon began to include others who had contributed to American independence.[52] His sentiments echoed those of Jefferson: "The memory of very many of these men, for their united efforts to obtain our independence, deserve [*sic*] our grateful remembrance."[53]

Peale's and Jefferson's collections of worthy Americans were comparable in their objective of preserving history; however, Peale the artist created a more uniform and more extensive portrait collection. Jefferson's was available only to those who did business with him or were invited into his home, whereas Peale's gallery was open to the public for a small fee. This became his vocation, and his gallery would grow over the years to incorporate both portraiture and displays of natural history, and it would enjoy the claim as America's first museum. The function of his collection was to preserve the past and to influence the future, as he explained: "Ever fond of perpetuating the Remembrance of the Worthies of my time, I conceive it will be a means of exciting an Emulation in our Posterity."[54] Late in 1791 Peale requested the secretary of state to sit for a portrait and assured Jefferson, "I have a great desire to exert my abilities in this portrait and your indulgence will grately obligate"[55] (fig. 18).

For his gallery of worthy men Peale did not paint the cosmopolitan Jefferson as recorded by Mather Brown in the London portrait. Gone are the elaborately pleated double jabot on the shirt front and elegant striped waistcoat, although the dark blue frock coats with their fashionably tall collars are similar. In both portraits Jefferson's head is turned in three-quarter profile as he gazes away from the viewer in contemplation. Peale's practice of keeping his museum portraits to a uniform bust size with a neutral background eliminated any personal symbols and props such as the documents Jefferson holds or the Goddess of Liberty that can be seen over his shoulder

FIGURE 18. Thomas Jefferson by Charles Willson Peale, from life, 1791–92.

Peale wanted a portrait of the new secretary of state to display with his collection of American worthies at his gallery in Philadelphia. The color and details of the clothing and the simpler hair dressing make Peale's Jefferson notably distinct from Mather Brown's Minister Plenipotentiary Jefferson, who circulated among the Paris intellectuals and appeared at the French court.

in the Brown portrait.[56] Rather, Peale Americanized his Jefferson through grooming and the color choices of his clothing.

Peale chose to paint Jefferson with his natural, rusty-red hair simply brushed away from his face, without side curls. His version of Jefferson moves away from the European image of the Mather Brown and appears much closer to the American that Trumbull created as the central figure of his *Declaration of Independence* and in the resulting small, informal portrait made as a gift for Jefferson's daughter Martha. This Jefferson had let go the European folly but remained stylish without ostentation.

The colors of the coat and waistcoat, the blue and the buff, were significant to Americans. During the revolution Washington had chosen these colors for his own uniform and had required that his major generals wear a blue coat with buff facings over white or buff breeches.[57] He left some discretion in regimental uniforms, but from the beginning of actual conflict with the British, Washington was concerned with the "impolicy of any part of our Troops being Clothed in Red." He warned that unless the color was changed immediately, "our people will be destroying themselves."[58] The blue and the buff took on a wider connotation than just being the colors of the Continental army uniform and came to represent the American cause.

The blue and the buff infiltrated British politics and became a badge of political protest when Charles James Fox appeared in British parliament dressed in the colors adopted by Washington and his officers. Fox embraced the American cause, and in November 1780, at the beginning of parliament, he openly leveled the accusation against the king that "the present reign offers one uninterrupted series of disgrace, misfortune, and calamity!"[59] As described by Sir William Wraxall, Fox "constantly, or at least usually wore in the House of Commons, a blue frock coat, and a buff waistcoat, neither of which seemed in general new, and sometimes appeared to be threadbare. Nor ought it to be forgotten, that these colours . . . then constituted the distinguishing badge or uniform of Washington and the American Insurgents." Fox's political position was supported by Edmund Burke, but he did not go so far as to take up the blue-and-buff motif. According to Wraxall, "In his dress and exterior he was not less negligent than Fox: but, the spirit of party did not blend with the colour of his apparel; and he rarely or never came to the House in Blue and Buff."[60]

The color combination of blue and buff continued to hold significance after independence. The coat and waistcoat shown in Peale's portrait of Jefferson match in color those that Jefferson ordered from his New York tailor, Christian Baehr. In August 1791 Jefferson wrote Baehr from Philadelphia with a request: "If either now or at any time hence you can find a superfine French cloth, of the very dark blue which you know I wear, I will be obliged to you to make and send me a coat of it." This would suggest that this was not the first dark blue coat he had ordered from Baehr. Two weeks later he sent another letter adding additional items to the order: "When I wrote you lately desiring some clothes to be made, I omitted to desire a gilet (sleeveless waistcoat) and a pair of breeches of buff Casimir, a very light buff, not a yellow one."[61] He settled his account with Baehr in January 1792 but apologized for the delay in payment as the invoice had missed him in Virginia and just reached him in Philadelphia.[62] These dates would make the clothing available to Jefferson at the time of his December 1791 meeting with Peale.

Peale's was the first Jefferson portrait taken from life that was publically exhibited in the United States. It remained on view in Peale's Philadelphia museum but was available only to museum visitors, for Peale never made prints or copies from this portrait as he had his paintings of Washington.[63] Another artist and engraver, William Birch, made a proof print in 1795, which he placed in a Philadelphia exhibit. In the exhibition catalog Birch identifies his print as "Mr. Jefferson" and states that it was taken from the portrait in Peale's museum gallery. The print was to serve as a sample for a projected series of twenty-five print portraits of "celebrated personages in the American Revolution." All would be created from images in Peale's collection. There were not enough subscriptions, however, to move the project forward, and neither the proof nor subsequent copies of Birch's Jefferson prototype are known to have survived.[64] Birch's choice of Jefferson to lead off his portraits series speaks to Jefferson's image becoming more firmly linked with the American Revolution and in particular with the Declaration of Independence by the mid-1790s.

The failure of Birch's proposed series was not caused by his inabilities as an artist. Five years later, in December 1800, he completed his Philadelphia views, which proved very successful. Jefferson was among the initial subscribers to *The City of Philadelphia, in the State of Pennsylvania North America*, which consisted of twenty-eight plates of views of the city in 1800. The revolution was seminal in the history of the United States, and the events and people who took part in it were still toasted and recognized regularly, but the series of prints that would make a name for William Birch celebrated instead an American city.[65]

Shortly after Jefferson sat for Peale, another image of him was created by the noted Italian sculptor Giuseppe Ceracchi. Unfortunately, the final product of Ceracchi's work, a larger-than-life marble bust of Jefferson in classical costume, did not survive the 1851 fire at the Library of Congress, where it was on display in the reading room. Ceracchi's terra-cotta maquette, made from life during Jefferson's Philadelphia years, went with the sculptor back to his studio in Italy, and its whereabouts remain unknown. Due to these losses, the Ceracchi bust has not provided a lasting image of Jefferson, but it was appreciated during the years it was displayed in the entrance hall of Monticello and then later at the Library of Congress. The family judged it an excellent likeness, and it was favored by Jefferson himself. One visitor called it "superb"; another said it was "exquisite" and masterfully done. Jefferson did not receive the bust until 1795 at Monticello, and so it was not fully available to the public during his lifetime, although it would have had a wider viewing audience when it was on display at the Library of Congress.[66]

It is unfortunate this additional likeness of Jefferson as secretary of state has not survived, but that it existed at all is testimony that his reputation and position placed him among those Ceracchi chose to sculpt. Ironically, a marble copy of Ceracchi's bust of Alexander Hamilton has survived from Jefferson's collection (fig. 19). According to his grandchildren, Jefferson sat

FIGURE 19. Alexander Hamilton after Giuseppe Ceracchi, 1794. Marble.

Unfortunately, Ceracchi's bust of Jefferson in the antique style no longer exists, but his marble bust of Hamilton affords us some idea of the quality and style. According to a family member, the two Ceracchi busts faced one another across Monticello's entrance hall and allowed Jefferson to quip that they would be opposed in death as in life.

Hamilton's bust across the Monticello entrance hall from his own. One story relays that when guests noticed the busts facing each other, Jefferson would wryly comment, "opposed in death as in life."[67]

Though there were no images of the secretary of state in circulation, Jefferson's name was placed before the public in print. Part 1 of Thomas Paine's pamphlet *The Rights of Man* was published in England in 1791, and Paine shrewdly—and probably sincerely—dedicated it to George Washington. Paine's work was scheduled for publication in the United States, and Jefferson was loaned an advance copy. When he returned the borrowed pamphlet to the publisher later than promised, Jefferson felt he should add a brief, cordial message to express his pleasure that the pamphlet was to be printed in the United States. He maintained that he did not intend to endorse the work, or foresee that a note from the secretary of state provided a perfect testimonial for Paine's writings. The publisher used this opportunity to add a preface that claimed the author of the endorsement was "eminent in the councils of America," and then became even more specific by adding that his past diplomatic post at the court at Versailles made him "conversant in the affairs of France." This was especially significant to a work supporting the French Revolution; however, the sentences taken from Jefferson's note related to current politics in the United States, not France. The controversy arose around Jefferson's statements, "Something is at length to be publicly said against the political heresies which have sprung up among us. I have no doubt our citizens will rally a second time round the standard of Common Sense."[68]

In his explanations to family members and close friends, Jefferson claimed that he did not anticipate the "dust Paine's pamphlet has kicked up here." He admitted in a letter to James Monroe that although he agreed with Paine's principles, he "never meant to have entered as a volunteer into the cause."[69] It became apparent that Jefferson owed an explanation to Vice President John Adams, as the leading assumption was that the "heresies" Jefferson referenced related to the pro-British "Discourses on Davila" that had been appearing in the newspapers and were known to have been authored by Adams.

Though Adams accepted Jefferson's written explanation of the incident, the debates over Paine's work grew increasingly more public. The rebuttal of Paine's *Rights of Man* that began appearing in the Boston *Columbian Centinel* under the pen name "Publicola" was assumed to be by Adams as well, although it was actually the work of Adams's son John Quincy. Publicola's first article linked the "parent of this production" (i.e., Paine) and "the gentleman who has stood its sponsor in this country" (Jefferson).[70]

Jefferson was obviously uneasy with the public attention being given his approval of *Rights of Man,* but in personal correspondence he continued to promote the work positively. He wrote a correspondent in London that if the British were allowed to read Paine, it would be "a refreshing shower to their minds" and could bring England to "reason and revolution"—the latter exactly what the British government feared.[71] In 1791 Jefferson saw the events in France as determining the future of Europe: "The success of that [revolution] will ensure the progress of liberty in Europe." In addition, it served as a corollary to the continued advancement of republicanism in the United States: "The failure of that would have been a powerful argument with those who wish to introduce a king, lords and commons here."[72] The French Revolution and Paine's work were both factors in holding the American monarchists at bay.

Jefferson was equally enthusiastic when he received six copies of *Rights of Man Part Two* from Paine in the summer of 1792. He wrote Paine expressing his pleasure and returned to his initial theme, the need in the United States for Paine's "lessons in republicanism." Jefferson continued to be anxious about those he viewed as monarchists and posed a question to Paine: "Would you believe it possible that in this country there should be high and important characters who need your lessons in republicanism, and do not heed them? It is but too true that we have a sect preaching up & pouting after an English constitution of king, lords, & commons, & whose heads are itching for crowns, coronets & mitres." He saw great benefit in Paine's writings and the positive effect of having them before the public, reprinted in American newspapers. The readership proved to Jefferson that the American people were essentially republican and those who preferred a closer model of the British government stood in the minority. He encouraged Paine to continue with his pen and promised to remain a "sincere votary" and "ardent well-wisher."[73] Yet in the coming years Jefferson would temper this promise.

Jefferson may have been disturbed by the "dust kicked up," but he did not deny his agreement with Paine's sentiments. He displayed Trumbull's portrait of Paine in his Philadelphia residence, apparently giving it a place prominent enough that it was noticed by the British legation attaché. Edward Thornton remarked with disapproval that "a miniature of Payne has a place in Mr. Jefferson's collection."[74] On a later visit the busts by Houdon caught his attention in the drawing room, as well they might. He evinced no recognition that the work was by this superb French artist but did recognize the subjects. He observed, "In the Drawing Room of Mr. Jefferson, there are three busts of Franklin, Paul Jones and La Fayette, three Gentlemen, the first of whom had talents without virtue, the second deserved hanging, and the last, not improbably, may meet with that fate" (fig. 20). Thornton also observed a Houdon bust of John Paul Jones in Washington's residence; however, its presence was less egregious as it was placed in the hall instead of the drawing room. Thornton reasoned, "A bust of the latter *Gentleman* [John Paul Jones] is admitted into the hall of the President's house; no farther—he could not, I conceive, decently think of introducing him among Gentlemen." The placement of portraits made a difference. Thornton followed these observations with the comment, "The French principles are gaining ground fast in this country."[75]

Jefferson's display of art, in this instance at least, made the impression that he could have wished. The British secretary reported to associates at home the seeming American favoritism towards England's chief political rival, France. This was not totally true, of course, as international allegiances remained divided, and March 1793, the date of Thornton's letter, marked a turning point for some Americans, as the news of the execution of Louis XVI reached the country late in the month.[76] Some Americans applauded the death of a monarch, even a monarch that had once been an

FIGURE 20. Benjamin Franklin (*top left*),
John Paul Jones (*top right*), and Lafayette
(*bottom*), modern copies after Jean-Antoine
Houdon. Plaster, originals, 1778 (Franklin),
1780 (Jones), and 1789 (Lafayette).

These bust portraits by Houdon were some
of the first pieces Jefferson obtained in Paris
for his collection of worthies. They followed
him to Philadelphia, where British legation
secretary Edward Thornton disapprovingly
noted their presence in the drawing room
of the secretary of state. At Monticello they
became a part of his "most honourable suite"
displayed in the Tea Room.

ally; some were revolted by the execution of the French king and reports of
the growing violence in France.[77]

Trusting to Jefferson's memory, another incident occurred in which his
collection of portraits of worthies came under scrutiny. In an 1811 letter to
Benjamin Rush, he vividly recalled that he was hosting a dinner attended
by the secretaries of the departments plus Vice President Adams. This was
convened at Washington's request to discuss a pending issue in the presi-

dent's absence. The business was concluded and after-dinner conversation continued over glasses of wine. Jefferson remembered specifically a point in this conversation that served to "delineate Hamilton's political principles." Jefferson described the dining room as "hung around with a collection of the portraits of remarkable men, among them were those of Bacon, Newton & Locke." He continued, "Hamilton asked me who they were. I told him they were my trinity of the three greatest men the world had ever produced, naming them." According to Jefferson, a long pause ensued before Hamilton responded: "The greatest man, said he, that ever lived was Julius Caesar."[78] This incident remained important for Jefferson, as it illustrated the difference between his and Hamilton's personal sensibilities as represented by Enlightenment thinkers versus the Roman statesman and military-leader-turned-dictator who ended the Roman republic. But this was a private dinner attended by only colleagues. What truly upset Jefferson at the time was being named and placed in full public view through Hamilton's newspaper essays. This was an open threat to his personal image and reputation.

Hamilton, under the pseudonym "An American," was more direct than John Quincy Adams's Publicola. The younger Adams used only Jefferson's title, secretary of state, but did not name him directly, even though there was no doubt as to who was Thomas Paine's sponsor. John Quincy's main thrust was against Paine's pamphlet, not Jefferson, whereas Hamilton was intent on raising questions as to Jefferson's character, virtue, and ambition. His editorials began August 4, 1792, in the *Gazette of the United States* with "An American No. I." By the second paragraph Jefferson was named and identified as the head of a political party. The editorial proceeds to accuse him of opposing the Constitution, the provisions for public debt, and the Bank of the United States, without which a strong and secure nation could not be built. Jefferson was a threat to the permanent welfare of the country.[79]

The following month, writing under the name "Catullus," Hamilton struck out at Jefferson again and assigned him an image of duplicity. He informed readers that "Mr. Jefferson has hitherto been distinguished as the quiet modest, retiring philosopher—as the plain simple unambitious republican." This description could fit Peale's portrait of Jefferson, which hung in his gallery and was available to the public. Hamilton wanted it known that this was not the true Jefferson. In actuality he was "the aspiring turbulent competitor." He illustrated his point with examples of "characters of artful disguises" who have been "unveiled." He described Jefferson as appearing in "the plain garb of Quaker simplicity," but when the outer garb was stripped away, there was the "concealed voluptuary." With this reference to Jefferson disguised as a simple Quaker, Hamilton made a surprising juxtaposition with an analogy of Caesar refusing the diadem and the royal trappings of government but "tenaciously grasping the substance of imperial domination."[80] This allusion to his refusing diadem and royal trappings operated as an analogy to Jefferson's opposition to any hint of aristocracy in government protocol. Yet Hamilton suggested that this was just another ruse, as Jefferson secretly desired power. Curious that many years after the fact, Jefferson remembered Hamilton claiming Caesar to be the greatest man to ever live when viewing his portraits of Enlightenment philosophers, but in September 1792 Hamilton positioned Jefferson as an ambitious and deceitful Caesar. These articles were the beginning of negative pen portraits of Jefferson that would become more frequent and vitriolic as the decade progressed.

But Catullus did not go unchallenged. In January 1793 a writer under the pseudonym "Gracchus" confronted "the thunder of Catullus and his glittering host." Gracchus was explicit that "Mr. Jefferson has *uniformly* observed a conduct which harmonizes with the purest principles of republicanism." By placing "uniformly" in italics, he subtly countered the charge of "duplicity" as alleged by Hamilton. Gracchus asserted that Jefferson was "the early and steady friend of his country; the firm but dignified opponent to the trappings of royalty, and the baubles of nobility." In defending Jefferson, he aimed at President Washington and his levees. Gracchus wrote, "It is said that an officer of government cannot mix indiscriminately with citizens, because it will employ too much of his time, and the affairs of state will be neglected—for this reason he has fixed days for all to gaze upon him." He pointed out the discrepancy that "those persons who are received as guests, and are distinguished by a particular attention, seem to be a privileged order of men in our government, and are, at least, a grade removed from common citizenship."[81] Jefferson was gaining notice as the champion of the common citizen, an image that did not seem compromised by his gentlemanly lifestyle complete with carriages, a full staff directed by a French maître d', elegant furniture, art, and books. Meanwhile, Washington was beginning to receive open criticism. The British legation secretary, Edward Thornton, mentioned in one of his letters to England the "attacks upon the President himself for his levees and other appendages of *Monarchy and Aristocracy*."[82]

Political acrimony began to strain friendships. Jefferson and Adams's relationship suffered with publication of Paine's *Rights of Man* and the resulting articles by Publicola. Jefferson's patronage of and friendship with John Trumbull came under political tensions as well. Jefferson and Trumbull resumed the friendship they had established in Europe soon after their return to the United States. Trumbull wrote almost immediately to confirm Jefferson's safe arrival and to express his pleasure to learn that he would soon be in New York as secretary of state. Jefferson in turn continued to support Trumbull's career with letters of recommendation, as the artist set out through Virginia and further south to Charleston, taking portraits along the way for his *Declaration of Independence* and *Surrender at Yorktown*. These paintings had Jefferson's special interest, but he also encouraged subscriptions to Trumbull's prints of *Bunker's Hill* and *Death of Montgomery*.[83] Trumbull did not forget his promise to give Jefferson a study of *The Surrender of Lord Cornwallis at Yorktown*. A note arrived with the painting in October 1791 that assured Jefferson, "I wish it were now a more valuable testimony than it is of the Gratitude and Esteem of D[ear] sir Your obliged friend & Servant."[84] Presumably this joined Jefferson's art collection at his Philadelphia residence, for it was later listed in Jefferson's catalog of art he owned and displayed at Monticello. This catalog was compiled between 1809 and 1815 and showed "The surrender of York by Trumbul" as hanging in the Monticello parlor. It was placed on the lower tier alongside "The Medals given by the revolutionary Congress to the officers who distinguished themselves on particular occasions."[85]

Trumbull became disillusioned with Jefferson "the apologist," while he felt "revolted from the atrocities of France." In addition, while he revered Washington, he believed Jefferson opposed him and according to Trumbull "a coldness gradually succeeded." The final break came at a dinner party hosted by Jefferson at his Philadelphia residence in 1793. Trumbull engaged in an argument with Virginia congressman William Branch Giles, who very openly opposed Hamilton and his policies. The dinner table discussion, however, revolved around points of religion. Trumbull felt put on the defensive in arguing for the place of the established church and was offended that his host did nothing to deter Giles's attack. Trumbull concluded his account by stating, "From this time my acquaintance with Mr. Jefferson became cold and distant."[86]

Later in the decade Jefferson wrote, "The passions are too high." Perhaps he thought of Trumbull when he added that due to the political climate, "men who have been intimate all their lives cross the streets to avoid meeting, & turn their heads another way, lest they should be obliged to touch their hat."[87]

"My great wish is to go on in a strict but silent performance of my duty: to avoid attracting notice & to keep my name out of newspapers, because I find the pain of a little censure, even when it is unfounded, is more acute than the pleasure of much praise."[88] Jefferson had written these words before leaving France, but his feelings had not changed in the ensuing years. He was very sensitive to open confrontation, especially when it appeared in the full public view offered by the newspapers. His term as secretary of state had not toughened his feelings, and he resolved to leave. He believed a logical exit would be at the conclusion of 1792, as this was the end of the first "epoch" for "periodical change" as designated by the Constitution.[89] However, Washington convinced him to remain for at least another year.

The situation did not improve. In August 1793 he explained to Washington that he was uneasy with his current situation, "where the laws of society oblige me always to move exactly in the circle which I know to bear me peculiar hatred." He identified this circle as "the wealthy aristocrats, the merchants connected closely with England, the new created paper fortunes."[90] He admitted to his discomfort with those who bore him "a peculiar hatred," but Jefferson had made no secret as to where he stood on issues that affronted this circle of wealthy and prominent men. He was pro-French, opposed to the banking system, and strongly outspoken against any appearance of aristocracy and elitism that he feared might infringe on the liberties of the citizenry. British attaché Edward Thornton discerned Jefferson's biases and reported, "This gentleman is or affects to be a most rigid republican; a warm admirer of Thomas Payne, and a vigorous stickler for revolutions and for the downfall of an aristocracy." And he observed Jefferson's dilemma: "He meets however frequently with most determined defenders of aristocracy and regal power, and often receives a blow through the sides of his *friend* T.P. [Thomas Paine] to whom no mercy is shown by such persons."[91]

Jefferson believed he was disliked and was being falsely represented in the newspapers. In this volatile political atmosphere, he was convinced that his "words were caught, multiplied, misconstrued, & even fabricated & spread abroad to [his] injury."[92] When Jefferson took his position as secretary of state, he did not attempt to disguise his preferences for France, whether in personal style or political alliance. Even when uncomfortable with the publicity he received over Paine's *Rights of Man*, he did not remove the author's portrait from his display of American worthies. This image as Francophile and supporter of a radical writer would not be forgotten by those who chose to use it against him in the political contests to come. But he did not list this in his reasons for wishing to retreat from his national position and return to his Virginia estate, Monticello. His character was threatened. It was time to retire.[93]

Word was about that Jefferson would be leaving his position at the end of 1793. John Adams wrote to Abigail concerning their formerly close friend: "I am told Mr. Jefferson is to resign tomorrow. I have so long been in an habit of thinking well of his Abilities and general good dispositions, that I cannot but feel some regret at this Event." He went on to predict, "If he is neglected at Montecello he will soon see a Spectre like the disgraced States-man in Gill Blass, and not long afterwards will die." Adams was referring to the *The Adventures of Gil Blas* and was comparing Jefferson to the count in the story, who after losing position and reputation retires to his gardens only to be haunted to an early death. Adams concludes his thought: "For instead of being the ardent pursuer of science that some think him, I know he is indolent, and his soul is poisoned with Ambition."[94]

Jefferson left Philadelphia for Monticello on January 5, 1794, where he would spend the next three years redesigning his house and focusing upon his farms. He did not die like the count in *Gil Blas*, but then he was hardly neglected or forgotten. Alexander Hamilton recognized in 1795 that "there are three persons prominent in the public eye, as the successor of the actual President of the United States [Washington] in the event of his retreat from the station, Mr. Adams, Mr. Jay, Mr. Jefferson."[95] Hamilton was not mistaken. Jefferson would rejoin Adams in Philadelphia as his vice president.

4

CAMPAIGNING FOR CHANGE

A cannon salvo and a banner reading "Jefferson the Friend of the People" welcomed the vice president–elect upon his arrival in Philadelphia on March 2, 1797.[1] Jefferson had lost the presidential office to John Adams by three electoral votes, but he claimed indifference and wrote, "The second office of this government is honorable & easy, the first is but a splendid misery."[2] He had another purpose in Philadelphia. On the day before the national inauguration, he would be invested as president of the American Philosophical Society.[3] Serving as president of the oldest learned society in the country would be an honor as meaningful to Jefferson as public office. This dual image as man of the people and man of science would work both for him and against him as he remained at the center of political controversy.

The election of 1796 had been close. Even with his loss, Jefferson remained the leading republican contender for the presidential election of 1800. This made him the target for Federalist commentaries in the newspapers and in print culture. Federalist writers were ready with their pens, and favored themes appeared and reappeared: Jefferson the timid philosopher and Francophile, Jefferson the hypocrite, Jefferson the enemy of the Constitution, and Jefferson the atheist. Each characterization was aimed at creating doubts among voters and raising the question before the electorate: Was Thomas Jefferson qualified to be president of the United States?

During Jefferson's three-year hiatus at Monticello, the larger issue had not changed. Would this experiment in democratic-republican government be a success? The Federalists saw anarchy as the greatest threat and believed strong leadership a necessity. This belief framed their pen-portraits of Jefferson as the timid, whimsical intellectual who would be unable to keep the country on course. It would be up to Jefferson to take strong political stands and hone an image that would reassure the electorate of his leadership abilities, all the while remaining the enlightened gentleman who would still be the Friend of the People.

If Jefferson is to be believed, he did not seek the nomination for the presidential office in 1796. As the rumor began to spread that Washington intended to step down from the presidency at the conclusion of his current term, James Madison confided to James Monroe, "The republicans knowing that Jefferson alone can be started with hope of success mean to push him." But based on his recent correspondence with Jefferson, Madison feared that if openly approached, Jefferson would publicly decline standing for the office.[4] Conversely, Jefferson suggested that Madison, still active in the House of Representatives, should pursue the top office in the nation. Jefferson did not want to give up his own retirement "for the empire of the Universe" and admitted some guilt in requesting that Madison, "one, whose happiness I have as much at heart" should "take the front of the battle." He had not forgotten the "battles" that he had experienced in Washington's cabinet or the humiliation at seeing his name put before the public in unfavorable newspaper essays. He may have felt some guilt in pushing Madison, but he was the one person with whom Jefferson felt comfortable taking the helm and guiding "the fortune of our political bark."[5]

Was this simply posturing to cover his ambition? Many opponents at the time would have argued so, but it is possible that Jefferson felt genuine reluctance to step once more into a national position after his experiences as secretary of state. He remembered the animosities laid bare in the press that aimed at his political ideas and even his character. He felt his gentlemanly requisite of public duty had been fulfilled, which left him free to maintain his honor and reputation by removing himself from the public sphere and indulging in the tranquility of his farms and the satisfaction of personal labor. Given his age, he was fully aware of the imperative of bringing his neglected estate into full operation, which he estimated would take four to five years. And as to ambition, he exonerated himself of the desire and claimed, "The little spice of ambition, which I had in my younger days, has long since evaporated, and I set still less store by a posthumous than present name."[6] He considered the question of his holding public office closed.

Even though alerted to Jefferson's reservations, Madison continued planning the presidential election of 1796. James and Dolley Madison often made an extended trip to Monticello during the summer months, but that year he decided it best to avoid Jefferson and confided to Monroe, "I have not seen Jefferson and have thought it best to present him no opportunity of protesting to his friend against being embarked in the contest." He was not overly confident and confessed, "Whether he will get a majority of vote is uncertain. I am by no means sanguine." Madison admitted, "His enemies are as indefatigable as they are malignant."[7]

By October, Jefferson would have known his name was being put forward and apparently was resigned to the possibilities of once again entering public service.[8] He made the following reflective comment as he responded to a letter from a supporter: "I have not the arrogance to say I would refuse the honorable office you mention to me; but I can say with truth that I had rather be thought worthy of it than to be appointed to it." He concluded, "Well I know that no man will ever bring out of that office the reputation which carries him into it."[9] Jefferson cared about his public image and knew that image was easier to maintain and direct when standing slightly back, involved in but not leading the fray. But in the election of 1796 he was spared the worries of the first office by his loss to John Adams.

Jefferson felt he could not avoid being in Philadelphia for the inauguration. Rumors circulated that he considered the second office as beneath him. Not only did he want to counter these as false, he also felt his attendance was important as a mark of respect to the people. However, he alerted Madison that he would "escape into the city as covertly as possible." He shared more detail with his son-in-law, Thomas Mann Randolph: "I mean to get into Philadelphia under shadow of the stage and unperceived to avoid any formal reception." He admitted that he had given a later arrival date than what he actually anticipated.[10] His efforts were not successful, as he was greeted with a banner and sixteen rounds fired by the Company of Artillery. The newspapers announced the return of the "tried patriot."[11]

He spent the first night with the Madisons before moving into John Francis's hotel, which would remain his residence while in Philadelphia over the next four years.[12] He employed only one servant for attendance while he was in the city and again did business with Henrietta Gardiner for washing, as he had done while secretary of state. Mrs. Gardiner, as he often listed her in accounting records, was the wife of William Gardiner, the freed former valet of James Madison.[13] He recorded regular payments to an unnamed barber, some on a monthly basis; thus the duties of shaving and hair dressing were not assigned to the one servant he employed. He resumed using Thomas Billington the tailor and may have needed to replenish his wardrobe, as he paid very little for clothing during his time at Monticello.[14]

Carriages and horses had been left at Monticello, and so he began to walk. He hired a coach for only one event in 1797, to greet the Monroe family, returning from France, at the Philadelphia harbor and to attend a diner for Monroe on July 1 at Oellers' Hotel. Otherwise he walked and began this practice immediately. Newspaper accounts of the inauguration described how following the ceremony and a brief bit of business with the Senate, the new vice president "walked home" accompanied by well-wishers. President Adams, also staying at Francis's hotel until Washington vacated the President's House, made the trip in his newly acquired carriage.[15] In subsequent years spent as vice president, Jefferson hired a horse if he needed to travel outside the city.[16]

Very practical explanations can be applied to these chosen living arrangements. As he foresaw his new office, "It will give me philosophical evenings in the winter, and rural days in summer."[17] On those "philosophical evenings," the new president of the American Philosophical Society could enjoy intellectual exchanges with other members, but this did not require a fully staffed residence, and he intended to divide his time between Monticello and his duties in Philadelphia. In 1796 he had begun the redesign and rebuilding of his house, which was a project that totally engaged his interest. When he served as secretary of state, his younger daughter, Maria, spent time with him in Philadelphia while she was enrolled in boarding school, but now he was alone. Maria was engaged to her cousin, John Wayles Eppes, and would marry in October 1797.[18] A room at John Francis's hotel was sufficient. His living arrangement left more resources available for his house renovation and building projects at Monticello.

These practical considerations could account in part for forgoing a carriage and taking room and board in a hotel, but then how did this play into his political profile over the next four years as vice president and, as placed by Hamilton, at the head of a party? This marked the beginning of a new image and a shift away from his self-presentation as secretary of state. Gone was the elegant residence with its French furniture, art, dinner parties, and a full staff to manage the household and entertaining. Vice President Jefferson's walks to and from the State House and about Philadelphia would have presented a very different impression than Secretary of State Jefferson in his carriage or phaeton with his personal servant, the young French boy

Joseph, following on horseback. By arriving in the public stage and walking to and from the inauguration, Jefferson immediately began constructing his image as the man of the people.

When Jefferson undertook the office of secretary of state, he professed that he entered into the new political scene as a stranger. Not so as he rejoined the national government as vice president. He was perfectly aware of the issues and had to know that greeting the Monroe family at the Philadelphia harbor in late June 1797, just four months after his inauguration, was sure to make news.

The Monroes were returning from France under a political cloud. Washington had assigned James Monroe as minister to France during negotiations for the controversial Jay Treaty, which tied the United States to an almost exclusive trade agreement with Britain. Monroe was instructed to reassure France of the United States' continued alliance even while negotiations with Britain were ongoing; however, his overzealous assurances to the French government, which extended to encouragement in their war with Britain, placed the Washington administration in an awkward position. Monroe had made some unfortunate choices, including harboring the notorious Thomas Paine after securing his release from a French prison. Monroe served in France for two years before receiving a sudden and humiliating recall that potentially could have ended his public career.[19]

Jefferson went on board ship to meet the Monroe family, and if this were not enough provocation to the Federalists, he was joined by Albert Gallatin and Aaron Burr. These men showed rising profiles among the republican faction, and both had openly challenged Alexander Hamilton and Federalist policy. Jefferson marked the occasion with a hired a coach, which he used again a few nights later at Oellers' Hotel for a dinner in Monroe's honor. This was not an instance in which quietly appearing on foot supported the statement he was making. Jefferson was the ranking political member at the dinner given for Monroe. He left the welcome speech to Judge Thomas McKean, but then Jefferson always avoided public speaking. Still, the first personal toast after those to the United States, their allies, peace, and liberty was to Thomas Jefferson, hailed as a "Man of the People."[20] He must have realized this would be covered in the press and could only be interpreted as a very deliberate demonstration against an action initiated by Washington and fulfilled under Adams's continuing Federalist administration.

The Monroe affair marked a decided shift in Jefferson's public role as the republican leader. His earlier wish—to "go on in a strict but silent performance" of his duty and to keep his "name out of newspapers"—was not an option if he and his colleagues were to bring about change in the next national election.[21] He had to accept that public criticisms were sure to be aimed at him. His name would appear in newspapers.

In the build-up to the election of 1796, a series of editorials appeared under the pen name "Phocion." This pseudonym assumed that the reader knew their Plutarch well enough to recognize Phocion as the Athenian general and statesman from the fourth century BCE who always responded when called by the people for service. He represented strong, serious, and sensible leadership.[22] Hamilton had used this pseudonym in the past, but from 1796 to 1800, when the letters were directed against Jefferson, it was more often the cover for William Loughton Smith of Charleston, South Carolina. Smith was a wealthy southern Federalist who published a series of letters under the name Phocion in the *Charleston Courier* that were picked up by other newspapers.[23] In 1796 he compiled these into a pamphlet titled *Pretensions of Thomas Jefferson to the Presidency Examined.* A degree of elitism shaded these Federalist writings, submitted under the names of famous classical figures of Greece and Rome, which made Jefferson hope they would not appeal to the average American. During the congressional debates over the Jay Treaty, he tested a piece he believed to be by either Hamilton or Jay and reported to Madison, "I gave a copy or two by way of experiment to honest sound hearted men of common understanding, and they were not able to parry the sophistry [in this instance] of Curtius."[24] These men made up the political base of the Democratic-Republicans, and Jefferson needed to know their reaction to the editorials by Smith and others that questioned his character and leadership abilities.

Jefferson's successful cultivation of his image as a *philosophe* while in France had reached the United States and could well have influenced his election as president of the American Philosophical Society. Jefferson the intellectual also drew the notice of Alexander Hamilton, William Loughton Smith, and other Federalist writers. Early in the decade, when conflicts first began to appear, Hamilton observed in a private letter that Jefferson "drank deeply of the French Philosophy, in Religion, in Science, in politics."[25] At the beginning of the French Revolution, Hamilton expressed to Lafayette his "dread" of France's "Philosophic politicians" and their misguided appraisals of the character of the people and what (or who) would best direct the French nation.[26] He obviously held these same feelings towards the "unthinking populace" in America as well. Early in their own revolution, he had expressed to John Jay his belief that "it requires the greatest skill in the political pilots to keep men steady and within proper bounds."[27] Strong leadership was extremely important.

In 1796 Smith picked up this theme in his series of editorials penned under the name Phocion. He stated clearly that Jefferson's pose as a philosopher should disqualify him for the presidency. Smith defined the characteristic traits of the philosopher as timidity, whimsicality, and a lack of "energy in action" should an emergency arise. He created a scenario in which the president's ministers called upon him, only to find him in his cabinet impaling butterflies. Interesting that he chose this analogy, as Jefferson never assembled a butterfly collection, but perhaps it suited as a delicate operation and so created a contrast to his proclamation: "The great Washington was, thank God, no philosopher."[28]

Other writers adopted the same theme. One pointed out that the factious men who would surround the "timid president" would compel him to adopt their policies.[29] But none wrote quite so colorfully as Smith's Phocion. In the same commentary in which he described Jefferson with his butterfly collection, he added comments on Jefferson's Whirligig Chair. This required recalling Jefferson's days as secretary of state when he lived at his fully furnished house on Market Street. The chair, according to Smith, "had the miraculous quality of allowing the person seated in it to turn his head without moving his tail."[30] The revolving chair must have struck Smith as particularly appropriate for philosopher Jefferson, as it gave physical form to the deceit and hypocrisy symbolized by the face and the body being turned in different directions. Jefferson purchased the revolving chair in 1790 from John Burlington, a furniture maker in New York, and it is still located at Monticello. The irony is that Burlington made a similar chair for George Washington.[31]

To address Jefferson the *philosophe,* Smith had to recognize Jefferson's one published book, *Notes on the State of Virginia.* In "Phocion I" he quoted heavily from *Notes* and called attention to Jefferson's discussion on slavery and race. He presented Jefferson's "extravagant project of emancipating all the slaves of Virginia" and his "more extravagant one of afterwards shipping them off to some other country" as highly implausible. Smith knew he had to be very careful in his discussion of the social and economic deliberations attached to emancipation or he could alienate some northern Federalists. He could more easily criticize Jefferson for his racist views, and so he launched into a long extract from *Notes.* He included Jefferson's aversion to the intermixing of races and his doubts as to the ability of the master and his former slaves to live together under the same government.[32]

In "Phocion IV" Smith resumed his discussion of emancipation. He did not reiterate his claim of Jefferson as racist but made a point against "philosophical politicians" and warned the southern states of Jefferson's hypocrisy—yes, he is a Virginia slaveholder, but he believes in emancipation, which can hold very dangerous consequences. Smith cast the French intellectuals marquis de Condorcet and Jacques Pierre Brissot among those influencing the idea of emancipation of slaves in the French West Indies, thus painting them as participants in the slave revolt in Saint-Domingue (now Haiti). In Smith's estimation the bad judgement of these two French *philosophes* resulted in the massacre of many innocent people, and he suggested that the citizens of the southern states pay attention. Jefferson was a philosopher and a friend of Condorcet. Smith left it unsaid, but he certainly planted the idea that Jefferson's philosophical temperament could create such anarchy in the United States.[33] In "Phocion V" Smith continued to caution southern planters. He stated, "For my part, were I a southern planter, owning negroes, I should be ten thousand times more alarmed at Mr. Jefferson's ardent wish for emancipation, than at any fanciful dangers from monarchy."[34] This image of Jefferson the emancipator was far more sinister than the whimsical scholar impaling butterflies, but it raised the same question: Would you trust this man as your president?

In the presidential elections of 1796 and 1800, Jefferson's role as a slave owner and his views on race were placed before the public. Smith would not have taken up these issues had there not been some public interest. But his criticism was directed more strongly at the economic and social impacts that would result from emancipation rather than the ethical issues attached to chattel slavery. Smith was very open that he did not favor emancipation or mixing of the races. However, what appears more often in the newspaper essays was not the question of Jefferson's stand on slavery and emancipation but rather his ideas on religion. The next president of the United States might be a slave owner—but an atheist?

"But it does me no injury for my neighbor to say there are twenty gods, or no god. It neither picks my pocket nor breaks my leg."[35] This was Jefferson's bold assertion in *Notes* that some Americans found alarming. His name was attached also to the Statute of Virginia for Religious Freedom, which was often misconstrued as being aimed at limiting religious practice rather than its true purpose of safeguarding religious preferences from state regulation. An essay appearing in a Newport, Rhode Island, newspaper in September 1800 warned, "He ridicules the Bible, with wanton malignity. 'No matter,' says he somewhere, 'whether there be twenty Gods, or no God.' Is such a man fit to be President of the United States?"[36]

Smith chose Jefferson's quote of "twenty gods, or no god" as the focus for his "Phocion X." He was once again prowling through *Notes on the State of Virginia* for material that could prove the author unsuitable for the nation's highest office. Unlike the writer from Rhode Island, who only knew that Jefferson was reputed to have said this "somewhere," Smith could cite source and page number. In his essay he equated religious freedom with freedom *from* religion, claimed this attitude was more prevalent among philosophers educated in France, and suggested that most French philosophers were atheists. Smith brought the Statue for Religious Freedom into his discussion by questioning whether attendance at public worship in Virginia had improved with this statute. This led to his main point, which contended that patriotism was based on moral principles, and these were connected to religion.[37] Without active religious participation, patriotism in American could decline.

Some opposition voices were willing to acknowledge Jefferson's finer traits as a cosmopolitan intellectual and polished gentleman, but they were linked with a warning to beware. As in Hamilton's earlier accusations, Jefferson's charm was presented as a guise and a cover for duplicity. One Federalist described him thus: "Jefferson with his accustomed ease and elegance, Jefferson, the scholar and the gentleman." But having admitted to these qualities, the writer cautions the reader not to be disarmed by his polished, gentlemanly appearance. The ultimate message was still that Jefferson did not possess the qualities needed to be the American president.

An opposition writer concerned with Jefferson's religious beliefs admitted to his distinguished character traits and described "the elegant and refined philosopher of *Monticelli*, who has given a polish to the character of the American style, and who is master of the boldest, as well as the most beautiful imagery." But this elegant and bold style was misdirected. The writer proceeds to alert the reader to Jefferson's close following of the atheistic beliefs of French philosophers Voltaire and Jean le Rond d'Alembert.

Yet another writer addressed his comments directly to Jefferson and claimed: "Nature, Sir, in profusion gifted you with talents, a brilliant fancy, penetrating genius, with a native elegance of diction, combined with a thirst for knowledge, formed you a man of learning and taste, well acquainted with the classics, deeply read in the Philosophy of natural history, observant of men and things, and attentive in theory to political concerns." But here lay the problem. Despite admitting these admirable qualities, this writer questioned Jefferson's grasp of "political concerns." He continued: "But, to balance these singular favors, she denied you others, which, 'to move in a tempestuous sea of liberty,' or guide the helm of a great nation are of more utility and absolutely indispensable. — Your fortitude has been tried and found unequal to the task." Here was another critic who argued that Jefferson was too intellectual to be an effective leader and was better suited for a sedentary life that would not tax his delicate nerves. The writer took up the familiar argument that "when Governor of Virginia, you fled from your State because a storm was gathering."[38] This Federalist did not deny Jefferson's intelligence and talents but claimed he lacked the fortitude needed to be head of state.

Another Federalist counted Jefferson's gentlemanly self-fashioning and elegant bearing as a part of his cunning and allowed that Jefferson, "by the help of an insinuating address, a soft counter tenor voice, a civil and affected smile, and a happy flexibility in the vetribrae of his back bone, performed wonders amongst the unsuspected classes of citizens, by way of *electioneering!*" Self-promotion was not a gentlemanly trait, but in the opinion of this Federalist, Jefferson was cunning enough to cover his "electioneering" with that "ease and elegance" that distinguished him.[39] This description is especially interesting, as it gives Jefferson a "soft, counter tenor voice" that might explain his reluctance to speak in large groups.

The Federalists fostered the notion that even though Jefferson could so easily be the gentleman, the American aristocrat, yet his goals were to subvert the American republic. One writer believed Jefferson's aims were "to substitute a pure and unmixed democracy, in place of our well-balanced Republic." Following this, Jefferson meant "to Jacobinize, revolutionize, and of course, demoralize the people of these happy United States."[40] To be too democratic was to be dangerous and radical.

Jefferson supporters were not idle. They responded and countered with rebuttal after rebuttal to reassure voters that Jefferson was their principal safeguard of republican standards and their staunchest opponent to the threat of monarchical government. He had written the Declaration of Independence and pushed for important amendments to the Constitution. He was not the Jacobin intent on selling out the United States to the French; rather, he was the enlightened citizen and patriot. His supporters gave as

FIGURE 21. "The Providential Detection," unidentified artist, c. 1799.

This anonymous political caricature encapsulates the Federalist propaganda aimed at Jefferson during the critical election of 1800.

well as they received in the newspapers, but not all Federalist accusations were published as written essays.

A political caricature titled "The Providential Detection" (fig. 21) visually encapsulated the major themes of the anti-Jefferson opinion articles appearing in the Federalist press and shared their purpose of alerting the public to the danger of placing Thomas Jefferson in a position of leadership. The caricature's origin, creator, and exact date are somewhat mysterious, but the identity of the principal figure and the message are quite clear. Clues in the print place it late in the 1790s, most probably a product of the build-up to the presidential election of 1800. Even if one did not recognize the face, the central figure must be Thomas Jefferson.

American caricatures took inspiration from those published in England. The satirical print had grown in popularity in London in the second half of the eighteenth century, possibly spurred by the greater political participation of the British populace along with the growth of the print industry. During the colonial period and in the years of the early republic, printing expenses prohibited a large number of caricatures from appearing in North America. When they did appear, they generally were printed as broadsides on individual pieces of paper, and in both England and the United States these were sold in print- or bookshops where sales were directed towards the elites and propertied middle classes.[41] With so little known about the production of "The Providential Detection," however, it is difficult to project how many people actually owned or saw the caricature, but it remains a valuable visual example of the Federalist campaign against Jefferson in the election of 1800.[42]

The title, "The Providential Detection," stretches across the lower edge of the print and visually supports and adds meaning to the overall design. In the drama unfolding in the caricature, the United States Constitution (and thereby American independence) is in danger of being destroyed. Only the diligence of the eagle—representing the American polity and watched over by the eye of providence—can avert disaster. Most viewers would have been familiar with these two symbols that comprise the Great Seal of the United States: the eagle on the obverse and the pyramid with the eye of providence in a triangle on the reverse.[43] The message proposed by "The Providential Detection" is that of danger. The freedom and virtue of this exceptional American republic could become victim to anarchy, Jacobinism, and atheism. Without diligence on the part of patriots, the figure kneeling at the "Altar to Gallic Despotism" could bring down the republic.

The most recognizable evidence of the figure's identity is the document titled "To Mazzei" dropping from his right hand. Jefferson had written a letter to his Italian friend Philip Mazzei dated April 24, 1796, and after relaying necessary business he launched into a summary of current politics, charging that "the aspect of our politics has wonderfully changed since you left us. In place of that noble love of liberty and republican government which carried us triumphantly thro' the war, an Anglican, monarchical and aristocratical party has sprung up." But the political storm whipped up by the letter arose primarily over its negative implication of the great Washington. Jefferson suggested that "men who were Samsons in the field and Solomons in the council . . . have had their heads shorn by the harlot England."[44] Mazzei shared portions from this letter, resulting in its publication in a French newspaper early in 1797. By May of that year it had made its way back to the United States, where it appeared first in the New York *Minerva* before quickly being picked up by other publications.[45] Jefferson asked Madison's advice, although he had all but decided "to be entirely silent," as he had done regarding his endorsement of Paine's *Rights of Man* when it caused a similar controversy. Some of his original language had become twisted in translation and reprinting, but disentangling and explaining his meaning would only draw attention to his aspersions against Washington. Jefferson was enough the politician to realize that it would publicize "a personal difference between Genl. Washington and myself, which nothing before the publication of this letter has ever done: it would embroil me also with all those with whom his character is still popular, that is to say nine tenths of the people of the US."[46] Jefferson requested that Madison come for his summer visit to Monticello and bring Monroe so the three of them could discuss this and other political matters. This triumvirate of Jefferson, Madison, and Monroe continued to grow tighter and stronger.

The reprinting of the letter in the United States would set the date for "The Providential Detection" at some point after May 1797. The Mazzei letter not only provided a favored topic for the Federalist press prior to the election of 1800; it also would continue to dog Jefferson throughout his career. As John Marshall expressed to Alexander Hamilton, "The morals of the Author of the letter to Mazzei cannot be pure."[47] The Mazzei letter was the political caricature's boldest link to Jefferson, as the scraps of paper fueling the flames intended for the Constitution are not so much an identification of person as an identification of character. They contain names that to some were heretical and reflected Jefferson's all too liberal and philosophic attitudes that Hamilton had warned against. It was as though the artist had access to Jefferson's personal library. Prominent is the name of the English writer William Godwin, whose doctrine on the perfectibility of mankind predicted a lessening need for government.[48] The American edition of Godwin's *Enquiry concerning Political Justice* was published in Philadelphia in 1796 and remained a part of Jefferson's library until sold to Congress in 1815. Then there is the French philosopher Helvétius, whose views on public ethics Jefferson commended; he described him as "the most ingenious advocate of this principle." (While in Paris, Jefferson had frequented the intellectual salons of Helvétius's widow.)[49] More conservative thinkers could interpret both Godwin and Helvétius as anarchists in their views that less government would be beneficial to society; Godwin openly professed to be an atheist.

Not surprisingly, the title of Thomas Paine's most recent work, *Age of Reason*, is visible on the altar. Many of Jefferson's political opponents would remember Jefferson's endorsement of Paine's earlier work, *Rights of Man*, with his bold assessment that "something is at length to be publicly said against the political heresies which have sprung up among us." By the time the first part of *Age of Reason* was published in 1794, followed by the second part in 1795, Jefferson was far more circumspect and cautious as to any public connection. Still, in the 1796 presidential election, Smith recalled Jefferson's link with Paine. His "Phocion X" warned the American public that if Jefferson were elected president, undoubtedly Paine would return to America and join Mr. Jefferson at the presidential dinner table, "where the enlightened pair of philosophers would fraternize, and philosophize against the *Christian religion* and the absurdity of *religious worship*."[50] Paine's *Age of Reason* was extremely controversial with its criticism of established churches, so when "The Providential Detection" combines his name with Godwin's and Helvétius's, it definitely suggests that Jefferson himself was an atheist.

Another name on the Gallic altar with a more local and immediate connection to Jefferson is that of "Munro," referring to James Monroe, who published a controversial pamphlet refuting his recall from France during Washington's administration.[51] The pamphlet was critical of Washington, while it was well known that Monroe was a close friend and political colleague of Jefferson's. The dinner given for Monroe after his return where a toast was drunk to Jefferson as "Man of the People" was reported in a Federalist newspaper that suggested he should be toasted as "Man of the French People."[52] Jefferson as Francophile threads through the caricature. Then there are the republican newspapers on the altar—the *Aurora* of Philadelphia and the *Chronicle*, most likely indicating the Boston *Independent Chronicle*—that supported Jefferson and his political colleagues in opposition to the Federalist press. The skulls and crossed bones circling the base of the altar indicate the poison in this thinking that feeds the flames. Behind all of this lurks the devil.

These thrusts of negative propaganda were aimed at the public character and virtue of Thomas Jefferson, which were of critical consideration when evaluating leadership, especially in a republic where government corruption could bring downfall. With no recognition of hereditary superiority, leadership must be based on merit.[53] Thus Jefferson's actions, philosophy, friends, and associates all were evaluated. The creators of "The Providential Detection" did not overlook physical appearance and the message that could be projected through clothing, facial features and expression, deportment and mannerisms. These tools of self-fashioning became a means of projecting the Jefferson image.

Although the central figure kneeling before the altar is readily identified by the document he holds labeled "To Mazzei," the face in profile would have been recognized as Jefferson's by those who knew him personally or perhaps had seen a formal portrait or print of him. There was the public display of Jefferson's portrait in Peale's gallery, yet the caricature's features bear an especially good likeness to the Houdon bust portrait of Jefferson in profile. No Houdon bust of Jefferson is known to have been on public display in the late 1790s; however, Jefferson brought back at least one, and possibly more, from Paris. One that he presumably had at his residence in Philadelphia was presented to David Rittenhouse in January 1793 with a note explaining: "Th: Jefferson, beginning to pack his useless furniture, finds nothing more so than the article he now sends to Mr. Rittenhouse." He goes on about the "uselessness of the thing" but says that it is presented with "the sincere affection of the giver; as a testimony of which he desires Mr. Rittenhouse to give it house-room."[54] At the time the gift was given, Secretary of State Jefferson was in the process of downsizing his residence in Philadelphia, preparing for his retirement to Monticello. His comments to Rittenhouse make it sound likely that he did display his own bust alongside the others in his collection, although it did not elicit the caustic remarks from the British secretary Thornton as had the busts of Franklin, John Paul Jones, and Lafayette. Rittenhouse provided the bust the house-room Jefferson requested until after his death, when his daughter donated it to the American Philosophical Society in 1811.[55] And so at the time in which "The Providential Detection" was created, there would have been a Houdon of Jefferson in Philadelphia, although not on public display. Whatever the source, "The Providential Detection" offers a reasonable likeness of Jefferson that did not have the exaggerated features that often appeared in caricatures.

For "The Providential Detection" the artist depicts a very slim figure dressed in fashionable clothing that fits the body very snugly. This coincides with Senator William Maclay's first impression of Jefferson, whose "cloaths seem too small for him," and underscores his comment that Jefferson displayed "more than Parisian politeness."[56] Certainly "The Providential Detection" seeks to link Jefferson with France through many allusions, and the slim cut of the clothing could serve as one more visual link.

The interpretation of the cut and fit of clothing must always allow for personal taste and thus some subjectivity; however, one clothing element made very visible in the caricature definitely links with revolution and reform. This is the footwear. The figure of Jefferson wears ankle-high shoes or boots that are tied with strings rather than closed with the usual buckles. Various contemporary references describe this change in men's shoes. In 1792 the duc d'Orléans, a sympathizer with the revolutionary faction in France, was described as wearing his hair cut short and unpowdered and shoes tied with strings.[57] This style began appearing in England as well and was noted by British parliamentarian and writer Sir William Wraxall. In his memoirs he looks back at this period of revolutions and comments on the "discredit on dress" making its way into England, but he maintains that "dress never totally fell till the era of Jacobinism and of equality in 1793 and 1794. It was then that pantaloons, cropped hair, and shoe-strings, as well as the total abolition of buckles and ruffles, together with the disuse of hair-powder, characterized the men."[58] The figure in "The Providential Detection" still wears the older fashion of knee breeches, and his hair is pulled into a queue and from the tonalities in the print appears very light and so possibly powdered. But the shoes tied with string are a feature that points to revolutionary ideas coming to Jefferson via Europe.

The long cloak draped about the figure adds a sense of drama and for a contemporary viewer would have been appropriate to the theme. Late in the eighteenth century the cloak was no longer as fashionable for men's outerwear, its place taken by the greatcoat; however, cloaks were still worn for funerals, a custom that extended back to the Middle Ages.[59] The long, dramatic cloak could be interpreted as yet another symbol of Jefferson's preparation for the funeral of the Constitution and thereafter the death of American stability and independence, should he be elected to the presidency.

The assertion that Jefferson was a dangerous Francophile is skillfully incorporated into this political print through the appearance of the figure and the props that surround him. This theme appeared and reappeared in the press to the degree that an anonymous essay in a New York paper of June

1798 proposed that Jefferson and other leaders of the republican faction intended to work with France to overthrow the US government and set up a Directory on the French model.[60] Another anonymous article listed reasons why Thomas Jefferson, supporter of the Jacobin faction, was unfit for the presidency: he was a Deist, he opposed an energetic government, he opposed the laws, and his object was the subversion of order and destruction of religious principles, and, lastly: "His household is *French*—his language, his dress, his manners, his associates are *French*—his library and Philosophy are *French*.—Such a number of *French* dishes might be unpalatable to the *American* taste."[61]

Another opposition essay printed in a New England newspaper in July 1797 echoes so very closely the points made in "The Providential Detection" that it raises the question if one inspired the other. The writer expresses his pity for the American people if Jefferson is "their man." If so, then they should "strike their colours," "attend the funeral rites of Liberty and Independence," "assume the tri-coloured cockade" (which represents France), and "establish the French festivals as their days of worship." The writer predicts that "Thomas Jefferson would then dispense the rites of the Altar, with pious alacrity, and Thomas Paine would be his proper deacon to distribute the sacrament of the devil's communion table."[62]

The drama taking place in "The Providential Detection" casts Thomas Jefferson as an anarchist with a dangerously radical philosophy that reflects his French preferences in both thought and appearance. His aim is to sabotage the American Constitution. It is true that upon first seeing a draft of the new Constitution he expressed concern that there was no bill of rights and no term limits set for the president. When he received a draft in Paris, he complained to Adams in London that "their President seems a bad edition of a Polish king. He may be reelected from 4. years to 4. years for life." As an officer for life who controls the military, it would be hard to "dethrone" him. Adams held a very different view. "You are apprehensive the President when once chosen, will be chosen again and again as long as he lives. So much the better as it appears to me. . . . Elections, my dear sir, Elections to offices which are great objects of Ambition, I look at with terror." These very early remarks reflect their differing opinions on the structure needed to create a stable, functioning republican government. Adams feared anarchy; Jefferson feared monarchy.[63]

As early as 1789 Jefferson had found himself needing to explain his views on the Constitution. He wrote to Francis Hopkinson, "You say that I have been dished up to you as an antifederalist, and ask me if it be just." He stated flatly, "I am not a Federalist," and was equally adamant that "I am much farther from that of the Antifederalists." The Antifederalists had fought the ratification of the Constitution, and even though Jefferson had felt strongly that the Constitution should be amended to include a bill of rights, once he was assured it would be so done, he added his support for "the great mass of good it contains." That left unsettled the question of term limits for the office of president, but the recent inauguration of Washington left time to resolve this issue. The matter could rest until he left office, as Jefferson felt Washington's name and integrity offered the stability needed by the new government.[64]

His early reservations regarding the Constitution came back at him magnified, as he increasingly became the focus of the political debates of the 1790s. In his first essay aimed at Jefferson, Hamilton, writing as "An American," contended that as the Constitution was being debated and placed before the people, "Mr. Jefferson, being in France, was opposed to it."[65] In another of his letters, Hamilton did not name Jefferson specifically but opened with the question, "What is the most sacred duty and the greatest source of security in a Republic?" His self-supplied answer was, "An inviolable respect for the Constitution and Laws."[66] In his estimation contempt invariably led to anarchy. Other Federalists followed Hamilton's lead, which pushed Jefferson's defenders to remind readers that it was not true that he did not zealously support the Constitution.[67] But his defenders could turn to another document of national importance as proof of Jefferson's patriotism—the Declaration of Independence.

The Fourth of July evolved in the 1790s from a locally celebrated event into a national holiday that by mid-decade began to take on partisan overtones. Early in Washington's administration, festivities were often led by local chapters of the Society of the Cincinnati, and Federalists fully participated. By 1793 celebrations began to divide into two factions: those held by elite Federalist organizations and those led by the republicans, who used the occasion to demonstrate their opposition to Federalist policy and to champion what they claimed to be "true republicanism." Along with the parades, cannon fire, and ringing bells, the republican celebrations supported the revolution in France with liberty poles and red liberty caps.[68] These celebrations were often accompanied by a reading of the Declaration of Independence. Some Federalists questioned the propriety of recalling the not-so-distant conflict with Britain considering the improved relations under the Jay Treaty. By its very origins the document was linked to revolution, which disturbed some given the ongoing upheaval in France.[69] Sentiment showed divisions along political lines.

By 1794 Jefferson and Madison began to be toasted as a part of Independence Day celebrations, and by 1800 acknowledgement of Jefferson's role as author of the declaration was a part of the republican electioneering. The *Independent Chronicle* in Boston described how, "at an early age, he had the glory of conceiving and of composing . . . the great charter of our national independence." Another pro-Jefferson editorial advised, "We hold it to be clear that the fate of America, in a great measure depends upon placing at the head of our Federal Government at the next ensuing election, the author of that celebrated declaration which secured to America her freedom and happiness."[70]

As Jefferson's name became more firmly attached to the declaration and the Independence Day celebrations began to be dominated by the republicans, the Federalists backed away from any participation. Jefferson received a private letter describing the Federalist boycott that made the Fourth of July parade "a parade of republicans only; the other party gave no demonstrations of joy, the church bells were silent, & the[y] were generally attending to their daily occupations." Jefferson's correspondent felt that "this was showing their true colors."[71] The Philadelphia *Aurora* validated what Jefferson learned privately: the Fourth of July 1800 "was celebrated by republicans—and by them only."[72]

The Jefferson of "The Providential Detection," who would destroy the constitution; or the Jefferson described in newspaper editorials as a whimsical philosophe incapable of firm leadership; or the Jefferson depicted as the dangerous Jacobin—all ran counter to the image that republicans needed for the upcoming election. Jefferson as the American patriot dressed in the blue and the buff still hung in Peale's gallery, but this portrait was painted in 1791. As the election began in earnest at the end of the decade, a new formal portrait—one that projected a Jefferson who was steady and capable of strong, decisive, and responsible leadership—would be timely and help combat the image projected by the Federalists.

Jefferson would have denied any electioneering, but from late 1799 into mid-1800, he sat for four different artists.[73] He only commissioned one himself, which was from the acclaimed Gilbert Stuart, who was working in Philadelphia at the time. The other requests came from the artists, which Jefferson could have refused, but he made time for the sittings. Of

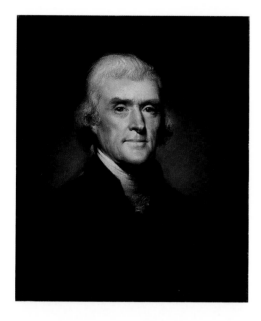

FIGURE 22. Thomas Jefferson by Rembrandt Peale, 1800. Oil on canvas.

Rembrandt Peale's portrait became the definitive image of Jefferson during the election of 1800 and was widely reproduced in prints. Peale depicts Jefferson in the black suit that was gaining popularity among well-dressed American men.

the resulting portraits, the one that would make Jefferson's facial image as familiar to the American public as the rhetorical images created in newspapers was created by Rembrandt Peale, the second son of Charles Willson Peale (fig. 22).

The younger Peale was eager to establish his reputation as a portrait artist. His newspaper advertisements played on his name: "Rembrandt" was set in bold type across the top of his notices. The artist-commissioned portrait was taken between Jefferson's arrival in Philadelphia in the last week of December 1799 and mid-May 1800, when he returned to Monticello. A sure gauge of Rembrandt's success in achieving a good Jefferson likeness was the number of prints produced from his portrait and the rapidity with which they appeared.[74] The interest shown in having a portrait of Jefferson that could be engraved and marketed as an affordable print confirmed his standing as a strong contender in the increasingly heated presidential election.

Rembrandt's Jefferson has a different demeanor than earlier extant portraits. In both the Mather Brown and in the C. W. Peale portraits, the figure of Jefferson gazes into the distance as though in contemplation rather than engaging the viewer directly; however, when these portraits were taken Jefferson was not being accused of being the whimsical, weak intellectual. Conveying a look of resolve had become important. Rembrandt gave the republicans a Jefferson who appeared calm, solid, and straightforward. This

FIGURE 23. George Washington by
James Heath after Gilbert Stuart,
1800. Engraving.

Gilbert Stuart's full-length image of
Washington was made available to
the general public through a print
produced in London by James Heath.

attitude was supported by depicting Jefferson dressed in sober black. The
public would remember former President Washington in his signatory black
velvet suit, or they might have purchased a recent print by James Heath
taken from Gilbert Stuart's full-length portrait of Washington (fig. 23). This
print had been published in London in January 1800 following Washington's death the previous December.[75] Even though the print is in gray scale,
Washington's suit, stockings, shoes, and hat (resting on the table) are of the
darkest tone, and as shoes and hat could be expected to be black, this interpretation could extend to the suit as well. As was usual for Western clothing, the fashion impetus for somber menswear was coming from Britain
and France, but its reception in the United States was growing, especially
after it was adopted by Washington.

This could account for its American popularity, but the color black also
has symbolic meaning that goes far back in Western culture. It has indicated mourning for centuries, and certainly Jefferson and Adams had experienced the court protocol surrounding black as the color for official

mourning when they served as ministers at Versailles. These requirements extended to all classes, and Louis-Sébastien Mercier, in his popular *Tableau de Paris*, derided the custom by suggesting that a permanent mourning might be welcomed: "These deaths suit everybody, since black clothes go very nicely with mud, bad weather, thrift and a reluctance to devote hours to one's toilet."[76]

Linked with the occasion of mourning was the idea of sobriety. Perhaps due to this connotation, black clothing became identified with ecclesiastics and scholars, but on occasion it appeared in the higher social milieus. When Castiglione wrote his *Book of the Courtier* in the first quarter of the sixteenth century, he recommended black as the most agreeable color for the "ordinary attire" of the polished Renaissance man and advised leaving the brighter colors for special occasions. He made his choice based upon the "sobriety" associated with black and used as an example the soberness of the Spaniards and their preference for black.[77] From sixteenth-century Spain—and through Spanish influence, both political and economic— the use of black clothing was adopted in seventeenth-century Holland and became the dominant color among the Dutch merchants and burghers. Here it moved from the courtier to become the mark of the middle-class, professional man.[78]

The bourgeois of France adopted black, and by the eighteenth century it was the customary color for the clothing of lawyers and other professionals (fig. 24). Arthur Young, an English traveler and writer, visited Paris in 1787. He noted in his journal the predominance of black clothing among those of the middle class and attributed it to a need for practicality. The city was filled with dusty streets that could quickly turn to mud—Mercier's reasoning for black—and suffered from a lack of hackney-coaches and chairs for hire. Young observed, "To this circumstance also it is owing, that all persons of small or moderate fortunes, are forced to dress in black, with black stockings." He doubted this visual distinction denoting rank would be tolerated in England.[79]

Young made these observations just prior to the revolution in France, a time when the black suit was briefly pushed to the center of controversy. When in May 1789 the Estates-General were called to debate France's growing financial crisis, the grand master of ceremonies advised the deputies of the three estates on the protocol to be followed in dress. The First Estate, the church, required their clergy to appear in ecclesiastical vestments appropriate to their position in the church. The Second Estate, the nobility,

FIGURE 24. Antoine-Laurent Lavoisier and his wife, Marie-Anne Pierrette Paulze, by Jacques-Louis David, 1788. Oil on canvas, 102¼ in. × 76⅝ in.

Lavoisier was a noted French chemist. When he was inducted into the American Philosophical Society as an honorary member in 1787, Jefferson forwarded his certificate of membership, and Lavoisier responded with a letter of gratitude. In this portrait by David, Lavoisier and his wife, Marie-Anne, are both fashionably dressed. As a wealthy bourgeoisie, Lavoisier wears the black suit and black stockings that had become associated with the professional classes of France.

were to appear in black silk suits trimmed in gold, white silk stockings, lace jabots, hats trimmed with braid and plumes, and, as gentlemen, they would carry a dress sword. The Third Estate, one half the delegates representing the commoners, were to wear black suits as well, but made of wool, not silk, and untrimmed; black stockings, plain muslin cravats with no lace, and untrimmed hats finished their costume. As they were not members of the aristocracy, they were not allowed to carry the gentleman's dress sword. Controversy grew, and for a brief while the plain black suit signaled alliance with the Third Estate—the deputies of the people—and emerged as an emblem of political loyalties.[80] Jefferson noted the effect of the "mode" after attending the early sessions of the Estates-General before leaving France. He reported, "Mode has acted a wonderful part in the present instance. All the handsome young women, for example, are for the tiers etat, and this is an army more powerful in France than the 200,000 men of the king."[81]

Rembrandt Peale's portrait depicts Jefferson's transition towards two new fashions: the black suit and the latest style in men's hairdressing. In Rembrandt's portrait, Jefferson's hair is cut on the crown so that it can be brushed towards the forehead. This reflects the eighteenth century's renewed interest in the classical world and its art.[82] The style visually relates

FIGURE 25. Roman coin showing a profile of the Emperor Titus, c. c.e. 80–81. Copper alloy.

Titus was made a character in Voltaire's play *Brutus* and was popularized by the French actor Talma. As the cropped hairstyles visible on Roman coins, medals, and sculptures began to be mimicked, the style was often called *à la Titus* or *à la Brutus*.

to the Roman world and became known across Europe through statuary, coins, and medals (fig. 25). Its popularity in Paris was credited to the actor Talma and his role as Titus in Voltaire's *Brutus,* which he played to great acclaim in 1791.[83] The hairstyle came to be called *à la Titus* or *à la Brutus* and carried political connotations, as it was associated with those supporting the revolution in France.[84]

Jefferson may have adopted this style before 1800, as a small pastel portrait by James Sharples taken in 1797 shows a similar hairstyle. This profile portrait provides a more complete view of Jefferson's hair, which is pulled back into the traditional queue with the updated crop across the forehead (fig. 26). Sharples reveals that Jefferson had not gone so far as becoming a "cropped head," as had some of the more adventuresome young men in Britain and France. As previously noted, William Wraxall in his memoirs blamed the "era of Jacobinism and of equality in 1793 and 1794" for cropped hair and the disuse of hair powder among men.[85] During his presidency there is written evidence that Jefferson cropped his hair, but as he prepared for the election of 1800, he is depicted with a fashionably updated hairstyle but not a radical one. Sharples has his hair still dressed with the queue, and both Rembrandt and Sharples show him with a light dusting of hair powder.

The other portraits of Jefferson taken in the 1799–1800 preelection period support Rembrandt's rendering of Jefferson. Madison was responsible for sending Charles Peale Polk to Monticello to take Jefferson's portrait in November 1799. Polk was a nephew of Charles Willson Peale and had lived in the Peale household following his parents' deaths, but unfortunately his

FIGURE 26. Thomas Jefferson by James Sharples, c. 1797. Pastel on paper.

In Sharples's pastel profile of Jefferson, his clothing is not unlike that recorded by C. W. Peale six years earlier: a blue frock coat and buff waistcoat—although a second underwaistcoat in light blue is added. However, Sharples portrays Jefferson with an updated hairstyle, cropped across the forehead.

skills as a portrait painter did not match those of his uncle or cousins. His portrait of Jefferson bears some resemblance to the features captured by Charles Willson Peale for his gallery but without the sophisticated modeling of light and shadow or the suggestions of expression and character (fig. 27). Polk made three copies of his original and advertised these in the *Virginia Gazette,* but there is no evidence that engravings were made, which would have allowed a wider audience. Madison may have had hopes that Polk's portrait would assist in popularizing Jefferson's image, but there is no indication that his work generated a great deal of interest.[86]

Two of the portraits made during this period are believed no longer extant. In Philadelphia, Jefferson sat for Edward Savage; however, the whereabouts of the original portrait are unknown. Savage created an engraving from his original painting that he advertised in the Philadelphia *Aurora,* which suggests some market for Savage's image of Jefferson, but it did not enjoy a lasting popularity.[87] Gilbert Stuart's portrait taken in May 1800 would undoubtedly have been the work to spread Jefferson's image, but according to Jefferson, "He was yet to put the last hand to it, so it was left with him."[88] This was one of Jefferson's few personal commissions, and a work by the most eminent American portrait artist would be guaranteed

FIGURE 27. Thomas Jefferson by Charles Peale Polk, 1799, replica of original.

Charles Peale Polk arrived at Monticello in November 1799 at the recommendation of James Madison to take Jefferson's portrait. The election of 1800 was not that far away, and a fresh image of Jefferson would be timely. Unfortunately, Polk's portrait did not gain wide recognition.

an audience. It was a wise political move, but unfortunately Jefferson never received this particular portrait from Stuart, and the commission remained unfilled until 1821.[89]

This left Rembrandt's portrait to set the Jefferson image as the election got underway in earnest. He projected the Jefferson that his republican supporters could have wished, one who did not appear the Francophile Jacobin and atheist that had been proclaimed in the many Federalist newspaper editorials, nor the whimsical and timid philosopher. Rather, Jefferson meets the viewer with a direct gaze as he sits solidly clad in a black coat and waistcoat with hair in an updated but powdered style. The overall look is not so unlike the widely circulated images of the great Washington. This would be reassuring to many Americans.

When Jefferson reentered the national political arena as vice president following the election of 1796, he displayed a new level of determination as his party's leader. He knew what to expect when he joined the national government a second time—his name would appear in newspapers. The political climate had not become calmer, but this time there could be no retreat. His new resolve included the construction of a new public image. The art and French furniture that had surrounded him and created a part of his image as secretary of state remained at Monticello. When he left his Philadelphia boarding house as vice president, he did not travel in one of his carriages pulled by blooded Virginia horses; he went on foot. Towards the end of his term as vice president, his changes in clothing became a topic of public discussion.

As proof of his support for American manufactures, he was publicized as wearing only clothing produced in the United States. One optimistic republican writer predicted that under a Jefferson administration, American-made clothing would be the national choice. He wrote that already the *"Jefferson shoe* and *hat* are become a fashion of our own; and we soon expect to hear of the *Jefferson coat,* &c."[90] The "Jefferson shoe" was most likely the laced, ankle-high bootee as shown in "The Providential Detection," which would gain more notoriety during his presidential years. The style of the hat is more uncertain, but quite possibly it could have been some version of the round hat that had ascended from working-class, practical beginnings to fashion status (see fig. 2, p. 14). During his retirement, Jefferson was described as wearing "a common round hat."[91] Perhaps this choice began in the late 1790s, as ideologically it suited a new image that visually placed him among the people. During the revolution in France this style was borrowed from England to become a part of "republican" dress.[92] These changes in his self-fashioning and in his lifestyle cast him as a man of the people without negating his claim as a man of science. His appearance could connect him with the relaxed style associated with either.

As the presidential election of 1800 began in earnest, the Federalists were worried. The republican candidate was an increasingly strong contender. What was to be expected from a Jefferson who could appear steady and solid, fashionably dressed in black as pictured by Rembrandt Peale, but who could also be seen walking from his boarding house wearing clothing styles that had become associated with reform and change? To some observers, Jefferson and the political change he represented were welcome; to some it was very disconcerting. Many would agree with the apprehension expressed to Hamilton by elder statesman Charles Carroll of Carrollton: "His fantastic tricks would dissolve this Union."[93]

III

The Presidency

It has been the greatest of all human consolations to me to be considered by the republican portion of my fellow citizens, as the safe depository of their rights. The first wish of my heart is to see them so guarded as to be safe in any hands.
— Thomas Jefferson to John Vanmetre, September 4, 1800

5

A NEW PRESIDENTIAL PROFILE

Manasseh Cutler, Federalist representative from Massachusetts, was curious: "What events are to follow the *new order of things.*" Word was about that changes were afoot in the protocol observed by the presidential office. Rumor held that the new president would host no levees nor give an opening address to the first session of congress, as he claimed that such elitist receptions and formal speeches were antirepublican and followed too closely a monarchical model. Cutler suspected that this break with the procedures established during the Washington administration and then continued by Adams was "to gain the applause of the multitude." But newly elected President Jefferson saw his goals as extending beyond just popularity. Prior to the election he stated, "I am decidedly against degrading the citizen in his own eye, exalting his functionary, & creating a distance between the two which does not tend to aid the morals of either. I think it a practice which we ought to destroy & must destroy."[1] He believed that the changes in protocol that he intended to introduce would help narrow the gap between the citizen and his elected officials. These changes would include his own self-fashioning and presentation as president, and he put his plans in motion immediately with his inauguration (fig. 28).

Jefferson stepped out of Conrad and McMunn's boarding house at noon on March 4, 1801, to walk to his inauguration at the unfinished Capitol building in the newly laid out town of Washington. The walk was short. The streets, as they existed, were extremely uneven, and so there was a practicality in just walking and not bothering with a carriage. But it also set a tone. He was unable to eliminate all fanfare. Local militias provided an escort, congressional supporters and local citizens joined him on his walk, and rounds of

FIGURE 28. Thomas Jefferson by Rembrandt Peale, 1805. Oil on linen, 28 in. × 23½ in.

Jefferson was at the apex of his political career when he sat for Rembrandt Peale for this portrait following his landslide victory for a second presidential term.

artillery were discharged. This was the first presidential inauguration in the new capital city of Washington.[2]

Edward Thornton first came to know Jefferson as secretary of state. Now he was back in the United States after a brief return trip to England and was serving as the British chargé de affaires.[3] He supplied a description of the inauguration of the new president in his report to the foreign office in London and alluded to the "republican spirit" that ran through this "performance." He confirmed that Jefferson went "on foot, in his ordinary dress, escorted by a body of militia artillery from the neighbouring State, and accompanied by the Secretaries of the Navy and the Treasury, and a number of his political friends in the House of Representatives."[4]

Local newspapers were more respectful of the ceremony itself but confirmed Thornton's observations that "his dress was, as usual, that of a plain citizen, without any distinctive badge of office."[5] Though neither Thornton nor the newspaper coverage was explicit, Jefferson's choice of clothing did strike both as "ordinary" and representing a "plain citizen." The small bit of additional information included in the newspaper account was that his dress lacked "any distinctive badge of office."

Even though titles and manner of address had been debated in Congress, there had never been a consideration of state robes or other distinguishing insignia assigned to the American president. Jefferson could have followed the example set for American leadership by Washington, as shown in the full-length portrait by Gilbert Stuart (fig. 29) and made available to

FIGURE 29. George Washington (Lansdowne portrait) by Gilbert Stuart, 1796. Oil on canvas.

The image of Washington in a black suit was becoming well known to Americans. This elegant portrait was commissioned by William Bingham for Lord Lansdowne and served as the prototype for the print by James Heath that hung in many American homes (see fig. 23).

the public with the engraving by James Heath. Jefferson could have worn a gentleman's dress sword, retained a touch of lace at throat and wrists, and attached a cockade to a dress hat. But the Washington image in dress, policy, and protocol was what he would be deconstructing. Contemporary observations of the presidential inauguration of 1801 implied that Jefferson avoided even these elite accessories and appeared quite plain as he walked to the capitol, where he stressed his position as a republican citizen.

FIGURE 30. Thomas Jefferson by Cornelius Tiebout after Rembrandt Peale, 1801. Engraving.

Engraver Cornelius Tiebout presented newly elected President Jefferson as both statesman and man of science.

These accounts give only a very general notion of Jefferson's appearance at the time of his inaugural ceremony; however, as he took office, two Philadelphia engravers were at work creating prints that offered full-length impressions of the new president (figs. 30 and 31). These were executed by engravers and printers working in competitive pairs: printer George Helmbold employed David Edwin, and printer Augustus Day worked with Cornelius Tiebout. Neither print was taken directly from life, and each

FIGURE 31. Thomas Jefferson by David Edwin after Rembrandt Peale, 1801. Engraving (second state).

Edwin chose to render President Jefferson as a statesman and used elements of the Louis XVI portrait in the Philadelphia statehouse for background inspiration.

contains slightly different information. The Rembrandt Peale portrait of 1800 provided the model for the head and facial features in both engravings, and so they underscore again the popularity of Rembrandt's portrait. More importantly, they provide visual references for what must have been the popular concept of Jefferson at the time of his first inauguration, as their goal was to produce an image that would sell among the American public.

"The Man of the People" was the title printer George Helmbold chose for his forthcoming print. Augustus Day intended to represent Mr. Jefferson as "a philosopher and statesman."[6] Neither of these titles was new; both had been attached to pro-Jefferson references in the 1790s, and he was hailed a man of the people as vice president in Philadelphia. Earlier in the decade, while secretary of state, he began to establish his reputation as man of science. Various news articles coupled his name with that of Dr. Franklin, and he was identified as a gentleman of eminence in both "politics and literature" and recognized as "amiable and philosophic."[7] These references were offset, however, by the many Federalist references to Jefferson the "philosopher," but with negative connotations. But the Helmbold and Day prints aimed at positive interpretations of the new president, offering profiles as the representative of the people as well as a man of science and learning. He was still the president of the American Philosophical Society, and *Notes on the State of Virginia* continued to be reprinted. Printers Helmbold and Day chose to build their interpretations of Jefferson and their subsequent marketing strategies around profiles used in the previous two elections. This pointed to the degree of success achieved by Jefferson and his supporters in creating an image that was believable and acceptable to the American public.

George Helmbold began advertising for subscriptions for his forthcoming full-length print of Thomas Jefferson as early as September 1800. His initial plan was to produce a companion portrait of republican vice presidential candidate Aaron Burr, but this plan changed once it became apparent that the two republican candidates were tied in the number of electoral votes and Burr did not step aside, making his actions questionable to his republican constituents. Helmbold very astutely announced that he was withdrawing the proposal for a Burr portrait.[8] A subsequent letter to Jefferson assured the president of his support of the "republican cause," as he inquired about a possible government appointment.[9] His advertisements, which extended though a number of cities along the eastern seaboard, always appeared in the prorepublican press, and he attempted to undermine his competition by stating that Augustus Day's "republicanism was doubtful."[10] Day did not respond to this charge directly, but he included in his advertisement that his engraver, Mr. Tiebout, was "an *American* artist of the first abilities."[11] This alluded to the fact that Helmbold's engraver, David Edwin, was from England and an American resident of just over three years.[12] Even art did not escape current politics. The contest between Helmbold and Day to produce the first full-length print of the new president was a draw, as both prints became available to the public on July 4, 1801.

These prints celebrated the inauguration of a new American president who based his reputation on upholding a republican form of government free from shades of monarchy, and who in his inaugural address described the United States' relationship with Europe as "kindly separated by nature and a wide ocean."[13] Yet the new republic's artistic ties to Europe were not easily broken and were evident even in these commercial prints. Very early in the formation of the republic, Jefferson explained his enthusiasm for the place of the arts: "Its object is to improve the taste of my countrymen, to increase their reputation, to reconcile to them the respect of the world & procure them its praise."[14] He looked towards every means to gain validity and respect for this new, experimental republic positioned at the edge of Western civilization.

Engravers Edwin and Tiebout did not hesitate to employ Old-World traditions in creating the settings for the image of the new American president. In both works the figure of Jefferson stands among massive columns and drapery, balustrades and richly patterned carpets. These were the elements of the grand manner style in portraiture and had supported state portraits and served as backdrops for European monarchs and nobles for two centuries.[15] Edwin and Tiebout could consult impressive examples of European state portraits in Philadelphia, as the portraits of Louis XVI (fig. 32) and his queen, Marie Antoinette, hung in the senate chamber of the statehouse.[16]

On the occasion of Washington's second inauguration in 1793, which took place in the senate chamber in Philadelphia, Edward Thornton of the British ministry had attended and commented upon the portraits. He assumed they had been presented during the war for independence, as he had noticed them before, but felt it strange that during the inauguration they were covered with draperies. To his thinking, this was "trifling" but nevertheless indicative of the American mindset that seemed to find the visual presence of monarchy at an American presidential inauguration somehow inappropriate, even when that monarch had been an ally.

FIGURE 32. Louis XVI by
Charles-Clément Bervic after
Antoine-François Callet, 1790.
Engraving.

Both Jefferson and Washington had
been presented with prints of the
state portrait of Louis XVI by Callet.
A copy of the portrait in the Philadelphia statehouse would have been
available to David Edwin for study.

David Edwin's print shows the more direct influence of the Louis XVI portrait. He places Jefferson before a column and balustrade with drapery suspended from above. On the far wall behind the figure, he even incorporates an image that replicates the frieze depicting the prow of a warship that is discernable in the portrait of Louis XVI.[17] Edwin moves away from the royal state portrait by mitigating the grand scene with books, writing implements, and a globe. Tiebout borrows elements from the grand manner but makes the setting more specific to Jefferson through select props that suggest the theme of philosopher-statesman. Beside the books on the draped table stands a bust portrait of Franklin, and behind the Jefferson figure appears another reference to Franklin, the electrical machine, which Day's advertisements identify as a "philosophical apparatus."[18] A globe of the world sits on the floor at Jefferson's feet, while he holds a copy of the Declaration of Independence in his outstretched right hand and gestures towards it with his left. This becomes the major focus of the composition. Tiebout emphasizes the power of the ideas inherent in Jefferson's document, whereas Edwin relies on the more overt gesture of Jefferson wrapping a forearm around the globe. The two together underscore Jefferson's thoughts expressed in his inaugural address, as he pronounced the government of the United States to be "the world's best hope."[19] No evidence has come to light, however, of Jefferson commenting directly on either engraving, yet the concept of American republicanism enveloping the world would have appealed to him.

Edwin and Tiebout looked to the portrait of Louis XVI for inspiration, while another obvious influence was the James Heath print of Washington taken from Stuart's full-length portrait. This print became popular quickly and prompted George Helmbold to announce in his initial advertisement of September 1800 that his print of Jefferson would be "22 inches in length and 14 inches in breadth, in order to make it a match for Stuart's print of Gen. Washington."[20] Helmbold was mistaken in labelling the print as Stuart's: the engraving was not authorized by the artist, and he felt his portrait had been pirated, much to his financial loss.[21] Even though Stuart claimed the likeness inadequate, Heath was true to the composition and detail of Stuart's painting.

The Washington portrait is both congruent and incongruent with the European tradition of state portraiture. In his original painting, Stuart gives the figure a background suitable for a king, featuring columns and floating drapery, and has Washington adopt a classic pose, his right hand extended in the oratorical gesture. Yet the American president is without crown or scepter. Denied luxuriant state robes like those worn by Louis, Washington does not fill the space in the same manner as the French king. In his *Psychology of Clothes*, J. C. Flügel notes that "clothing, by adding to the apparent size of the body in one way or another, gives us an increased sense of power, a sense of extension of our bodily self—ultimately by enabling us to fill more space."[22]

This extension of the bodily self, the duty performed by robes of state, related in principle to the republican controversy that occupied Jefferson and his colleagues. How were power and authority to be expressed without elevated titles or other insignias of position? Abigail Adams was convinced that President Washington "ought to have more state," whereas Jefferson was equally convinced otherwise, and as president his goal was to eliminate any vestige of Washington's republican court.[23] By 1802 he was pleased to write his good friend, Polish patriot Thaddeus Kosciuszko, that "we have suppressed all those public forms & ceremonies which tended to familiarize the public eye to the harbingers of another form of government."[24] These were the forms and ceremonies begun under Washington's administration that had so disturbed Secretary of State Jefferson. He continued in his conviction that the breach between the citizen and his functionary that began under the first administration must be eliminated.

The Jefferson figures in the Edwin and Tiebout prints share similarities with that of Washington in the Stuart-Heath portraits, yet there are subtle but important differences as well. Both Washington and Jefferson are depicted in dark suits; however, the figure of Washington in the Stuart-Heath print displays greater formality, as his hair is dressed so that the queue disappears into a dark bag topped by a rosette that can be seen partially resting at the nape of his neck. This styling was generally reserved for very formal occasions, even in Europe. There is lace at his throat and wrists, and he carries a dress sword ornamented with a tassel. A formal hat with a cockade rests on the table. In comparison, the Jefferson figure does not appear with anything as elegant as a gentleman's dress sword, hair-bag, lace, or even a hat. Even the pose of the Stuart-Heath Washington is more formal than either Edwin's or Tiebout's portrayal of Jefferson. Stuart may have chosen this pose to suggest Washington addressing Congress, perhaps in conjunction with the controversial Jay Treaty.[25] This would not be appropriate for Jefferson. He believed a direct presidential address to Congress resembled too closely the old, monarchical tradition of the British king addressing parliament. The gestures employed by Tiebout and Edwin of Jefferson pointing towards the Declaration of Independence and embracing a globe of the world were more fitting. The most notable distinction in the dress of the two figures is in the footwear. Washington's shoes are fastened with elegant buckles, while in both prints Jefferson wears the same ankle-high, laced shoes that began to be associated with his name in the late 1790s and were a means of identification in the political caricature "The Providential Detection." Edwin and Tiebout were working as competitors, not collaborators, yet each identified this type of shoe with Jefferson.

The notice given Jefferson's footwear continued during his presidency and elicited comment by members of the Federalist faction, who called attention to the fact that rather than displaying elegant buckles, their president wore shoes that laced. With a tone of sarcasm, one Federalist remarked that Jefferson's shoes "closed tight round his ankles, laced up with neat leathern strings and absolutely without buckles." For this observer, Jefferson's footwear made the statement that buckles were "superfluous and anti-republican especially when he has strings." Another Federalist attributed this style preference to Jefferson's deliberate attempt at "singularity." He claimed that "in every age of the world, rulers and philosophers have made themselves remarkable for the affectation of some singularity." The writer also speculated that "our philosophic president chooses to have his singularities as well as European kings—He prefers shoestrings, when other folks wear buckles."[26]

Jefferson's records show that during his first year as president, he purchased his "bootees" and shoe strings from John Minchin, a boot- and shoemaker who had relocated from Philadelphia to Washington. An invoice from Minchin to Jefferson in March 1801 lists charges for a pair of shoes, one pair of bootees, and silk strings. The bootees were six dollars and the strings twenty-five cents; the shoes only three dollars. Shoes remained in his wardrobe, but he was willing to pay double the price for the bootees with separate and more frequent orders for replacement strings. There were still orders for "boots" at almost double the price of the bootees, indicating that utilitarian boots remained a necessity.[27]

The visual interpretations of the new president engraved and printed by the teams of Helmbold-Edwin and Day-Tiebout leave the impression of a simply dressed President Jefferson, in a dark suit, wearing his laced bootees. The David Edwin print was meant to depict Jefferson as a man of the people, while Cornelius Tiebout's interpretation was as statesman and philosopher. Yet their Jeffersons appear quite similar. This may have suited Jefferson, as in his view "man of the people" and "man of science" could be one and the same. Understanding science and the progress that it promised represented the leveling process that would allow the bottom tier to better themselves and join those born to the privilege of a liberal education. Nothing in either print suggests that his appearance was not suitable for an American president, even if some interpreted the bootees as introducing a hint of the French Jacobin. Not far into his presidency, however, political opponents began to remark on an aspect of his appearance that many questioned and found inappropriate, as it ran counter to even the most understated dress for a gentleman.

As Jefferson's first year in the presidency concluded, a report reached leading New York Federalist Rufus King that the president had made himself accessible and "familiar with, the sovereign people" but was not holding levee days and observed no ceremony. Equally notable was that the president "often sees company in an undress, sometimes with his slippers on."[28] Later in the year a more detailed impression was recorded by Federalist senator William Plumer of New Hampshire upon his initial meeting with Jefferson. He wrote, "In a few moments, a tall highboned man came into the room; he was drest, or rather *undrest*, with an old brown coat, red waistcoat, old corduroy small clothes [breeches], much soiled—woolen hose—& slippers without heels." Plumer first mistook him for a servant, but following introductions he reached the conclusion, "I certainly dress as well as the first officer of the nation." Despite appearances however, Plumer added to his account that Jefferson was "easy of access, & conversed with great ease & freedom."[29]

Plumer was surprised that the president greeted him "undrest." Old clothing—mismatched in color and texture with woolen stockings and slippers—gave him the impression of a serving person, not a gentleman holding a position as head of state. Years earlier Lord Chesterfield advised his son that "dress is a very foolish thing, and yet it is a very foolish thing for a man not to be well dressed according to his rank and way of life."[30] In the half century since Lord Chesterfield's letters, attitudes toward the visual role of clothing had not changed. Clothing and personal appearance still served as visual indicators of rank and status. Jefferson was sending a confusing visual message by not greeting the new senator from New Hampshire in clothing that appeared well kept, clean, and of a quality that designated a gentleman.

Jefferson's new mode of presenting himself in undress and slippers provided gossip among the Federalists in Washington, but the whispers were magnified to international proportions with the arrival of the new British minister, Anthony Merry, in November 1803 (fig. 33). Soon after the minister arrived, Secretary of State Madison escorted Merry to the President's House to present his credentials. Former British secretary and chargé Edward Thornton had noted that President Washington seemed flattered that former British minister Hammond always called upon him in full dress.[31] Apparently Merry was given no warning that things had changed.

According to Merry's account, he arrived at the President's House dressed "in full official costume, as the etiquette of my place required on such a formal introduction of a Minister from Great Britain to the President of the United States." He was shocked to find the president "not merely in undress, but actually standing in slippers down at the heels" and wearing clothing that was "indicative of utter slovenliness and indifference to appearances, and in a state of negligence actually studied." Merry went on to conclude, "I could not doubt that the whole scene was prepared and intended as an insult, not to me personally, but to the sovereign I represented."[32]

Federalists delighted in Minister Merry's outrage. As the story was told

FIGURE 33. Anthony Merry after a painting by Gilbert Stuart, 1805. Reproduced from a glass negative.

British minister plenipotentiary Anthony Merry arrived for his initial meeting with President Jefferson in full diplomatic regalia, perhaps close to the formal attire shown in this glass negative of the lost Gilbert Stuart portrait. He interpreted Jefferson's undress and lax behavior as an affront not just to him but to his sovereign, George III.

and retold, Jefferson's attire sometimes varied. Samuel Taggart, the Federalist from Massachusetts, described the scene with Merry in "the robes of his office" while "our exalted chief magistrate received him in his gown and slippers; some add his night cap," but then—probably not the nightcap. Taggart had to admit that it was most likely "hyperbole." Nevertheless, Taggart reported that "it is whispered that the British Ambassador is not at all charmed with Democratic Majesty."[33] Another high Federalist added the news in a family letter that "Mr. Merry, the English Ambassador who arrived recently, is the news of the day in Washington. Tommy Jeff and his party don't care for him."[34] Things had not begun well with the new British envoy and would become worse.

In the weeks following his initial interview, Merry was further outraged at what he felt were improprieties that occurred at dinners hosted by the president and his secretary of state. As a former diplomat, Jefferson would have known that representatives of countries at war were generally not invited to the same social functions, but he had included in his dinner list M. Pichon, the French chargé d'affaires, and his wife. To add to this insult, when dinner was announced, Jefferson offered his hand to Mrs. Madison and escorted her to table rather than Mrs. Merry. A similar scene played out at the Madisons' dinner party, when Madison escorted Mrs. Gallatin, wife of the secretary of the treasury, leaving Mrs. Merry to be rescued by her husband and guided to a place at table.[35] Merry believed the actions of the president and secretary of state were intended as deliberate insults and aimed not just at him but at Great Britain. Insults to Merry, as the physical representative of his king, extended to George III.

Soon after the dinner party incidents, a brief executive memorandum, "Rules of Etiquette," appeared that summarized the order of initial visits and reiterated that no titles would be recognized nor differences of grade among diplomatic members. As to dinner seating, the rule of *pêle-mêle* would be observed, and this extended to dinners hosted by any member of the executive staff. The only precedence was given to ladies to pass before gentlemen from one room to another.[36] Had this memorandum been available upon Merry's arrival, the ensuing social debacles might have been avoided, or if Merry had been given some indication that full dress was not expected upon his initial presentation of his papers, another incident at least might have been lessened. Based upon the experiences of former ministers, Merry could have expected to be received by a US president looking much as the Washington of the Stuart-Heath engraving, and certainly Jefferson could have received Merry in his black suit had he chosen.

Minister Merry did not let go of his indignation quickly. After being recalled from the United States and given another assignment to Denmark and Sweden, he was still telling the story of his first meeting with the American president. On this assignment his undersecretary was Stratford Canning, who included Merry's story in his memoirs. Canning began by comparing Jefferson to Washington: "Jefferson helped materially to introduce that loose tone, which differed so much from his illustrious predecessor's. . . . It is reported of him that he received Mr. Merry, our first envoy to the independent States in his dressing-gown, seated on a sofa catching a slipper after tossing it up, on the point of his foot."[37] This description, as does Taggart's, has Jefferson in a dressing gown, though from Merry's initial account to his superiors, the encounter took place with Jefferson in casual daywear that, based upon the experiences of others, could have been somewhat worn and mismatched. Only the slippers remained consistent.

Jefferson's behavior was questionable, but Merry's attitude toward the new republic and its elected leaders was equally questionable. As the physical presence of the British sovereign, could he have felt on a level with an American president who had at one time been a British subject? When informed that Danish chargé Peter Pedersen had been received by Jefferson in slippers, Merry's response was that Pedersen was a minister of the third rank, whereas he was of the second rank, a minister plenipotentiary.[38] Certainly Merry acknowledged rank and position. It is also probable that he was aware of the unwritten rules of dress surrounding a gentleman receiving callers, especially morning visitors. A long-standing tradition allowed those of superior social rank to receive their equals or social inferiors in undress, which could be a banyan or dressing gown—but not their superiors. The reverse was not acceptable and could have played into Jefferson's motives as he prepared to greet the new minister.[39]

When chargé Edward Thornton applied to return to England, he strongly suggested that his position should be filled by a minister with more rank. He advised the Foreign Office to send someone to the United States with title and social standing who had a background in diplomacy; someone, therefore, of enough self-assurance to function in a society that was still quite fluid and at times unpredictable. Anthony Merry did not meet Thornton's suggested qualifications. He was the son of a wine merchant and had worked his way up from a consular position. The United States was his first assignment as a minister plenipotentiary.[40] Obviously he was a sensitive man, as his predecessor, Thornton, was certainly no admirer of Jefferson but had registered no complaints. Jefferson held a reputation among British diplomats of favoring France and bearing resentments towards Britain.[41] Nevertheless, upon Merry's arrival Jefferson initially agreed that he appeared a reasonable and good man.[42]

Jefferson defended his actions towards Merry and explained himself in a letter to James Monroe, then serving as the American minister at the Court of St. James. He maintained that he depended on the wives of his four cabinet secretaries to assist when needed as hostesses, and on these occasions he would escort his acting hostess to table. Dolley Madison carried this duty at the unfortunate dinner with the Merrys. He was adamant as well that Merry must understand United States' protocol: "The principle of society, as well as of government, with us, is the equality of the individuals composing it. That no man here would come to a dinner, where he was to be marked with inferiority to any other."[43] This addressed the issues arising around dinner etiquette, but it made no reference to Merry's displeasure with Jefferson's personal appearance.

Despite his strong statement about American protocol and equality, Jefferson seemed uneasy with the situation. He encouraged Monroe to make their position on protocol clear and to counter misrepresentations by Merry.

Madison sent a similar request, as he advised Monroe that applying "an antidote to this poison will require your vigilant and prudent attention."[44] James Monroe was alert to any change in attitude but could hardly be sure that his dinner invitations refused and visits not returned were related to the Merry affair, as some of these refusals occurred prior to Merry's introduction. He questioned whether he had been snubbed by the queen at her drawing room, as she walked directly past him with no pause. The incident occurred about the time the "etiquette story" was circulating, but then Monroe rationalized that the queen was old, her sight was poor, and her drawing room was always a "confused multitude."[45] Monroe was not pleased with the occasional derogatory remarks regarding the United States made within his hearing but decided a better course was to ignore them. By not taking them personally, he could disregard any insinuations of inferiority either as a nation or as an individual. He took the larger view of the situation—that "it was the impulse of antient feelings excited at present by light causes."[46]

Indeed, much weightier causes of concern troubled both Britain and the United States from the time of Merry's arrival in November 1803 through the etiquette crisis that continued through the early months of 1804. Monroe was joined at the Court of St. James by William Pinkney to negotiate a new treaty with Britain that would secure American commerce and shipping rights as a neutral nation in the global wars led by Britain and France. The treaty was joined to the ongoing grievance surrounding the impressment of American seamen. These issues were all intertwined with Britain's need to guard against an invasion by Napoleon, a threat that would not be relieved until the defeat of the French navy at the Battle of Trafalgar in 1805.[47] It is understandable that Merry's displeasure with his treatment in the United States was not given more attention by the London Foreign Office. British poet Thomas Moore had become friends with Minister Merry and his wife on his American tour and in a letter home mentioned that "they have been treated with the most pointed incivility by the present democratic president, Mr. Jefferson." He expressed the opinion that "it is only the precarious situation of Great Britain which could possibly induce it to overlook such indecent, though, at the same time, petty hostility."[48]

The new British legation secretary, Augustus John Foster, arrived in Washington during the protocol disputes with Minister Merry. Twenty-four years old when he assumed his duties in December 1804, Foster was well educated and had traveled Europe, where he was introduced to some of the best of European society. His mother was a member of the British aristocracy, and he brought with him the polish, experience, and confidence lacking in Anthony Merry. He quickly sided with the British minister, however, and was more comfortable with the Federalist members of congress in the political and social controversies.[49] He remained critical of Jefferson, disdainful of Washington society in general, and left some interesting (often critical) observations.

From his initial encounter with the president, Foster concluded that Jefferson looked much like "a tall large-boned farmer." He described him as "a tall man with a very red freckled face and grey neglected hair, his manners good natured, frank, and rather friendly though he had somewhat a cynical expression of countenance." Foster listed his clothing as "a blue coat, a thick grey-coloured hairy waistcoat with a red under-waistcoat lapped over it, green velveteen breeches with pearl buttons, yarn stockings and slippers down at the heel."[50] Jefferson greeted the new attaché in much the same apparel he had worn when he welcomed the British minister and Senator Plumer, and he was still wearing those down-at-the-heel slippers that were becoming as notorious as his laced bootees.

Foster placed Jefferson's political game against the backdrop of the new capital, in that he felt the president could not have behaved as he did were the government still in Philadelphia or New York. Only the remote, rural nature of the current capital allowed him to receive guests in yarn stockings and old slippers. Foster thought the issues surrounding the location of the capital not only played a part in the political divisions but also underscored divisions in the levels of society. In Foster's view, the wealthy and "more respectable" congressmen would have voted to return to Philadelphia or another of the larger cities, whereas the majority, "being composed of rough and unfashioned persons," were more comfortable in the rural setting of Washington, where servants were not mandatory or even expected. He believed that without this remote location, Jefferson could not play this role of the common citizen, presenting himself in public wearing clothing and adopting a demeanor that could define him as one of them, a man of the people.[51] This is an interesting supposition that cannot be disproved, even though Jefferson had begun creating an image that allied him with the general public while still in Philadelphia as vice president, but there he never pushed his image as far as when president in Washington.

This was when Foster concluded that Jefferson was "playing a game" in his deliberate disregard of appropriate protocol and dress and that "Mr. Jefferson knew too well what he was about."[52] Foster joined many of the

Federalists in the belief that the main object of Jefferson's game was to retain the highest office in a land where, in Foster's estimation, manners were not esteemed by the mass of society. This game allowed Jefferson to appear and behave in a fashion beneath the station that he held in order to appeal to the common man.[53] Foster agreed with Federalist Manassah Cutler that Jefferson was playing to the masses.

Jefferson would continue to greet both friends and opponents in similar clothing. Even though Senator William Plumer had been startled with the president's appearance on his initial meeting, on subsequent visits he seemed to link this dressing-down to time of day. He wrote of a visit in November 1804: "I found the President dressed better than I ever saw him at any time when I called on a morning visit." Plumer described his clothing on this occasion: "Though his coat was old and thread bare, his scarlet vest, his corduroy small cloths, and his white cotton hose, were new and clean—but his linen was much soiled, and his slippers old." When Plumer made an 11:00 a.m. call the following summer, he simply stated, "The president was in an undress," which now seemed of little consequence, though he did note that Jefferson was wearing "slippers with his toes out."[54] The infamous slippers were deteriorating further. Someone outside the government, Jefferson admirer artist William Dunlap, had opportunity to call upon "the great man" at the President's House and assumed that he had interrupted Jefferson in study or pursuing business, as he appeared "*en dishabille* and slippered." Dunlap was hardly offended but rather pleased at being allowed the introduction.[55] Jefferson's appearance seemed to be disapproved or excused according to political leanings and eventually, as in the case of Plumer, became acceptable with familiarity.

Charles Willson Peale had a plan for his son Rembrandt's second portrait of Jefferson (fig. 28, p. 132). It was to be featured at an illumination of the Peale Museum that would coincide with the inauguration of the reelected Jefferson. Father and son arrived in Washington in January 1805 with the objective of obtaining Jefferson's portrait and with hopes of commissions from other members of government. On their first full day in the city, they called on Jefferson and were invited to attend the evening's dinner with several members of congress. On that particular evening, January 9, 1805, the dinner guests were all Jefferson's republican colleagues, and so the Peales would have made a very comfortable addition.[56]

Later in month Rembrandt and his father returned to the executive mansion for two sittings with the president followed by a final "touch-up" session.[57] Charles Willson Peale was pleased with the portrait of the sixty-one-year-old Jefferson and announced in a letter to the family in Philadelphia that it was completed on January 31 and "much to our satisfaction." He described it as a "charming portrait."[58]

This "charming portrait" captures a rather different image from that of Rembrandt's very successful 1800 portrait of Jefferson in the black suit. Rather than black, Jefferson appears to be wearing a red coat, although only a small portion of the high-rolled collar is visible. But the suit is not the major statement, as it is swallowed by the large fur-lined cloak that wraps the figure. It became the most provocative feature in Rembrandt's work and raises the question of what message was intended with this very public portrait of the president at the peak of his popularity.

The simplest explanation for the cloak could be the extreme cold that the region was experiencing. In his diary C. W. Peale mentioned on several days that the weather was severe and uncomfortably cold. He displayed his humanity by observing that "the intense cold here I think must be severely felt by the poor inhabitants of this large wilderness of City," but Peale the businessman went on to speculate that the cold was deterring commissions, as no one wanted to travel out to inspect the examples of Rembrandt's talent that were set out for viewing in their rented rooms.[59] Jefferson expressed many times his sensitivity to cold. He wrote in 1801, "When I recollect on one hand all the sufferings I have had from cold, & on the other all my other pains, the former preponderate greatly."[60] Cold may have accounted for the presence of the cloak but not its inclusion in the finished portrait. Jefferson could have posed wrapped comfortably in the fur through most of his sitting and then put it aside as Rembrandt laid in the clothing. But then the artist may have encouraged the cloak, as it gave a marvelous opportunity for Rembrandt to display his skills in rendering fur. Certainly it made for a different look from the suited and uniformed men generally seen in the Peale Museum, and it removed Jefferson further from the well-known images of Washington in his black suit.[61]

The choice of using the cloak may have rested with the artist or with his father, as the portrait was actually the senior Peale's commission; however, Jefferson did own a cloak such as the one pictured that had an interesting provenance. One of the most colorful accounts of the fur cloak was written by a close friend and admirer of Jefferson, Margaret Bayard Smith. She set down a reminiscence that she titled "The Fur Cloak" that is valuable in dating when Jefferson used the cloak in Washington, which coincides with

FIGURE 34. Thaddeus Kosciuszko by
Christian Josi after Joseph Grassi, c. 1796.
Engraving.

There is substantive evidence that Kosciuszko presented Jefferson with the fur-lined
cloak that he wears in his 1805 portrait by
Rembrandt Peale. It appears similar to the
garment Kosciuszko wears in this print;
however, Kosciuszko's garment is sleeved and
not a cloak.

the Peale portrait. The story also makes a credible link to Polish-American
hero Thaddeus Kosciuszko (fig. 34). Jefferson loaned Smith his cloak for
the carriage ride home on a cold winter evening of 1805 following a dinner
party at the President's House. "It was in the winter of 1805, that I was dining at Mr. Jefferson's, when soon after leaving the table, I was seized with an
ague." Her imagination was stirred to think that "I, an obscure individual in
America, should be wrapped in the same mantle that once enveloped the
Czar of Russia—that was afterwards long worn by the . . . Hero, of Poland,
and now belongs to one of the greatest men alive!" The "Hero of Poland,"
Kosciuszko had gained high regard during the American Revolution. His
military engineering skills were significant in the American victory at Saratoga, and he was then called to fortify West Point on the Hudson River.
Smith had heard the history of the fur during Kosciuszko's second trip to
America (1797–98), when he stayed with some of her relatives prior to his
arrival in Philadelphia and meeting with Jefferson.[62]

The legend of the cloak began with Kosciuszko's failed insurgency
against the Russian army occupying Poland and his subsequent imprison-
ment in Saint Petersburg. After an eighteen-month incarceration and the
death of Catherine II, Kosciuszko was personally released by the new Russian Emperor, Paul I, with the stipulation that he could not return to his
native Poland. Kosciuszko refused to accept money from the emperor, and
according to Smith's recounting of Kosciuszko's story, Paul presented his
own fur cloak to the Polish hero as a parting gesture.

Upon Kosciuszko's return to the United States in 1797, he was greeted as a returning hero for his participation in the American Revolution and his gallant though failed attempts in repelling the Russian armies occupying Poland. As he arrived in Philadelphia, the horses were removed and citizens pulled his carriage into the city. Newspapers announced his arrival, and articles and biographies appeared that defined him as a man of character, a hero, a statesman, and a philosopher. A story reprinted in several America newspapers stressed his participation in revolutions—American, French, and Polish—and went on to label him a "leveller": "If Kosciusko be a leveller, (which by the bye every revolutionist who exerts himself for the benefit of humanity ought to be) he is a leveller who . . . wishes to level, as it were, in order to raise all to the same height, but not to trample every thing under foot."[63] This was a description Jefferson might wish for himself. It aligned closely with his belief in maintaining the ideals of the American Revolution and establishing a government that existed for the people.

Kosciuszko remained in the United States for only ten months before returning to Europe. During this time the men formed a lasting friendship and continued to correspond until Kosciuszko's death in 1817. In gratitude for Jefferson's aid and friendship, Kosciuszko wrote a brief note just prior to his leaving in which he requested, "Give me leave to present you a Fur."[64] Smith concludes her own story with this and wrote, "On leaving this country for Europe, Kasioskio, left this cloak, with his revered friend Jefferson."[65] In her version the fur cloak had dramatically transitioned from a monarch to a Polish revolutionary to an American patriot.

Neither Smith's story nor Kosciuszko's brief note specifies the type of fur, but following Kosciuszko's departure a fur begins to appear in Jefferson family correspondence and through the years became more clearly defined. Jefferson first mentioned a fur garment in December 1798 following Kosciuszko's departure in May. He reported to his daughter Martha that the weather was extremely cold on his return to Philadelphia from Monticello, yet he assured her that he stayed as comfortable as if he had been in a "warm bed . . . thanks to my pelisse." Here Jefferson uses the term "pelisse," which at that time would have designated an outer garment, cut either as a cloak, coat, or jacket and distinguished by a fur lining or fur trim; thus the term could be used interchangeably with the fur cloak described by Margaret Bayard Smith.

Years later, well into his retirement, Jefferson made another reference to his pelisse that identified the type of fur. He had suffered from the cold on the three-day trip from Monticello to Poplar Forest, his retreat home in southern Virginia. He requested that Martha send his "wolf-skin pelisse and fur-boots." She would find the items in the closet over his bed, and he was specific as to how the items should be packed. "The pelisse had better be sowed up in a striped blanket to keep it clean and uninjured," he suggested, but it would suffice to package "the boots in any course wrapper." Jefferson's request reveals not only the type fur that lined the cloak, but also that he obviously regarded the wolf-skin pelisse as valuable.[66]

After Jefferson's death the cloak that Margaret Bayard Smith had contemplated with such awe came once more into her care. In January 1837 his grandchildren took an inventory of furniture items, probably in relation to their mother's death the previous October. Their correspondence related that "Mary says Kosciusko's wolf skin pelisse is at Mrs. H[arrison] Smith's who suggested it would be well to give it to some society which she named (but Mary had forgotten). She thought they would go to the expense of having a glass case made for it to preserve it from the moths." No one knows what ultimately became of the Kosciuszko-Jefferson wolf-skin pelisse, but this exchange among grandchildren confirms that Jefferson's wolf-skin cloak connected to Kosciuszko.[67]

These collected references from Jefferson himself, and his family and friends, regarding the provenance of the cloak lead to a probable Kosciuszko connection. The cloak may have interested Peale because Philadelphians who still remembered Kosciuszko's triumphant return in 1797 could relate the cloak to the Polish-American hero. But provenance aside, the cloak in Rembrandt's portrait serves another function. It strengthens the figure and acts much as do robes of state in supplying that "extension of the bodily self." Visually it creates a solid base around Jefferson as he looks straight at the viewer from a three-quarter profile. The cloak presents an interesting analogy to European nobility, who often posed in ermine, while the American president sat wrapped in wolf skins.

Jefferson presented himself in a fur that despite its possible European origins offered a visual connection to an important American resource and suggested the potential of opening exploration and trade in the trans-Mississippi region. The newly purchased Louisiana territory had been an important accomplishment of his first administration, and just over a month after his sitting with Rembrandt, he would remind the country of its value in his second inaugural address. Even though some had opposed the purchase, Jefferson asked, "Is it not better that the opposite bank of the

Mississippi should be settled by our own brethren and children, than by strangers of another family? With which shall we be most likely to live in harmony and friendly intercourse?" Before the Louisiana Purchase Treaty was completed, he had already organized the Lewis and Clark Expedition. As Rembrandt painted his portrait in January 1805, Jefferson anxiously awaited news from Meriwether Lewis as the expedition worked its way up the Missouri River and towards the Pacific Ocean. He would not receive the first shipment of objects and data until the following August.[68] Whether or not the fur surrounding Jefferson served as a reminder of the new western territory, the purchase of Louisiana added to the look of confidence that Rembrandt recorded in Jefferson's portrait.

Jefferson was very aware of another founding leader who had used fur successfully as an insignia of America. People on both sides of the Atlantic were familiar with the popular print by artist Charles Nicolas Cochin and engraver Augustin de Saint-Aubin of Franklin in his well-publicized fur cap worn over his straight, undressed hair. Equally famous was the Joseph-Siffrèd Duplessis image of Franklin wearing a fur-collared coat (see fig. 11, p. 45). A copy of this famous portrait, which Jefferson believed to be painted by Jean Valade, was one of his early acquisitions as he began building his portrait collection while in Paris.[69] Not only does Franklin appear with a fur collar in the Duplessis, but his coat and waistcoat are red, as is the coat Rembrandt shows Jefferson wearing under his fur cape. A print of the Duplessis portrait by Juste Chevillet was completed in 1778, soon after the original painting, and it enjoyed wide sales even as it supported the American cause in France. Many copies were painted besides the one owned by Jefferson, and through prints and copies the portrait had a wide distribution.[70] A visitor to Monticello mentioned Jefferson's copy as "Franklin in the dress in which we always see him."[71] It was an image familiar to many Americans.

Jefferson's name was often linked to Franklin's, both politically and in the study of science. In his print of Jefferson as philosopher-statesman, Cornelius Tiebout depicted a bust portrait of Franklin on the table. He could have easily used an image of Washington, but the public was obviously aware that this was not an accurate pairing: Franklin's image was. For Jefferson, Franklin remained "the ornament of our country and I may say of the world."[72] Should viewers of the new Rembrandt portrait be reminded of Dr. Franklin's famous portrait in which he wore a fur-lined coat, Jefferson would not have objected.

Not far into his presidency, another eccentricity in dress began to be attached to Jefferson, as he was described as wearing "red breeches." By 1801 red as a color choice for men's breeches was far from fashionable, and popular taste inclined more toward buff, black, or other neutral colors. The origin of these stories is impossible to determine with certainty; nevertheless, the red breeches became a symbol for Jefferson himself. In the opposition press it was a means of ridicule that in some instances even bordered on lewdness and barely disguised sexual innuendo. Jefferson supporters downplayed any significance and pointed to the pettiness of applying such an image to the president. An example was an imagined dialogue published in an Alexandria, Virginia, newspaper in 1804 titled "Confabulation between a Federalist & a Democrat." The Democrat attempts a conversation around the benefits for the United States in the accession of the Louisiana Territory and the benefits to the new territory of good laws and light taxes, while the Federalist wants to dwell on the gossip surrounding the president's red breeches and rumors that he had received foreign dignitaries in old red breeches. He knows that George Washington had always worn black breeches. In the Federalist's eyes, "Any man that can say red breeches are constitutional, I say he is a Jacobin! a disorganizer, a blood thirsty French cut throat."[73]

As this example illustrates, Jefferson's red breeches were linked with his slovenly dress and his pro-French sympathies. An apocryphal story set shortly after Jefferson's return to the United States from Paris places Secretary of State Jefferson at a dinner party in New York as the guest of Vice President John Adams. One dinner guest is said to have commented that "Mr. Jefferson, who has just returned from France, was conspicuous in his red waistcoat and breeches, the fashion of Versailles." This story, titled "Reminiscences of New York," was published in an 1830 edition of *The Talisman* as a memoir. It follows many historical events of the time but contains some inconsistencies alongside the facts. Jefferson was placed at the same dinner table as the French minister, the comte de Moustiers. Jefferson knew Moustiers while in Paris, but the count was returning to France as Jefferson was sailing back to the United States. The two never met at an American dinner party. But even with this and other discrepancies, we can wonder if the allusion to Jefferson dressed in the fashion of Versailles was totally fabricated or had some basis in fact.[74] The one visual record of Jefferson in red breeches and waistcoat was Trumbull's oil study for *The Declaration of Independence*, which was painted in France. Trumbull could have been influenced by Jefferson's Parisian clothing, but the red plays an important compositional role in creating focus on the central group of figures and so may or may not have been taken from reality.

The French connection to the red breeches appears again in an early Jefferson biography by George Tucker. The 1837 publication excuses his "supposed predilection for red breeches" with the claim that "this, indeed, was a part of his official dress when minister to France."[75] But at the time of Jefferson's tenure, there was no "official dress" for a United States minister other than that prescribed by the protocol of the French Court. In his own memoirs, Jefferson's grandson, Thomas Jefferson Randolph, dismissed any political connection by reminding his readers that red was quite popular for men's clothing at one time and added that "Mr. Jefferson changed his fashion slowly hence doubtless was the origin of his red breeches known to fame in their day."[76]

It is questionable how often Jefferson actually wore red breeches. A 1792 order placed with his New York tailor, Christian Baehr, requested "a waistcoat and pair of breeches of best scarlet *French* cloth"; however, most of his payments to tailors in his accounting records are ambiguous, and if a color for breeches is specified in an existing tailor's invoice, the favored colors are more frequently buff or black.[77] Various descriptions of Jefferson, especially in his more radical dress, do not mention him in red breeches—a red waistcoat occasionally, but not breeches.

What could have begun as an emblem of Jefferson's pro-French sympathies, through his years in political office, took on broader connotations and became a symbol for Jefferson himself. On the date of his retirement from the presidency, March 4, 1809, a leading Federalist newspaper, the *New York Evening Post,* was pleased to report an incident that had Jefferson hanging in effigy from the city's liberty pole. According to the *Post,* "Last evening between 10 and 11 o'clock, a sailor was perceived by one of the City Watch to make several attempts to climb the Liberty Pole, planted in the *Republican Square.* . . . At length he succeeded in ascending, and suspended from the top of the pole, a pair of *Red Breeches,* stuffed with straw, in honor of the 4th of March, the day which reduces Thomas Jefferson 'to the level of private citizen.'"[78]

The political opposition seized all opportunities to challenge Jefferson's character and national loyalties. A political caricature titled "A Philosophic Cock," believed produced in 1804 and attributed to caricaturist James Aiken, used the cock as a dual symbol (fig. 35). The cock had come to represent revolutionary France and made obvious reference to Jefferson's

FIGURE 35. "A Philosophic Cock" by James Aikin, c. 1804. Aquatint engraving.

This caricature was likely produced for the 1804 presidential election. The symbol of the cock referenced the rumors of Jefferson's liaison with his slave concubine, Sally Hemings, as well as his affections for the French. "A Philosophic Cock" raised questions regarding Jefferson's character and allegiances.

initial support of France and its revolt against the Bourbon monarchy.[79] A "philosophic" cock made a specific connection to his attraction to French scientific and enlightened thought, and it brought up again a question posed in the past two elections: Could the intellectual possess the traits necessary to lead a nation? A secondary theme was introduced by the small hen alongside the cock, who looked up at him with a very attractive face.

The caricature alludes to a story first published in September 1802 in the *Richmond Recorder* and picked up by other newspapers. It told of Jefferson and his slave concubine "Sally" and was written by a radical journalist named James Callender who had supported Jefferson and the republicans. Callender was imprisoned under the Sedition Act passed during the Adams administration and had fully expected to be rewarded upon the Jeffersonian success. He was bitter when a government position was not forthcoming and subsequently published his story of Jefferson and his slave Sally.[80] He identifies Sally as the slave who accompanied Jefferson to France with his two daughters in 1784. This bit of information identifies the slave as Sally Hemings; however, Callender's retelling is not totally accurate, as she did not accompany Jefferson but rather was the nurse and personal servant for his younger daughter, Mary, when she was sent to join her father in 1787. Sally's identity was not important to Callender. His objective was to question Jefferson's character by making the case that he placed his concubine before the eyes of his two daughters. Callender supplies no details about Sally and only refers to her as the "African Venus" and states that she bore Jefferson children.

"A Philosophic Cock" literally puts a face to Sally Hemings, but we have no way of knowing how accurate the caricaturist's rendering may be. He places a turban on the hen to represent the headwear used by some African American women, but in 1804 the turban was quite a fashion item and was popular among many well-dressed women, regardless of race. Nevertheless, it is more likely an attempt to create a visual definition of her slave status. He gives her an oval, well-proportioned face, but there is no evidence that Aiken ever saw Sally Hemings. Jefferson's face, atop the cock, appears to be an unflattering adaption from Rembrandt's 1800 portrait, showing the hair cut straight across the forehead. If the caricature was produced in 1804 in conjunction with the election, prints made from Rembrandt's portrait would be the major Jefferson image in circulation.

Rather than answering questions about Sally Hemings, the caricature remained aimed at Jefferson by suggesting his continuing ties to revolutionary France and alluding to his practice of miscegenation, despite his racist remarks in *Notes on the State of Virginia*. As argued by all of the Federalist political rhetoric, Jefferson was not a man to be trusted. Nevertheless, he won the election of 1804 by a wide margin. The popularity of the Louisiana Purchase, the tax reductions, and the general prosperity of the country in 1804 countered the questions of character launched by the Federalists and illustrated by "A Philosophic Cock."

Jefferson's dressing down functioned as part of his reshaping of presidential protocol and connected him to a larger cosmopolitan movement. Reports coming from France, such as the journals of British travel writer John Moore (published in 1793 and 1795), included dress as a part of the changes taking place. Moore was dubious that "Republican manners would have been much to the taste of the French nation." Yet he observed, "There is however in Paris at present, a great affectation of plainness in dress, and simplicity of expression, which are supposed to belong to Republicans." As an example he related an encounter with a young Frenchman trying on republicanism who joined him one evening in his box at the theatre. Moore stated, "He was in boots, his hair cropt, and his whole dress slovenly: on his being taken notice of, he said, 'that he was accustoming himself to appear like a Republican.'" In his 1795 work Moore noted that "a great plainness or rather shabbiness of dress was . . . considered as a presumption of patriotism."[81]

Psychologist J. C. Flügel points to the upheaval in France as a major influence in the radical shift in men's clothing that occurred at the end of the eighteenth century. The major purpose of decorative splendor in clothing was to visually establish rank and wealth, but with the French Revolution and "its world-echoing slogan of 'Liberty, Equality, Fraternity,'" these visual distinctions had to be abolished. "The doctrine of the brotherhood of man was obviously incompatible with garments which, by their very nature and associations, emphasized the differences in wealth and station between one man and another."[82]

In England these experiments in appearance were exploited by those who favored government reform, and one of the most notable exponents was Charles James Fox.[83] As previously discussed in relation to Jefferson's laced bootees, Sir William Wraxall blamed the "discredit" placed on dress in England with "Fox and his friends" and their casual attitude towards appearance as a means of calling attention to their political agenda. He seemed to feel that in "affecting a style of neglect about their persons, and manifesting a contempt of all the usages hitherto established" the Foxites "first threw a sort of discredit on dress."[84] Jefferson was aware of Charles James Fox and his politics, although he never made reference to Fox in relation to dress or his adoption of the blue and buff as a supporter of the American colonies. After Fox became foreign secretary in February 1806 in the Grenville ministry, Jefferson wrote to American minister James Monroe in London: "The late change in the ministry I consider as insuring us a just settlement of our differences, and we ask no more. In Mr. Fox, personally, I have more confidence than in any man in England, and it is founded in what, through unquestionable channels, I have had opportunities of knowing of his honesty and his good sense. While he shall be in the administration, my reliance on that government will be solid."[85] He had hopes that Fox would facilitate an equitable treaty with the United States, but unfortunately Fox died in September after taking office in February, and the United States lost whatever support he may have offered. (However, Fox did recall Minister Anthony Merry during his brief months as foreign secretary.[86]) Even though the more radical changes in clothing were never as pervasive in England as they were France, their adoption by Fox could have served to encourage Jefferson's emulation. Fox also carried the title "Man of the People."[87]

The descriptions of the clothing in revolutionary France worn to express republican ideology—plain, shabby, even slovenly—and Wraxall's description of Fox and his circle and their deliberate negligence in matters of dress sounded similar to the claims about Jefferson. His use of something as simple as shoe laces rather than buckles was not lost on those watching

Jefferson closely as leader of what some pejoratively labeled a "democratic" faction. As he sat for Rembrandt a second time, the recent results of the election had confirmed that a majority of the polity approved the direction and image he had placed on the executive branch of government. Like Franklin and Kosciuszko, he could claim a continued reputation as "leveler" and man of the people.

Jefferson appears confident of the statement he makes as he sits solidly in his fur cloak looking straight out from the canvas; however, the viewing public may not have been as receptive of this rather exceptional look for their president. As Alfred Bush compiled his catalogue of the life portraits of Jefferson in 1962 and then again in 1987, he found there were no prints made of this portrait in the nineteenth century, and only one copy that appeared traceable to Rembrandt, even though the portrait remained on display in the Peale Museum.[88] The look Jefferson and the artist achieved may have been somewhat perplexing to American viewers, even when a majority supported his policies and elected him to a second term as their president. Public interest (or perhaps curiosity) in the latest image of their president caused C. W. Peale to extend the number of evenings that the portrait was featured during the illumination of the museum, yet it was Rembrandt's first portrait of Jefferson in the black suit that was copied and remained in circulation.

Rembrandt's 1805 portrait moved Jefferson's image away from the iconic archetype of Washington in his black suit with lace and dress sword to test an alternative interpretation of the presidency. With hair not formally dressed and powdered, and wearing a very utilitarian fur that suggests the natural resources of the nation, he appears ready to "destroy" the distance created by the Federalists between the citizens and their functionaries. As Jefferson had advised George III in his "Summary View of the Rights of British Americans," the chief executive's duty was to keep the "great machine of government" effectively running without ever forgetting that he was simply the servant of the people. Rembrandt's portrait assisted his goals by providing a visual declaration of his democratic ambitions for the nation.

Yet Jefferson's self-fashioning could shift and change. He would not always appear as the simple workman operating the machinery of government. He could step forward, when he chose, as the polished patrician in the black suit and white linen so favorably pictured by Rembrandt Peale during the contest of 1800. His image as man of the people was Janus-faced.

6

BUT ALWAYS THE COSMOPOLITAN GENTLEMAN

On the day of Jefferson's second inauguration, March 4, 1805, British attaché John Augustus Foster noted in his journal that "he was in high spirits, dressed in black and even in black silk stockings."[1] Here was the other side of Jefferson's Janus face. His personal self-fashioning could change dramatically from unkempt—what some labeled slovenly or even radical—to the gentleman in the stylish black suit. This latter image was enhanced by his small but elegant dinner parties, where the food was prepared under the supervision of a French chef and served by a liveried staff, even if the seating was pêle-mêle. As one dinner guest commented, "He is accused of being very slovenly in his dress, & to be sure he is not very particular in that respect, but however he may neglect his person he takes good care of his table. No man in America keeps a better."[2] These dual images, from extremist to patrician, coexisted and were used by Jefferson on different occasions throughout his presidency, although not always in a predictable pattern. He never explained his choices in style, but he made clear his belief that as president he was simply the "safe depository" for republican principles of government. During the election of 1800 he expressed to John Adams his conviction that it was not a contest between two men: rather, it was a contest of two differing "systems of principles" which they each represented. "Were we both to die to-day, tomorrow two other names would be in the place of ours, without any change in the motion of the machine. it's motion is from it's principle, not from you or myself."[3] The man was distinct from the machine, but as the elected chief officer of the nation, he was responsible for keeping this experimental machine in republican government in motion. Jefferson seemed prepared to adopt whatever image might best suit his responsibilities as guardian and advocate of American republican principles.

William Plumer, Federalist senator from New Hampshire, noted in his journal on November 26, 1804, that the new minister from Napoleonic France, General Louis Marie Turreau, had just arrived in Washington. The Frenchman appeared very attentive to dress and equipage and inquired as to the "court-dress." Plumer may have chuckled at this inquiry, as he thought of how he was received by President Jefferson earlier in the month at the President's House. Not much had changed in the president's appearance from their initial meeting two years previous, when Jefferson had worn an old, threadbare coat, soiled linen, and old slippers, although "his scarlet vest, his corduroy small cloths, and his white cotton hose, were new and clean" Except now, "His hair was cropt & powdered."[4] Plumer seemed surprised when exactly a week after this journal entry, he accepted a dinner invitation from the president and found him dressed in "a new suit of black—silk hose—shoes—clean linen, & his hair highly powdered." Plumer's observations presented one example of the dichotomy in dress employed by Jefferson in his role as president. The senator's account of this presidential dinner gives further insights into Jefferson's balancing of his presidential image.

Plumer added to his notes on Jefferson's appearance his impressions of the dinner itself. He seemed impressed that "his dinner was elegant & rich" and was accompanied by eight different wines. One, an excellent Tokay, was much to Plumer's liking, but he was taken aback to learn that Jefferson had paid a guinea a bottle, which he believed extravagant, considering it was "little more than a quart."[5] What first aroused Plumer's curiosity was the dinner invitation itself. "His cards of invitations are unlike those of former President's—their's issued in the name of *The President of the United States*." He thought it odd that the card he received said only, "*Th: Jefferson* requests the favor of Mr. Plumer to dine with him on monday next at half after three, or at whatever later hour the *house* may rise. The favor of an answer is *asked*."[6] This was simply an invitation from Thomas Jefferson, but Plumer reasoned that if the invitation were not being extended due to their roles in government, Jefferson's as president and Plumer's as senator, there would not have been an invitation at all. He inquired of Virginia senator and friend of Jefferson, William Branch Giles, who assured him that the invitation was simply from Thomas Jefferson, gentleman. For if invitations were issued as coming from the office of the president, he would be obligated to methodically invite each member of congress. Plumer accepted this answer, as he recognized that some congressmen publically opposed and ridiculed Jefferson and his policies from the floor of congress. However, over his two terms as president, few congressmen were not eventually invited for dinner.[7]

The egalitarian tone of the invitation was carried through in the seating at dinner. His entertainment of congressional members was usually confined to about twelve people (plus himself and his personal secretary), who were often seated at a round or oval table. Friend and admirer Margaret Bayard Smith noted the small numbers and the positive effect of seeing faces around the table and how it encouraged "the animating influence of looks as well as of words."[8] Jefferson explained that at these small and intimate gatherings, "I cultivate personal intercourse with the members of the legislature that we may know one another and have opportunities of little explanations of circumstances." In addition, he confided, "I depend much on the members for the local information necessary on local matters, as well as for the means of getting at public sentiment."[9] Obviously, these less formal gatherings suited not only his image of republican simplicity; they also facilitated his collection of information.

William Plumer may have been puzzled at the nature of the invitation he received, but he seemed pleasantly surprised by the abundant fine wines served and equally surprised to find the president dressed in a new black suit and silk stockings. Congressman Samuel Taggart shared in the same dinner with Plumer and noted as well the variety of foods and "very good wine." He remarked also on the improved appearance of the president, who "for once was dressed like a gentleman."[10]

Plumer and Taggart had only their own provincial tastes to judge the merits of food and wine, but Louisa Catherine Adams, wife of John Quincy Adams, had a broader base for comparison. She grew up in England, and as wife of Minister Adams, Catherine had lived and traveled in Europe and had dined at some very fine tables. She recorded in her journal impressions of one dinner at the President's House on a very cold Washington evening. She wrote, "The entertainment was handsome. French servants in livery, a French butler, a French cuisine, and a buffet full of choice wine." Although she was not fond of Jefferson, her only complaint was about the weather, as she wrote, "Had he had a tolerable fire on one of the bitterest days I ever experienced, we might almost have fancied ourselves in Europe."[11]

Even though Jefferson sought to steer the nation away from the patterns and influences of Britain and Europe, and in his appearance often strongly emphasized the idea of simplicity in dress, yet he obviously appreciated and enjoyed the comforts accorded by his experienced maître d'hôtel, Étienne Lemaire, and chef, Honoré Julien. These two Frenchmen headed a staff of approximately ten to twelve through most of the years Jefferson was in Washington. Frequent guest Margaret Bayard Smith wrote of Lemaire and Julien: "His maître d'hôtel had served in some of the first families abroad, and understood his business to perfection. The excellence and superior skill of his French cook was acknowledged by all who frequented his table." Lemaire brought skills gained in Europe, and at Jefferson's table "republican simplicity was united to Epicurean delicacy." She remarked as well that "the whole of Mr Jefferson's domestic establishment at the Presidents House exhibited good taste and good judgment."[12] Threads of European cosmopolitanism continued to be incorporated into the process of weaving together a unique republican nation. In Smith's opinion the two could blend as long as good judgment was in place. In his efforts to exorcise what he felt was excessive state ceremony, Jefferson put aside the formality of large state dinners in favor of small, frequent groups that were treated to excellent food and wine. He complained to his eldest daughter about the "fatigues of the table in such a round of company" and perhaps exaggerated in naming his entertaining "as the most serious trials I undergo."[13] Yet his private dinners were possibly his most effective method of introducing Old World quality within the bounds of a republican environment.

Those invited to Jefferson's dinners—and there were many, from congressional members to local residents and visitors—would have experienced this blend of European-American cuisine as hosted by the nation's leading republican.[14] But those not invited to the president's table had two occasions during the year to sample his food and wine. These were on January 1 or July 4, when the President's House was opened to the populace. Margaret Bayard Smith wrote about these special days, "The doors of the Presidential mansion were thrown open for persons of all classes, where abundance of refreshments were provided for their entertainment. . . . There was little form or ceremony observed at these re-unions. Every one as they entered shook hands with the President."[15]

Opening the President's House on New Year's Day may have recalled the elegant but exclusive celebrations Jefferson had experienced at Versailles. The event in Washington was not as elegant and far from exclusive, but there was a parallel in the tradition of calling on the monarch or on the president as a show of respect and good wishes. Senator Plumer still considered it as pleasant and agreeable. He was aware that this had been the practice in the United States since the establishment of the constitutional government, but he knew that some of the Federalists did not intend to call on Jefferson. Despite his Federalist affiliations, he felt these occasions acted as part of a ceremony and exchange of respect between the members of congress and their chief. At the 1806 celebration he found that despite the boycott, nevertheless a handsome crowd had assembled. The ground-floor rooms were thrown open and the president greeted and bowed to each visitor as the Marine band played. Plumer observed that the "side boards were numerous & amply furnished."[16]

That same year, August John Foster attended the New Year's Day open house with British Minister Merry and Mrs. Merry. Foster noted that this was one of the occasions at which Jefferson wore the black suit. According to Foster, "He was dressed in a suit of black, his gala dress on those occasions when it was the custom for him to speak some little while to members of the diplomatic corps." But he did not speak long enough to suit Minister Merry. After greeting them Jefferson moved away to engage with a visiting group of Native Americans. He "appeared wholly taken up with his natives" remarked Foster, and so once again Jefferson offended Merry, who left quickly.[17]

At other times local residents might see Jefferson riding alone around Washington with no attendant and in very common clothing. Senator Plumer and British attaché Foster shared similar opinions on this view of the president. Plumer wrote, "I have never seen the President of the United States when he rides horseback, which is almost every pleasant day that I am here, accompanied with a servant. . . . I do not know the cause of this singularity—for gentlemen of rank & consequence here are usually attended when they ride, by their servants—It may proceed from affectation—& it may arise from other causes." But in Plumer's opinion, "The appearance ill accords with the dignity of the Chief of a great nation."[18]

This habit also drew Foster's criticism. He believed Jefferson and his Democratic-Republicans took advantage of the location of the national government in the remote and undeveloped City of Washington. Jefferson's riding without attendants would have been unacceptable in a more cosmopolitan environment. Foster cited an occasion when Jefferson was "fastening his horse's bridle himself to the shop doors (as I have once witnessed his doing, when his nail was torn off in the operation)." This to Foster was as undignified as receiving visitors in yarn stockings and slippers.[19] These were the views expressed by political opponents. As could be expected, admirer Margaret Bayard Smith took a much more generous view of Jefferson's solitary rides. She suggested, "When he took his daily ride, it was always on horseback and alone. It was then he enjoyed solitude, surrounded only by the works of nature of which he was a fond lover and great admirer." She attributed these lonely rides to his love of botany and the many plants available for study along the Potomac River bordering Washington.[20] Yet an attendant would not necessarily preclude his botanical studies and might even assist. When Jefferson served as secretary of state, one of the duties of his personal servant, Joseph, was to follow on horseback, but this was before Jefferson's metamorphosis while vice president, when he stepped into the role of man of the people.

Smith felt uneasy about his riding alone on the less frequented roads and in the woods around Washington, but Jefferson assured her there was no danger. He confessed that "not a week elapses in which I do not receive letters threatening me with assassination, & it is about three days ago, since I received a letter announcing to me, that I was soon to be assassinated." He felt that no one would make such a threat if he intended to carry through. And who would dare do something that would be so quickly discovered? She was even more alarmed to learn of actual threats and exclaimed to herself, "And this is the man accused of cowardice!!"[21]

Accusations of cowardice were attached to his name during the British invasion of Virginia when he had fled Monticello before Bannister Tarleton's dragoons. Federalist opponents deemed this action a reflection of character and continued to remind the public that as governor he had fled "because a storm was gathering," and he "did not display either much firmness or patriotism."[22] Supporters attempted to parry this accusation by reminding readers that he had been exonerated and thanked by the Virginia assembly following the invasion.[23] Nevertheless, the label of coward and the charges leveled at him following the British invasion remained a sore spot with Jefferson.

Jefferson was truthful when he revealed to Smith that he had received anonymous death threats. Generally in the form of scribbled notes, they arrived through the post. One he received in December 1804 was from a supposed "friend" with the warning that there was "a plot formed to Murder you—before the Next Election." This was to be carried out by a "hardy band of Fellows" with daggers and pistols, some of whom were already in Washington.[24] These were not publicized, since Smith clearly had not known of the threats, and her husband was editor of the main Washington newspaper. Riding alone displayed courage, and perhaps Jefferson wished to challenge those making the threats and suggest to the scribblers of the death notes that he would not change his routine.

Despite these reports of Jefferson riding alone on horseback, in his first year as president he had a new carriage built in Philadelphia with plated harness for four horses at a cost of $1,206.[25] His son-in-law John Wayles Eppes assisted him in purchasing some fine Virginia horses, and the correspondence indicated he was intent on bays of matching height and color.[26] He added to his staff an Irish coachman named Joseph Dougherty, who served him the full eight years of his presidency.[27] According to Margaret Bayard Smith, however, "The place of coachman, was little more than a sinecure, as his handsome chariot and four beautiful horses, were never used except when his daughters visited him."[28]

Unfortunately, his daughters' visits were extremely limited. They made a visit together in late fall 1802 and remained until January 1803, but sadly the younger daughter, Maria, died in 1804. The elder, Martha, made only one other visit in late 1805, remaining in Washington for five months.[29] The 1802 family visit included Jefferson's ten-year-old grandson Jeff Randolph, who in his memoirs remembered his mother going out in the coach and his own adventure of being taken to the navy yard by the coachman and gaining immediate entry due to the recognition of the president's equipage.[30] But how could the gateman recognize a presidential coach that the president never used? Perhaps the gateman recognized the coachman, Dougherty, not the coach itself.

Congressman Samuel Taggart was unaware that the president even owned a coach. He was another Federalist who commented on Jefferson's riding alone and unattended, writing, "He keeps no carriage but when he goes abroad it is on horse back and commonly without any servant to attend him, which is more strange in this country than in New England, for here it is very rare for any man affecting the stile of a gentleman to ride out without a servant."[31]

Taggart made further reference to the importance of a carriage as a part of a gentleman's image in his observations of Vice President Aaron Burr. He seemed surprised that when Congress reconvened in the fall of 1804, Burr took his place as president of the senate: the previous July he had killed

Alexander Hamilton in their famous duel.[32] But Taggart noticed a change. "He assumes but very little state. His appearance is different from last winter. He has no carriage. He has taken lodgings more than a mile from the Capitol, and usually walks to and from it on foot. I believe he is treated by all parties with a great deal of neglect."[33]

A man on foot projected a very different impression from one in a carriage or even on horseback. Jefferson began to incorporate the more egalitarian image of walking about Philadelphia when vice president. In the very rustic, unfinished capital of Washington he gave up walking and was seen on horseback, no doubt astride a very fine horse, but the carriage remained in the stable. But it was there. He could revert to the "stile of a gentleman" whenever he needed. In truth, the carriage may have been purchased in hope that his daughters would be able to join him more often in Washington, and he would not want them seen in anything less. Even though the coach received little use, Jefferson sold it at quite a loss when he left Washington in 1809.[34]

A coach and four, a black suit with silk stockings, a command of scintillating conversation while hosting a dinner with fine food and wine— Jefferson could always step back into the acceptable image of a gentleman as needed. And it was needed when he was asked to sit for an official portrait with Gilbert Stuart that was a result of one of his diplomatic appointments.

William Plumer made a routine entry in his journal on November 20, 1804, that the president had nominated and the Senate endorsed the appointment of James Bowdoin of Massachusetts as minister plenipotentiary from the United States to the court of Madrid.[35] Bowdoin had been awaiting an appointment for three years. In a letter dated a week after the election was decided in 1801, he wrote congratulating Jefferson and commending his sound political principles and character. Within this he added that if his "feeble aid" could contribute in any way to the success of Jefferson's administration, he was more than ready to offer his services.[36] Jefferson responded promptly to Bowdoin's letter but did not suggest an appointment; rather, he mentioned the respect he held for his late father, James Bowdoin II, and seemed aware that Bowdoin himself was following the example set by his affluent family as both a cultural and political leader in Massachusetts.

Jefferson gave careful thought to Bowdoin's appointment, as this diplomatic mission to Madrid was important. Attorney General Levi Lincoln vouched for Bowdoin as a good republican, and Secretary of State Henry Dearborn was personally acquainted with him.[37] Tension with Spain was high. Jefferson was intent on obtaining the territory called West Florida that extended along the coast of the Gulf of Mexico between the Perdido and Mississippi Rivers. He believed this area was important to the commerce and security of the United States and held more immediate rewards for growth and prosperity than the far western territories just obtained through the Louisiana Purchase Treaty. Jefferson tried to claim that the Floridas (East and West) were a part of the retrocession from Spain to France and therefore included in the recent purchase treaty. Spain resisted and maintained that the Floridas were still Spanish territory. Jefferson thought he would get the support of Napoleon in this dispute but knew negotiations must be handled carefully and that a show of resolve was necessary on the part of the young United States. Bowdoin was accepting a very sensitive assignment.[38]

As a part of Bowdoin's preparations for his ministerial assignment in Madrid, he wished to obtain two portraits. He wrote Dearborn, his long-term acquaintance in Washington, requesting that he act as his intermediary in commissioning the portraits of the president and Secretary of State James Madison. He obviously had a very clear idea of the images of leadership that he wanted to display at the American legation in Madrid, and he wished them done by Gilbert Stuart if possible. In his letter to Dearborn he requested, "I shall be much obliged to you to procure me the portraits of Mr. Jefferson and Mr. Madison if a good painter can be found at Washington, and they should be willing to take the trouble of sitting therefor." After a short explanation of where in Spain the paintings were to be shipped and how payment should be collected, he became more explicit as to the painter he would prefer and stated, "I should like to have them done by Stuart, could he be induced to execute them, as well he is able." He specified that they need not be framed as he could obtain finer frames in Europe. As to the paintings themselves, he wanted them to be half-length and a matching pair.[39] Bowdoin's comment, "as well he is able," commended Stuart's abilities, as Bowdoin had developed discernment through his own travels and collecting. American-born Stuart's success as a portrait artist in Britain (before he returned to the United States in 1793) earned him credibility with an American audience that still looked to Europe for reassurance that they were selecting the best, and admittedly, Stuart was a very fine portrait artist. His abilities at executing an ambitious state portrait were known through his full-length portrait of Washington and the subsequent copies.[40]

The role of the portrait in diplomacy was well established in Western tradition. The diplomat could stand as the physical presence and voice of the distant leader, but the portrait served as a visual reminder and provided a virtual presence of authority. Although this was Bowdoin's first diplomatic assignment, he was obviously familiar with this concept. Growing up in prerevolutionary Boston, he had the opportunity to see state portraits at the city's council chambers, where portraits of royal governors were hung alongside those of the British monarchs.[41]

Jefferson would have understood Bowdoin's request. For his own diplomatic assignment in 1784, he had secured the portrait of General Washington by American Joseph Wright for his residence in Paris, and he then furthered the republican statement with added portraits of other worthy Americans. Bowdoin apparently recognized the importance of this concept and requested this pair of paintings of the president and secretary of state. He would not be representing a single, royal monarch as in the European diplomatic tradition. The pendant portraits would emphasize that the American republic did not place authority in a single, permanent leader. Power was balanced among many bodies: Congress, the chief executive counseled by his secretaries, and a judiciary. In the European tradition the state portrait of the monarch might be paired with a portrait of his consort, such as the life-sized portraits of Louis XVI and his queen that had hung in the state house in Philadelphia.[42] But for the United States there would be no dynastic heir or royal spouse. An appropriate show of stability and strength was the needed message in the portraits commissioned by Bowdoin. The virtual presence of President Jefferson and Secretary of State Madison would serve to reinforce Bowdoin's authority as he negotiated for territory important to the commerce and security of the expanding United States.

Exactly when and by whom Jefferson's sitting with Stuart was arranged is uncertain. The artist may have called on the president himself, but it could have been more easily negotiated through Dearborn. As a cabinet member he was in frequent contact with both Jefferson and Madison and was often a dinner guest at the President's House.[43] In fact, Bowdoin's polite wording, "[if] they should be willing to take the trouble of sitting therefor," could be interpreted as instructions to Dearborn to deliver a direct and personal request. A sitting for Madison would not be necessary. Stuart had completed pendant portraits of James and Dolley Madison just the previous year, so a current original or copy was available. This was not the case with Jefferson. Preparing for the election of 1800, he had sat for Stuart in Philadelphia, and his accounting entries show on May 12, 1800, he had "paid Stuart for my portrait 100.D," but he had never received the final work.[44] According to Jefferson, the work was not collected from Stuart because "he was yet to put the last hand to it, so it was left with him." After Stuart relocated to Washington, the artist claimed that he was dissatisfied with the portrait. It is possible that it no longer remained in his possession; nevertheless, he needed another siting with Jefferson.[45]

Jefferson agreed to sit for Stuart promptly. By June 27 Dearborn was able to report to Bowdoin's Boston agent that the portraits would soon be on their way. Stuart was relocating to Boston from Washington and would personally transport the paintings. Dearborn advised, "Mr. Stuart has nearly completed them and will take them with his other effects to Boston and when completed will deliver them to you, to be forwarded to Mr. Bowdoin."[46] Given his close relationship with Dearborn, it is probable that Jefferson arrived at Stuart's studio fully aware that a version of his new portrait was destined for Europe to serve diplomatic purposes.

Stuart's resulting portrait of Jefferson comes closest to resembling an official state portrait of any made during his presidency (fig. 36). A state portrait traditionally came soon after a coronation or at the beginning of reign, yet Jefferson was commencing his second term. However, he was at the zenith of his administration's accomplishments, including the successful annexation of the Louisiana Territory and the port of New Orleans through the purchase treaty with Napoleon in 1803. Now the United States just needed to acquire the Floridas to secure the entire Gulf Coast.

Perhaps it was fitting, given the circumstances and requirements of this portrait, that Stuart employed many of the same elements that he used in his highly successful portraits of President Washington.[47] True to the formula often employed in European state portraiture, the figure is placed in a portico-like setting with a large column offering a sense of stability. Vibrancy and richness are added by a swag of red drapery framing the figure, red drapery covering the table, and the red upholstery of the chair. A sense of atmosphere deepens the background, as Stuart adds a glow to the sky that could be interpreted as a new day beginning, thus encouraging an analogy with the new nation.[48] The usual books sit on the table, and the papers under Jefferson's hand imply a man of learning and statecraft. The setting for the figure is grand, but with a timelessness that lifts it out of the ordinary and provides an elevated dignity. The portrait is missing the richness of detail, however, that distinguished Stuart's Lansdowne Washington and its

FIGURE 36. Thomas Jefferson by Gilbert Stuart, c. 1805–7. Oil on canvas.

Upon his appointment as minister to Spain, James Bowdoin commissioned a portrait of the president and secretary of state from Gilbert Stuart. The resulting image of Jefferson is the closest to a state portrait of any taken and shares some details with Stuart's portraits of Washington and echoes the European grand-manner style.

many replicas. The titles on the books are indistinguishable, and the table holds far fewer objects. Both Stuart's Jefferson and Madison appear to have been executed more hurriedly than the Washington portrait. Stuart was much in demand during his eighteen months in Washington, and by the time he took up Bowdoin's commission, he was preparing for his move to Boston.[49]

Bowdoin had specifically requested the portraits be half-length, not full-length, which placed limitations on more elaborate poses, so both men are pictured seated alongside elegantly draped tables. Stuart turns Jefferson slightly away from the picture plane but fixes his gaze directly towards the viewer. His eyes are level, and his entire expression appears calm, firm, and collected. Stuart modified his copy of his original portrait of Madison to better suit the purpose of the new commission (fig. 37). He left the angle of the head unchanged but moved Madison's focus from the viewer to the right, towards the companion portrait of Jefferson, and opened the body to a more frontal positon by moving the arm over the back of the chair.

More interesting is the change Stuart made to Madison's expression. The hint of a smile that appeared in the original portrait—intended to hang alongside that of his wife, Dolley—has vanished, and his look is intensified by the addition of a slight frown. Even the lighting is made dramatic, and the shadowing of the face is more pronounced. Did these slight changes better reflect Madison's political responsibilities and the diplomatic purpose of the portrait? The secretary of state negotiates directly with foreign representatives; the chief executive must remain resolved and unwavering in securing the national goal. Madison appears ready to leap from his chair into action, while Stuart places Jefferson solidly anchored, with his hand resting on the draped table. Stuart was experienced in suggesting position and responsibility through portraiture, given his long career that had included painting the titled of Britain. Now he applied his expertise to well-placed republican Americans.

Stuart depicts both Jefferson and Madison in black suits that followed the Washington prototypes but without lace or dress swords. This color choice in the wardrobe of the well-dressed western man of the late eighteenth century formed a visual link to revolutionary politics and underscored the rising influence of the commercial middle class and the spread of Enlightenment thought. It visually supported the concept of a natural equality and countered notions of sumptuary laws that defined class distinctions and rank through clothing. Americans had not embraced the

FIGURE 37. James Madison by Gilbert Stuart, c. 1805–7. Oil on canvas.

For the Bowdoin commission Stuart used his recently completed portrait of Secretary of State Madison that was painted as a pendant portrait for his wife, Dolley. For the official portrait that was to travel to Europe, Stuart shifted Madison's pose to face the viewer and gave him a graver expression.

European tradition of insignia for their national leaders, such as velvet and ermine robes of state. Any man could wear the black suit. It fulfilled the understated dignity considered appropriate for a republican leader. Americans would prove far more comfortable with a leader whose appearance was comparable to that of a successful, bourgeois man of business, but in this instance, as Jefferson sat for Stuart, the business was nation building.

Unfortunately, Stuart's portraits of Thomas Jefferson and James Madison were never tested before the Spanish, with their long history of monarchical rule. James Bowdoin was ill when he reached the coast of Spain, and rather than travel to Madrid, he sailed for London to consult with doctors there. By the time he regained his health, Napoleon's dominance over Spain meant any negotiations could be more effectively conducted from France. Bowdoin was instructed to join American minister plenipotentiary John Armstrong in Paris, but this did not prove to be a compatible working relationship, and Bowdoin's health was still unstable. In May 1807 he petitioned Jefferson to be released from his post, and by April 1808 he arrived back in Boston. Meanwhile, Bowdoin had instructed from Paris that the portraits not be shipped to Spain but rather delivered to his Boston residence. Following Bowdoin's death in 1811, the portraits were taken to Bowdoin College along with much of his art collection.[50]

These two portraits did eventually appear before a public audience, but an American one rather than European. Stuart painted five copies of Jefferson's portrait, including the one for Bowdoin, and in 1807 artist Robert Field made an engraving of the image that began to eclipse the popularity of the prints taken from Rembrandt Peale's 1800 Jefferson portrait.[51] In March 1807 Field advertised in Boston: "This day published, price 1 dollar—a Print of THOMAS JEFFERSON—engraved by Robert Field, from a Picture by Gilbert Stuart"[52] (fig. 38). The column in the background links the print to the Bowdoin version, as some of Stuart's copies did not show this detail. Field made Stuart's work available to a broad audience, and Stuart's became the dominant image of Jefferson as president.[53] Apparently, this was a look easier for Americans to accept than Jefferson in wolf skins. They may have attended Peale's Museum illuminations in March 1805 that featured the latest portrait by Rembrandt celebrating the reelection of Thomas Jefferson, but this image of their president gazing at them wrapped in a rustic, fur-lined cape did not generate a general appeal. Rembrandt advertised his willingness to make copies, but only one is known to have been painted, and there were no prints made in the nineteenth century. The portrait

FIGURE 38. Thomas Jefferson by Robert Field after Gilbert Stuart, 1807. Engraving.

Field made his engraving after the work of Stuart, and the column in the background links it to the portrait for Bowdoin. This very fine engraving allowed the public to have an updated image of their president.

continued to be exhibited at the Peale Museum until the dispersal sale of 1854, but it could never claim the popularity of Rembrandt's 1800 portrait.[54]

Jefferson's second commission with Stuart produced a portrait that is unique and revealing as to the image Jefferson wished preserved. This commission was placed during the time he was sitting for Bowdoin's 1805 portrait and was still waiting to receive the portrait he had paid for in 1800. A note accompanied his $100 payment to Stuart for this second commission: "Mr. Jefferson presents his compliments to Mr. Stewart, and begs leave to send him the inclosed for the trouble he gave him in taking the head *a la antique*" (fig. 39).[55] Evidently this was Jefferson's idea and perhaps one that did not particularly excite Stuart, as Jefferson mentioned later that "I got him to sketch me in the Medallion form, which he did on paper with Crayons. altho a slight thing I gave him another 100.D. probably the treble of what he would have asked." He concluded, "It is a very fine thing altho' very perishable." Nevertheless, the resulting profile set within a medallion pleased Jefferson, and he agreed with the opinion that it was "deemed the best which has been taken of me."[56] This was far more praise than he would attach to any of his other portraits.

This portrait is distinctive from Stuart's usual style in both format and in the medium used. Rather than oil, it is a blend of gouache (an opaque watercolor) over a crayon drawing on hand-laid paper that was then mounted on thin linen with glue sizing.[57] He may not have been eager to take Jefferson in profile, as this format, appearing less complex than a full-face

FIGURE 39. Thomas Jefferson (medallion portrait) by Gilbert Stuart, 1805. Grisaille, oil, and egg mixture on blue-laid paper on canvas.

Jefferson commissioned Stuart to take his portrait *à la antique* and was pleased with the result. He kept the portrait in the President's House, and in Jefferson's retirement years, visitors commented on seeing it at Monticello.

portrait, was not as highly regarded. During the Peales' visit to Washington in the winter of 1805 when commissions were not forthcoming, C. W. Peale wrote in a letter to the family that Rembrandt "is yet unwilling to shew his talents at the profile." He still hoped that once his full portraits were seen, he would generate commissions with no compromises necessary.[58] Yet the profile portrait linked directly to classical traditions and had been preserved especially in coinage and medals.[59]

When rendered in the medallion format, the profile portrait carried a connotation of fame and immortality. Alexander Pope addressed the role of the commemorative medal in one of his poems, writing: "The Medal, faithful to its charge of fame / Thro' climes and ages bears each form and name." Pope's poem explains that "Ambition" chooses the medal over triumphal arches or columns that can crumble with time. The nature of the artefact, a disc cast in metal, made for a very durable piece that could be handed along over many years. It preserved the image of the great man, usually in profile, on the obverse and featured an allusion to his honorable deeds on the reverse.[60] The profile itself created more distance between the subject and the viewer than a full frontal or even three-quarter view of the face, and in this distance suggested immortalization.[61]

Jefferson's profile already had appeared on national medals prior to his portrait request of Stuart. At the beginning of his presidency, an Indian peace medal was struck in 1801 by Jacob Reich. Distributed through the War Department to military officers, Indian commissioners, and agents who worked on the frontier, these medals were used as presentation gifts for various transactions with Native Americans. Lewis and Clark carried the medals on their expedition of 1803–6 along the Missouri River. Reich struck a similar medal that same year to commemorate Jefferson's presidency, which was the first from the new United States mint (fig. 40).[62] Jefferson sent copies to his two daughters and sister-in-law, Elizabeth Eppes. He explained to Martha that he had not met with Reich and offered, "It is taken from Houdon's bust, for he [Reich] never saw me." Jefferson obviously approved and added, "It sells the more readily as the prints which have been offered the public are such miserable caracatures."[63] (This was before Robert Field's print from Stuart.) Jefferson seemed certain that Reich used the Houdon bust as a model; however, the hair brushed towards the forehead and the coat with the wide lapel more resemble the Sharples pastel. Another possibility would be that Reich studied Rembrandt's 1800 portrait or one of the many prints that Jefferson disparaged and through these later examples brought Houdon's 1789 hairstyle up to date.

Jefferson may have had no input into the medal's design, but he must have been pleased with the iconography chosen for the reverse. In one hand the goddess Minerva holds a staff topped with a liberty cap; with the other she places a copy of the Declaration of Independence on a rock labeled

FIGURE 40. American medal of Thomas Jefferson by Jacob Reich, 1801. Silver.

Jefferson approved this commemorative presidential medal created by Reich and felt it a better likeness than most of the prints then in circulation. He reported to family members that the profile was taken from Houdon's bust portrait, and certainly it looks very close to the Houdon except for the cropped hair across the forehead.

"Constitution." Meanwhile, the national eagle bearing a wreath hovers above. The inscription reads, "Under his Wing is Protection" and "To Commemorate July 4, 1776."[64] The reference to July 4, 1776, connects directly to Jefferson and follows the pattern of commemorating on the reverse side a memorable deed by the subject.[65] Whatever Reich's inspiration for the hairstyle, it follows the traditional eighteenth-century style in which the hair is pulled into a queue and tied with a ribbon. The Stuart portrait shows Jefferson far more in the *antique*, his bare neck and cropped hair lending to the idea of timelessness — and thus to fame.[66]

Jefferson's short hair was not invented by the artist to mimic the antique. The previous November Senator Plumer had mentioned that the president's hair was "cropt and powdered."[67] Cropped hair initially invoked associations with the "leveling" and reforms in England that were tied to the revolution in France. But by the time of Stuart's medallion portrait in 1805, cropped hair was growing in fashion and acceptability. In 1801 General James Wilkinson had issued an order to officers under his command: "For the accommodation, comfort & health of the Troops, the hair is to be cropped without exception." This was resisted by some of the Federalist officers, who believed it originated with the new republicanism that had taken control of the national government and represented the taste of President Jefferson.[68] In an 1804 profile portrait of Jefferson by Charles Févret de Saint-Mémin, Jefferson appears to be adopting the copped hair around the face yet still shows the traditional queue in back tied by a ribbon (fig. 41).[69]

By 1805 and Stuart's portrait, short hair for men was becoming much less controversial. Perhaps more interesting than the hairstyle is the black ribbon visible over Jefferson's shoulder in the more formal state portrait that Stuart created for Minister Bowdoin. Ribbon would have traditionally tied the hair back in the queue. Thus, in portraits created in the same sittings, the one intended for formal presentation in Europe adheres to traditional hairdressing, while the *Medallion*, as a private portrait, allowed Jefferson to indulge his taste for the classics and present himself in the purest republican manner.

This was the one portrait that Jefferson felt comfortable having at the President's House. Had he been able to collect his first commission from Stuart in September 1801, his plan was to send it directly to Monticello, as these were his instructions to his agent, John Barnes, who was attempting to collect the portrait on his behalf.[70] Apparently he intended that this

FIGURE 41. Thomas Jefferson by Charles Balthazar Julien Févret de Saint-Mémin, 1804. Charcoal, black, white, and grey chalks on pink prepared cream wove paper.

Jefferson's daughters encouraged him to have his portrait done when Saint-Mémin was in Washington in 1804. The profile portraits were produced on paper with assistance of the physiognotrace. From the original, Saint-Mémin made small engravings, perfect for Jefferson to distribute as presidential gifts.

formal portrait would join his collection of worthies at Monticello but not appear in a space as public as the President's House in Washington. How prominently the *Medallion* was displayed in the presidential residence is uncertain, but artist William Russell Birch commented on it when he called on the president late in 1805. Birch felt it the finest portrait he had seen of Jefferson and offered to make a print that would be suitable for presidential presentations. He borrowed the portrait, created his design for reproduction, and handed it off to engraver David Edwin. Unfortunately, the print was not completed until after Jefferson's retirement, and he did not receive copies from Birch until 1812. Jefferson's thank you note to Birch was not specific as to how many he received; nevertheless, they were too late to serve as presidential gifts. In his autobiography Birch confessed to accidentally ruining the plate after the few impressions he took to send Jefferson, and so a reproduction of Jefferson's favored image of himself never enjoyed the circulation he might have wished.[71]

Despite their difficulty doing business, Jefferson and Stuart shared a mutual respect. Jefferson addressed Stuart "with a high veneration" regarding his talents and encouraged him to move back to Washington, as Jefferson continued to believe that the national history should be illustrated with inspirational likenesses of its leaders. Of Jefferson, Stuart reportedly said "they had long been friends, tho' they differed in politicks." His remarks on his relationship with Jefferson indicated that he had attended dinner at the President's House, and based on his various exchanges with Jefferson, he observed that "Mr. Jefferson took very good care not to make a too great display of his learning."[72] Yet the "Medallion profile" demonstrated his understanding of the classical in art and its link to Western thought.

Jefferson's self-fashioning continued to fluctuate to the end of his presidency. Frances Few, the niece of Mrs. Albert Gallatin, visited Washington in the fall of 1808 and was invited to a dinner party at the President's House. She made notes of her experience and wrote, "I dined with the President— he is a tall thin man not very distinguished in his appearance but very agreeable in his manner." She went on to describe his clothing: "He was dressed in a pair of dark corduroy breeches—an old fringed dimity jacket that he brought with him from France which reached down to his hips—a blue cloth coat with metal buttons—worsted stockings nicely drawn up & a clean pair of leather shoes."[73] (At least the "down–at-the-heel slippers" had been replaced.) She said of the evening's conversation that Jefferson entered into it but never tried to monopolize it. The atmosphere was egalitarian, and she concluded that the president could only be distinguished from the other guests by his "shabbiness."

At the time of this dinner in October 1808, Jefferson was preparing to leave the presidency, assured that in all probability James Madison would be stepping into the office and therefore continuing a republican agenda. Presumably he could forgo receiving guests in mismatched and outdated clothing, but this was not the case. He continued to shift between the guise he had created as the representative the people had elected to keep the machine in motion and the gentleman in the black suit. He might just as readily have met Francis Few and the Gallatins in the black suit with hair powdered. This dichotomy in his personal fashioning was perplexing to many of his constituents and has remained difficult to reconcile.

He never lost sight of his theory, as expressed to John Adams during the election of 1800, that the presidency was really about exercising the principles of good government while keeping the machine in motion. He expressed this same idea to James Bowdoin following his first inauguration, when he stated that he served only as "the safe depository of the principle for which we were contending."[74] This self-effacing description of his role as president placed him as a conduit only. This distinction between the principles and the man allowed the "man" to issue his own dinner invitations that did not reference the office he held. He might own a fine carriage, but keep it from contributing to an image of state. The black suit could be the clothing choice when the occasion was celebratory or when he needed to make a more guarded appearance as head of state—such as in a formal diplomatic portrait. He could turn the Janus face when he needed to separate the private man from the man who was temporarily serving as president and guiding the motion of the machine.

But how successful were his efforts? British legation secretary Augustus John Foster, though not an admirer, admitted to Jefferson's popularity. He had accused Jefferson of "playing a game," and of "affecting to despise dress" as a part of this game. He saw Jefferson as a dreamer and a visionary, yet he also recognized Jefferson's practical and unrelenting ambition in working towards his vision for the American republic. Foster reached the conclusion that "if he lived, however, on illusions and mystic philanthropical plans for the benefit of mankind in the country . . . he was not the less awake or active in taking measures to insure the triumph of himself and his party." In these remarks Foster recognized a visionary who might seem to be playing a game but who never lost sight of where he wished to lead this game. He gave Jefferson credit for working towards the benefit of mankind without giving up his political agenda. Foster concluded, "I doubt that General Washington himself would so certainly have been elected for the third time to the presidential chair as he would have been, had he chosen to be put into nomination for it."[75] But Jefferson did not choose to continue in the presidency. The machine could be safely guided by his close friend and successor, James Madison. On March 11, 1809, Jefferson left Washington for Monticello, never to return to the city he had helped create.

IV

Retirement at Monticello

Putting to myself your question, Would I agree to live my 73 years over again for ever? I hesitate to say.
—Thomas Jefferson to John Adams, Monticello, August 1, 1816

7

CONTEMPLATING LEGACY

"Who shall write the history of the American Revolution?" This was the question Adams posed as he and Jefferson resumed their correspondence following more than a decade of silence. They had been coaxed into setting aside past differences through their mutual friend Benjamin Rush. He saw the estrangement of these two old patriots as not just a personal loss but a loss to the American republic.[1] A short note from Adams dated January 1, 1812, and a prompt and lengthier response from Jefferson began their correspondence and resumed a long-distance friendship, Adams writing from his home in Quincy, Massachusetts, and Jefferson from Monticello. It was Adams who stated directly, "You and I, ought not to die, before We have explained ourselves to each other."[2] This particular letter had a brief but lovely postscript from Abigail Adams "to add the regards, of an old Friend, which are still cherished and preserved through all the changes and vissitudes which have taken place since we first became acquainted."[3] Jefferson must have found the renewed dialogue with Adams bittersweet. Its invigorating challenge of philosophical debates called on the wide range of knowledge and reading shared by these two men, but the references to past disagreements never resolved and those unanswerable questions as to the future of the republic added an edge to their retirement correspondence.

Adams put forward a question that greatly concerned Jefferson. "Who shall write the history of the American revolution? Who can write it? Who will ever be able to write it?" Many of the documents, debates, and deliberations were lost or never recorded. The number of their colleagues who had shared in these world-changing events was diminishing. Jefferson was sensitive to this question as he worried about his image as presented in contemporary histories that cast doubts on his role in the American Revolution and the early formation of the nation. The first edition of John Marshall's five-volume *The Life of George Washington* had been completed in 1807. This work extended beyond being a biography of Washington and outlined American history from colonial settlement through the revolution and the founding of the republic. The final volume dealt with the rise of the partisan politics of the 1790s and unfavorably compared Jefferson and his political allies with the Federalists and their initial leader, Alexander Hamilton. This provoked from Jefferson a complaint against "the party diatribe of Marshall."[4] Jefferson's perceived pro-French sympathies were brought out and questioned as well.

Equally unsettling was an 1812 publication by fellow Virginian Henry Lee III. In his *Memoirs of the War in the Southern Department,* Lee resurrected the criticism of Jefferson as an incompetent wartime governor who reacted with cowardice during the British invasion of Virginia.[5] These accusations had haunted Jefferson throughout his public career, but now they threatened his reputation in history. To Jefferson these histories by Marshall and Lee were dangerous, not just to his own reputation but to American republicanism in general. Their retelling of early American history gave a more favorable impression of those who supported the Federalists and their ambitions for a more centralized and elitist government. Even though the Federalists had been in decline since his election to the presidency in 1800, Jefferson continued to fear his old enemies' monarchical leanings and the influence of their ideas on future generations of Americans.[6]

In his final years at Monticello, as he responded to the epistolary volleys from Adams and recalled the past, Jefferson was concerned as well for the future of the American republic. This connected directly with his insistence that its history be correctly remembered and recorded. In addition to a true and accurate understanding of the events of the revolution, subsequent generations needed to fully comprehend the character of the founders—their motives, actions, and concept of republican virtue. The future was irrevocably linked to the past; a correct understanding of history was, therefore, imperative.[7] He had to wonder what was to be his own legacy within that larger history?[8]

Another former friend, John Trumbull, held feelings similar to those deliberated by Jefferson and Adams. For him the question was not who could write the history but rather who would paint the history? Who could leave a visual record of the conflict with Britain for American independence? Even though future artists might be more skilled, they would not have had the direct experience nor have collected the likenesses of so many of the participants of the American Revolution now gone. He had recorded the faces of these important events and felt strongly that he should be the one to paint the history.[9]

The War of 1812 became the catalyst that reconnected Trumbull and Jefferson. The war had caught Trumbull back in London, but following the Treaty of Ghent, he sailed for New York and arrived in September 1815 to find patriotic fervor high. The public buildings burned in the City of Washington during the war were being rebuilt and expanded. The two wings of the Capitol, the only portions completed prior to the war, were to be connected by the rotunda that had been designed but never built. Trumbull recognized that the interior of the rotunda would need decorating, so this seemed an opportune time to resume his long-neglected series of history paintings. But Trumbull was known to be a Federalist, the Republicans held the majority in Congress, and such a project would require a congressional resolution of approval. James Madison was president; James Monroe was secretary of state. Trumbull was very much aware that they were Republicans and Jefferson men.[10] The support of Thomas Jefferson could prove helpful. A good friend of Trumbull's, Christopher Gore, observed that "Pericles could not advance himself at Athens without taking part with the Democracy against the Aristocracy."[11] Trumbull addressed a letter to Jefferson.

John Trumbull's letter arrived at Monticello the first week in January 1817. He very astutely began by recalling that twenty-eight years had elapsed since "under the kind protection of your hospitable roof . . . I painted your portrait in my picture of the Declaration of Independance," and he reminisced about how in the library of Jefferson's Paris residence they had planned together the composition for this painting. He quietly ignored his deliberate estrangement from Jefferson that arose amid the polarizing politics of the 1790s and their differing political opinions.[12] Rather, he proceeded to outline his current ambition of obtaining a commission from Congress to decorate the restored Capitol in Washington. *The Declaration of Independence* was his first consideration and would be the painting used to promote the series.[13] Certainly no painting could have interested Jefferson more.

Within the week Jefferson responded to Trumbull, assuring him that his affection for him was not diminished by the passing years and offering no hint at their estrangement. He used his letter to review old friendships and inquired of their "charming Coterie of Paris." He asked about their mutual friend Angelica Church, obviously not knowing that she had died in 1814. He and Maria Cosway corresponded occasionally, and he informed Trumbull that she was in Italy. He went on to inquire about Madame de Corny and expressed some sadness that their old acquaintances were so estranged and scattered. As to the government commission, he did not doubt that Trumbull could stand on his own reputation and talent; nevertheless, he was enclosing a letter for Trumbull to deliver to Secretary of State Monroe. In this letter to Monroe, Jefferson praised Trumbull's abilities and made the pitch that his paintings would be "monuments of the taste & talents of our country, as well as of the scenes which gave it it's place among nations."[14] Jefferson also wrote to Virginia senator James Barbour, recommending Trumbull and giving Barbour his permission to use Jefferson's name in promoting Trumbull—something that he rarely did willingly.

When Trumbull solicited John Adams's support, he received a brief sermon. Adams warned, "The Burin and the Pencil, the Chisel and the Trowell, have in all ages and Countries of which we have any Information, been enlisted on the side of Despotism and Superstition." In his estimation, "Architecture, Sculpture, Painting, and Poetry have conspir'd against the Rights of Mankind: and the Protestant Religion is now unpopular and Odious because it is not friendly to the Fine Arts." Adams was not alone in his views. For many Americans, art remained an extravagance associated with expense, and therefore luxury, and so could compromise the integrity of a republican state.[15] Nevertheless, following his admonitions, Adams concluded his letter by wishing Trumbull success in Congress "with all my heart."[16] Just as Jefferson, he would be visually linked forever with the Declaration of Independence in a prominent public space.

Trumbull was sincere in telling Jefferson that he intended to promote his series with his small study of *The Declaration of Independence*, which he would display in the House of Representatives as an example of his work.[17] By March 1817 he could share with Jefferson the good news that the House of Representatives had voted the funding for four of his paintings to be placed in the Capitol rotunda. He had arranged with President Madison that the paintings would be twelve by eighteen feet so the principal figures could be life-size. The subjects chosen in consultation with Madison were

The Declaration of Independence, which he would begin first, to be followed by *The Surrender at Saratoga*, *The Surrender at Yorktown*, and *The Resignation of Washington* (fig. 42). He would receive a total of $32,000 for the four paintings, considered a handsome fee.[18]

The following year, in October 1818, Trumbull reported again to Jefferson. *The Declaration of Independence* was completed "as far as it can be until I see it in place in the Capitol." Currently it was on public exhibit in New York.[19] He had received permission from President James Monroe to tour the painting with a twenty-five-cent admission fee per viewer. From New York *The Declaration* moved to Faneuil Hall in Boston; to Philadelphia, where it was displayed in the room of the Old State House where the signing took place; to Baltimore; and finally to Washington. The tour was quite a success, and approximately 21,000 patrons viewed the large painting. Trumbull followed with exhibits of his other paintings for this series, but none received quite the reception of *The Declaration of Independence*.[20]

Trumbull was honored that John Adams had come to view the painting when it was at Faneuil Hall in Boston.[21] Adams included in a letter to Jefferson that "Trumbull with a band of Associates drew me by the Cords of old Frienships to see his picture," but he made no comment on the painting itself nor gave his opinion of the work. Of more concern was that he "got a great Cold" in Faneuil Hall (he never used to catch a cold there) but closed his letter assuring Jefferson that "Sick or Well the frienship is the same of your old Acquaintance—John Adams"[22] John Quincy Adams, then serving as secretary of state, saw the "nearly finished" version of the *Declaration* at Trumbull's studio in New York prior to its trip to Boston. In his estimation, "The picture is immeasurably below the dignity of the subject." He added, "The old small picture [is] far superior to this large new one" but noted that Trumbull felt otherwise.[23] Jefferson never had the opportunity to see the final painting; he would have to wait for the print.

Trumbull began to negotiate publication of an engraving of *The Declaration of Independence* almost immediately, as the print could be made from his small study. He realized that of his series, *The Declaration* was of the greatest interest to the nation and that it was the image on which his reputation as patriot-artist primarily rested. Despite Federalist opposition in the 1790s, the Fourth of July celebrations grew, and many included a reading of the declaration. More Americans paid to see this painting on exhibit than any of the others on their way to Washington, which confirmed what Trumbull believed. He astutely had the names of Jefferson, Adams, Madison, and

FIGURE 42. Revolutionary War series by John Trumbull, placed 1826, US Capitol Rotunda. Oil on canvas, each 12 ft. × 18 ft. Top: *The Declaration of Independence, July 4, 1776* (1818); bottom: *The Surrender of Lord Cornwallis at Yorktown, October 19, 1781* (1820); facing top: *The Surrender of General Burgoyne at Saratoga, October 17, 1777* (1821); facing bottom: *The Resignation of General Washington, December 23, 1783* (1824).

Trumbull returned to his Revolutionary War series (begun when Jefferson was in Paris in the late 1780s) when he learned that a commission was to be awarded by Congress for paintings to decorate the new rotunda of the Capitol building. Jefferson fully supported Trumbull in his successful petition to Congress for the commission.

Monroe at the top of his list of subscribers for the print that would be completed in 1823.[24] His initial choice for an engraver was James Heath of London, who had so successfully engraved the Lansdowne Washington by Gilbert Stuart, but contract negotiations were never completed. In addition, Trumbull received some criticism that such an important American scene should be executed in Britain. Fortunately, a young but very capable artist and engraver named Asher B. Durand came to his attention.[25] Trumbull assured Jefferson that Durand had acquired his professional skills without any foreign instruction and so was American born and American educated. Even the print paper was of American manufacture, which allowed Trumbull to proudly claim that the engraving would be "completely American" and thus more worthy of the great scene it commemorated.

In this same letter informing Jefferson of the plans for the print, Trumbull announced that he would soon complete the last painting in the series, *The Resignation of Washington,* and confessed some liberties with the composition. Jefferson and Monroe had been in Congress at the time of the resignation and so could logically be included. Indeed, Jefferson wrote of "the affecting scene" of General Washington's final appearance before Congress as commander in chief as he handed in his commission and ceremoniously returned to private life.[26] But Trumbull decided to slip Madison in as well, so that "the picture will contain portraits of the Four Virginian Presidents."[27] He gave a similar explanation to Madison: "That I may have all the Virginia Presidents, I have taken the liberty . . . of placing you among the Spectators—It is a Painter's licence, which I think the occasion may well justify."[28] In actuality Madison was at his Virginia estate, Montpelier, on December 23, 1783, the date of Washington's resignation. Trumbull offered a second layer of history by adding the four Virginia presidents in his telling of this important event and must have thought the Virginia Dynasty would be of interest to Americans.

What concerned Jefferson personally as he read Trumbull's letter was that this dynasty was ending. He had left the presidency assured that the policies of his administration would continue as his good friends and political colleagues James Madison and James Monroe filled the office. This had allowed Jefferson a long-distance link to Washington while he enjoyed his retirement at Monticello. But many American citizens shared Jefferson's realization of changing times and knew as they greeted President Monroe—attired in the outdated knee breeches, buckled shoes, and tricornered hat—on one of his many tours through the states that he was providing them a visual reminder of their history. Monroe would be the last of the founders to serve as their president. When the Capitol rotunda opened in November 1826, displaying Trumbull's four large-as-life paintings, John Quincy Adams, representing the next generation, had stepped into the presidential office.[29]

Judging by Jefferson and Trumbull's exchanges, there was no hint of any lingering animosity from Trumbull, and it is questionable as to how much rancor was ever felt on Jefferson's part. He encouraged Trumbull to visit him at his home, and on paper Trumbull responded enthusiastically. But as Trumbull worked to finish the paintings and then negotiate their installation (and dealt with the death of his wife in 1824), a visit to Monticello never took place.

Even though Trumbull was unable to make the trip to Monticello, many others did. Jefferson's retirement years were full of visitors who came to call on the Sage, and their memoirs and letters offer impressions of Jefferson on his Virginia estate. Richard Rush, son of Benjamin Rush (who had brought Jefferson and Adams back into correspondence), visited in 1816 and described Monticello as "a sort of Mecca."[30] Jefferson's daughter, Martha Randolph, who alongside her daughters supervised the running of the house at Monticello during Jefferson's retirement, was not so romantic in her descriptions of the great number of visitors. Martha commented in September 1825 on "20 persons to Dinner in the Dining Room and 11 children & boys in My sitting room 31 persons in all," while her daughter Cornelia had noted just the month before, "My time is so completely occupied by serving & entertaining company . . . we had thirteen, fourteen & fifteen morning visitors & ten or a dozen perhaps in the evening."[31]

Visitors' descriptions of Jefferson suggest that he had carried his patriotic zeal for homespun and American manufacture into retirement. The idea of homespun fabrics as a political statement was not new to Americans and predated the revolution. What began as a means of resistance to the various economic measures imposed by Britain became a necessity during the revolution itself.[32] The embargo pursued by Jefferson during his second presidential term encouraged the use of homespun.[33] He appreciated a letter from a Virginia constituent, who informed him that homespun was already being worn in several Virginia counties to show patriotic resolve, but he encouraged the president to set an example and wrote, "I recollect that tho Tories found fault of the plainness of your dress a few years back, and should you appear in home spun now, I am apprehensive it would drive them out of the country in disgust, but in the eyes of the American people who delight in independance even in dress, the home spun would appear truly elegant."[34] Either Jefferson listened or was already of the mindset to pursue a simple domestic fabric. He informed his grandson, Thomas Jefferson Randolph, studying in Philadelphia, "We mean to exhibit ourselves here on New Year's day in homespun." He needed additional fabric for breeches to complete his outfit and requested Jeff send black cloth of either thick or corded cotton—either of these would do as long as it was homespun.[35] The War of 1812 curtailed imports from Britain and placed further emphasis on American manufactured textiles, but that period found Jefferson already engaged in home manufacture of cloth at Monticello, primarily for clothing his enslaved community.

In retirement he continued to dress down, although no one pronounced him as slovenly and indifferent to appearances as had his opponents while he was still in public office. In fact, when Congressman Daniel Webster visited Jefferson in December 1824, he commented, "His whole dress was very much neglected but not slovenly."[36] A visitor in 1816 reported Jefferson making the case that imports should be limited to only what was absolutely necessary and that Americans ought to manufacture all their own clothes and then not be too proud to wear them.[37] He went on to describe Jefferson wearing "a blue quaker coat, blue cloth vest, olive cotton cordyroy breeches with horn buttons on the whole—all homemade." The previous year, early in 1815, a gentleman calling at Monticello described Jefferson dressed in either the same clothing or something quite similar. Jefferson's coat and waistcoat were made of a blue, "stiff, thick cloth of the wool of his own merinos and badly manufactured."[38] This outfit included corduroy breeches with horn buttons.

Yet another account has him in a coat of a different fabric but again describes it as cut in a dated "Quaker" style: "His dress, in color and form, was quaint and old-fashioned, plain and neat—a dark pepper-and-salt coat, cut in the old Quaker fashion, with a single row of large metal buttons, knee breeches, gray-worsted stockings, shoes fastened by large metal buckles."[39] That Jefferson was described as wearing coats cut in the "old Quaker style" would suggest that he had not adopted the latest fashion of dress coats cut horizontal at the waist with narrow tails at the back, the forerunner of what came to be called the "tailcoat." Examples of affluent Quakers alongside fashionably dressed Philadelphians in the second decade of the nineteenth century are well represented in the work of artist John Lewis Krimmel

FIGURE 43. Details from *Fourth of July in Centre Square* by John Lewis Krimmel, 1812. Oil on canvas, 22¾ in. × 29 in.

Krimmel's painting of a Fourth of July celebration in Philadelphia offers examples of the variations in men's fashions in the early nineteenth century. The subdued "Quaker" dress on the man to the left contrasts with the more stylish dress of the two men at the far right. Notice their coat skirts shaped into tails, form-fitting pantaloons, and the tall crowns of their hats. From visitors' accounts, at Monticello Jefferson adhered to the older fashion preferred by the Quakers.

(see fig. 43). He recorded Quaker men in their broad-brimmed hats and knee breeches together with more fashionable young gentlemen wearing long pantaloons and coats with narrow tails.

These visitors described Jefferson in knee breeches, not the more fashionable pantaloons that reached the ankle. But when Daniel Webster visited in December 1824, Jefferson was wearing pantaloons.[40] His granddaughter Ellen Wayles Randolph confirmed that he did not adopt pantaloons until very late in life but found them more comfortable than knee breeches. She maintained that he dressed simply with the intent of "neatness and comfort" and admitted that he did nothing to conform with current fashion.[41] Certainly he did not seem bothered welcoming visitors in clothing that appeared homemade, from textiles generated at his own plantation.

Comfort may have been a factor, but his appearance also supported his long-held political convictions regarding American manufacture. During the election of 1800, one newspaper article identified him as a "patron of home manufactures," and certainly his opposition to British imports was well known.[42] The image that Jefferson created at Monticello was hardly as public as that of his former years when he held national office, yet visitors left records that were shared with others, whether in private correspondence or published accounts, in which Jefferson was given the role of the old patriot dressed as the modest American who relied on his own resources.

Two young gentlemen who called on Jefferson in early February 1815 caught him at a significant moment. George Ticknor and Francis Calley Gray arrived from Boston with letters of introduction from John Adams and found Jefferson planning for the shipment of his extensive personal library to Washington. During the second war with Britain, the War of 1812, the congressional library had been burned along with the public buildings in the capital. The loss prompted Jefferson to offer the sale of his own collection of books assembled over fifty years. When Ticknor and Gray arrived at Monticello on February 4, 1815, Jefferson had just received word that Congress had authorized the purchase of his books. Ticknor mentioned in his memoir of spending time among "this collection of books, now so much talked about."[43]

When Jefferson learned of the burning of the public buildings, he wrote Madison to express his outrage over the enemy's "barbarous achievements at Washington," perhaps forgetting that US forces had first looted and then torched York (now Toronto), the capital of Upper Canada, in April 1813.[44] The burning of Washington must have reminded him of his own situation as Virginia governor during the first war with Britain, as he expressed to Madison. "I have felt so much for you," he wrote, as "I know that when such failures happen they afflict even those who have done everything they could to prevent them."[45] He was correct that Madison was blamed for the burning of Washington in the Federalist press, who put forward the story that he had "scampered off at full speed with his whole court at his heels, leaving his army to follow or to fight, at their option." This was supposedly at the onset of a "paltry marauding party of the British." This account resurrects the stories told of Jefferson during the revolution and the British invasion of Virginia, describing how "Thomas Jefferson, then Governor and commander in chief of the armies and navies of the State of Virginia, fled from the capital of the State on the approach of the British forces, abandoned his command, and secreted himself in a place of safety."[46] The charges of cowardice against Jefferson were not let go, and now Madison stood accused as well.

Some things had not changed in the years that Jefferson had been away from Washington, but enough time had passed that he was no longer knowledgeable of who held various appointments. He called on his old friend Samuel Harrison Smith, former publisher of the *National Intelligencer* who now served as commissioner of revenue, to act as his intermediary in placing his library proposal with the chairman of the congressional Joint Library Committee. Jefferson began his letter to Congress: "I learn from the Newspapers that the Vandalism of our enemy has triumphed at Washington over science as well as the Arts, by the destruction of the public library with the noble edifice in which it was deposited." He then offered for sale his own library.[47] He did not suggest a price but enclosed a library catalog for an appraisal. The final offer and manner of payment would be left to Congress. There was only one point on which he was adamant—it was an all-or-nothing offer. He stated in his letter: "I do not know that it contains any branch of science which Congress would wish to exclude from their collection. there is in fact no subject to which a member of Congress may not have occasion to refer. but such a wish would not correspond with my views of preventing it's dismemberment. my desire is either to place it in their hands entire, or to preserve it so here."

In Congress the response to the library proposal fell very much along the usual party lines, and Jefferson's insistence that the library be accepted intact became an issue. Some critics questioned whether congressmen really needed "such as the Greek, Latin, Italian, Spanish and French authors."[48] An opponent to the purchase had to wonder, with the national treasury so depleted by the war, was Congress expected to purchase books such as Paine's *Age of Reason* or works by Voltaire, Condorcet, or Diderot? And would there be the manuscript copy of the letter to Mazzei or the original Declaration of Independence in the hand of the drafting committee?[49] Another writer simply announced that Congress had agreed to purchase Mr. Jefferson's library, "trumpery and all."[50] Those in favor of the purchase pushed back at the questions raised over the inclusion of philosophical works and books in foreign languages. One writer addressed the Federalist objections by questioning whether writings of notable philosophers that appeared in the great libraries of Europe were to be prohibited a place in the Library of Congress? The thought was developed further by posing the question that if books were regulated, would the Federalists next attempt to establish a set form of worship throughout the United States?[51] The library debate prompted the larger question of government controlling freedom of thought.

Ultimately, Congress voted to purchase Jefferson's library. A Georgetown book dealer, Joseph Milligan, was recruited to make an assessment based on Jefferson's catalog, and he reached the terms of sale: $23,950 for 6,487 volumes. President Madison signed "An Act to authorize the purchase of the library of Thomas Jefferson, late President of the United States" on January 30, 1815. The volumes were packed at Monticello and loaded on ten wagons for the trip to Washington.[52] The burning of Washington initiated Jefferson's library proposal much as it had spurred John Trumbull to begin painting again on his series of scenes from the first conflict with Britain. Both men in their own way looked to participate in the refurbishment of the capital and in so doing, to add to their own legacies.

Jefferson was adamant that a book he had compiled be included if his sale to Congress was successful. It was a collection of four different works that he had bound (in six volumes) under the title *The Book of Kings*. He had received from his Paris friend comte de Tessé a copy of what he referred to as the "Memoirs of the Margrave of Bareuth." To this he added the "Memoirs of the Comtesse de la Motte," "Trial of the Duke of York," and "The Book," which was subtitled, "The Proceedings and Correspondence upon the Inquiry into the Conduct of Her Royal Highness the Princess of Wales."[53] These works constituted a royal exposé. In thanking Tessé for the addition to his book collection, he referred to the other works and described them as a disrobing of royalty to expose their gross manners, coarse vices, and meanness. He intended his compilation to be "Medicine for Monarchists."[54] He pointed out his *Book of Kings* to George Ticknor during his 1815 visit, who found it curious but "expressive of his hatred of royalty."[55] Ticknor's remark illustrates that the former president's old antipathy toward monarchical systems was well known, and obviously Jefferson still held suspicions that lingering "monarchists" could even yet influence the national government. His compilation would present them lessons, some fairly recent, of the evils associated with royalty. In turn, many Federalists still distrusted Jefferson's ambitions, which they felt would destabilize the nation, and had not totally given up their campaigns against him in the partisan press.

As Jefferson's library sale was being debated in the newspapers, his name appeared in other political articles as though he had never left office. Of course, with Madison in the presidency many Federalists did not believe that Jefferson was totally gone. To the opposition he was still a threat to the nation. The Federalists tried to use the War of 1812 and the depletion of the national treasury as proof of Republican incompetence. The United States did not acquire Canada, and the war was essentially a draw as to territory gained. However, the nation was intact and the final major victory at New Orleans on January 8, 1815, left the Federalists little to stand on. This victory postdated the treaty concluded at Ghent on December 21, 1814, but it did contribute to American confidence and feeling that honor had been achieved. Yet an article appeared not long after the treaty was ratified that once more warned against Thomas Jefferson, offering arguments that had changed little since the partisan battles of the 1790s and his presidency.[56]

This article began circulating in newspapers in April 1815. Titled "Character of Jefferson," it raises the old accusations initially launched by Hamilton in 1792. Again there is the warning of duplicity—"He [is] cloaked under the garb of humility"—and readers are warned that he "can assume as suits his purpose the manners of a peasant or the exterior of a fine courtier." This recalls his self-presentation as president, whether the polished epicurean in a fine black suit or the slovenly and dressed-down executive leader greeting congressmen, foreign ministers, or the general citizenry that he might meet on a solitary ride. The writer then warns that he is "gifted with uncommon powers for conversation" and can be "insinuating to a charm." The writer admits that "he completely stamped the image of himself on the policy of his country" and concedes that he did this not through power, as would European rulers, but rather through "influence." The writer builds his argument to conclude that this was only possible because the country was young and unsettled and vulnerable—and it was "unprotected by privileged orders."

The library purchase raised again the old controversies over Jefferson's policies and his self-presentation. The "Character of Jefferson" article summarizes well the major points raised by the political opposition stretching back to the 1790s. The author's closing statement that the young country was more vulnerable in not having a designated elite class that could guide and protect—an aristocracy—gives a different perspective to Jefferson's insistence that his *Book of Kings* be a part of the congressional library. Jefferson's ongoing fear of a resurgence of an aristocracy and monarchy from the United States' colonial past was not as eccentric as it might seem with the distance of time. Some observers, such as the author of the "Character of Jefferson," still believed a defined, elite leadership was necessary for the safety and stability of the country. Even in retirement Jefferson rebelled against the old aristocratic establishment and supported the democratic leveling of society based on the abilities of the individual, not title or wealth. For the Federalists he remained the intellectual who lacked the energy and control needed to forge a strong national government; for his supporters his intellect stood for an enlightened breadth of thought that allowed the country to move forward with greater inclusivity than the Old World models—even if all did not enjoy full freedom and citizenship.

When Jefferson first took presidential office in 1801, Federalist congressman Manasseh Cutler had wondered what was to be the new order of things. The Federalist writer who explored Jefferson's character in 1815 felt the results were obvious. "The new order of things" had induced "national calamities." The evils of "an inefficient and disastrous war" were the result of Jefferson's innovative ideas, which were heavily influenced by French philosophy. Through his years in France, he drank too deeply at their "fountain of political science."[57] The old allegations were still there: Jefferson was the devious Francophile, the imposter who with his tricks and innovations would bring down the country. His fears for his legacy and place in history were not unfounded.

Another issue hovered that could color his legacy and impact his family. Weighing on Jefferson during his retirement was the worry of debt. During his last year in the presidency, as he reviewed his finances, he began to realize the amount of debt he had accumulated. He confided to his daughter Martha, "I have now the gloomy prospect of retiring from office loaded with serious debts, which will materially affect the tranquility of my retirement." But always the optimist, he continued, "I nourish the hope of getting along." Nevertheless, debt became an increasing worry.[58]

Jefferson's financial base lay in Virginia agriculture, and like many planters his estates had been in financial decline since the revolution. Years spent away from his farms and additional debt attached to holding public office had compounded his financial problems, but the real crisis came when the inflation bubble that followed the War of 1812 burst, causing many bank closures and drops in agriculture and land prices. The Panic of 1819 became a prolonged recession, and Jefferson would not live to see a financial reversal. He had never fully trusted Hamilton's banking system and had always opposed too much paper money in circulation, but he could take no satisfaction in the bank closures, as the financial panic threatened national well-being and thrust hardships on friends and family. It raised the very real possibility of his family becoming destitute.[59]

By early 1821 he was especially pressured by notes he had felt obligated to cosign for long-term friend Wilson Cary Nicholas, who was the father-in-law of his eldest grandson, Jeff Randolph, and who had assisted Jefferson previously with many loans. Nicholas died in October 1820 deeply in debt, with all his devalued property mortgaged, and Jefferson was faced with absorbing two notes of $10,000 each that generated an annual interest payment of $1,200. Jefferson pronounced this his financial coup de grâce; his estate holdings could no longer begin to cover what was owed, especially in the current deflated real estate market.[60]

The threat of becoming financially insolvent placed Jefferson in an extremely vulnerable position. As a gentleman and leader in his native Virginia, the loss of his estate—the land, the elegant house with its European furniture and art collection, and the support of an enslaved workforce—such a loss would compromise his dignity and station.[61] Even though much of the financial crisis whirled out of his control, a patriarch who could not protect those under his care would be suspect regarding the larger issues of leadership. He could apply to his own situation what he had observed so many years before while in France, which was so astutely summarized by sociologist Norbert Elias: "A duke who does not live as a duke has to live, who can no longer properly fulfil the social duties of a duke, is hardly a duke any longer."[62] The same concept applied to the Virginia gentry. Financial failure would greatly damage Jefferson's public image. Though his influence in national political decisions and policy making was receding, he had one final project that required his influence in Virginia. He regarded it as "the last service I can render my country"—the establishment of the University of Virginia.[63]

Jefferson believed strongly that education would support a "natural aristocracy among men" based upon "virtue and talents." This support would safeguard against the rise of a hereditary or landed aristocracy, a practice so closely linked to monarchy. It was a vital part of his vision for good government, and he asked, "May we not even say that that form of government is best which provides the most effectively for a pure selection of these natural aristoi into the offices of government?" Education was integral in forming this natural aristocracy, and he never let go his belief in the importance of education; he projected that "if the condition of man is to be progressively ameliorated, as we fondly hope & believe, education is to be the chief instrument in effecting it."[64] His earlier efforts to enact legislation in Virginia that would support public education had failed, so in these late retirement years he directed his thoughts towards higher education.[65] Ultimately these efforts resulted in the founding of the University of Virginia.

In his plans for the university, Jefferson was especially proud of his architectural designs. Rather than one large building, he drew a plan of smaller pavilions connected by arcades and facing a large, open commons. Each pavilion represented a different classical order, so the buildings could be used as tools for teaching as well as functioning as classrooms and housing.[66] He wrote Adams that he was directing the architecture and that "it's plan is unique, and it is becoming an object of curiosity for the traveller."[67] This open and admitted enthusiasm for his own architectural work was unusual. Even his beloved Monticello he referred to as "the curiosity of the neighborhood," but he made no further claims for the uniqueness of his house and its abundance of glass and openness to nature.

FIGURE 44. *The Declaration of Independence of the United States of America* by Asher B. Durand after John Trumbull, 1820. Engraving.

Jefferson ordered two copies of Durand's print of the *Declaration of Independence*. A visitor to Monticello commented on seeing one of the prints in the entrance hall.

Jefferson's invitation to John Trumbull welcoming him to visit Monticello included an offer to visit the building site of the university as well. He assured the artist that the buildings were unrivaled in the country as specimens of strict classical architecture. He wished Trumbull's artistic eye to see and evaluate his work and originality of design. Then he came to his real hope in encouraging Trumbull to make a site visit: he speculated that perhaps these buildings would be worthy of Trumbull's and Durand's skills in creating a print. Jefferson was sure that "it would be a very popular print."[68] If the proposed engraving of *The Declaration of Independence* were joined with a print of the University of Virginia, then two of his most treasured accomplishments would be visually immortalized and available to the public. Both endeavors were very important to him as a part of his final image and legacy.

But Trumbull did not make the trip to Monticello, and Jefferson would have to wait until 1823 for the publication of Durand's engraving of *The Declaration of Independence* (fig. 44).[69] Once received, a copy was hung in Monticello's entrance hall, and a visitor, the Reverend Henry Thweatt, noted in his travel diary that he questioned Jefferson about this historic scene. Thweatt asked: "'And how Mr. Jefferson did you feel amid—all being as you were—the author of the instrument—being thus signed by all'—'why my son'—(he very pleasantly replied with an arch look)—'pretty much as you may imagine with a halter around his neck to be hung—for such—doubtless would have been my fate—and that too of all who signed this instrument—had we been taken by the British.'"[70] No doubt Jefferson hoped for a wide distribution of this print as a reminder of this important event; however, subscriptions did not go well. Trumbull was quite disappointed and barely cleared the expense of Durand's fee and printing costs with only 275 subscribers by 1823.[71]

While Jefferson waited to receive his prints of *The Declaration of Independence,* he received a letter that announced another artist would be calling at Monticello to take his image for an important commission. In March 1821 young, up-and-coming portrait artist Thomas Sully arrived at Monticello. He came on behalf of the United States Military Academy at West Point to begin work on a full-length portrait of the retired president who had supported the need for a national military academy and then signed the bill establishing West Point as its home.[72] This portrait presented Jefferson with another opportunity to fashion a visual record of his legacy while telling a part of the American story.

8

A FINAL IMAGE

The request came in a letter penned in January 1821 by mathematics professor Jared Mansfield. He wrote on behalf of his fellow professors and the officers and cadets at the United States Military Academy at West Point. The request was straightforward; they wished to have a portrait of Jefferson that would be "an appropriate memorial of your person which may descend to posterity." The portrait would hang in the academy's library alongside that "of the great Washington, The Founder of the Republic and Col. [Jonathan] Williams the first chief of the Mil[itary] Academy."[1] This honor was being extended to Jefferson for both his service to the nation and his patronage of the academy, as it was on March 16, 1802, that as president he had signed the congressional bill officially establishing the academy at West Point. Feeling confident of Jefferson's consent, they had commissioned Thomas Sully, one of America's leading portrait artists, to call on Jefferson at his Virginia home to take the portrait; and in his letter Mansfield requested dates that would be convenient.[2]

Jefferson responded to the West Point letter in a true gentlemanly fashion by acknowledging the honor attached to such a request. He then graciously demurred, suggesting that the artist Sully might find the "employment of his fine pencil as illy bestowed on an ottamy of 78." But his modesty was short-lived, and he continued by recommending suitable dates for Sully's visit to Monticello.[3] Although his response was appropriately reserved, Jefferson must have realized the opportunity this presented. The portrait could become a lasting visual legacy, especially as it was intended to be hung in the academic library at West Point and thus would be available for public viewing. The tradition of displaying either sculpted or painted likenesses of writers, philosophers, theologians, and scholars in library reading rooms was a custom going back for many centuries in Western culture.[4] Jefferson qualified on several counts to have his image included in a scholar's library, and equally attractive in this proposal from West Point was that his portrait would hang alongside Washington's. This positioning would add legitimacy in the minds of most viewers to Jefferson's role as a vital participant in the founding of the American republic. He could justify this portrait not just as a contribution to his own legacy but as a record of early American history as well.

Jefferson had not met Thomas Sully prior to the artist's visit to Monticello in March 1821, but he would have known of his reputation as one of the country's leading portrait artists and proponents of the fine arts. In a May 1811 letter, Benjamin Henry Latrobe, the architect who had worked so closely with Jefferson on the Capitol and the President's House in Washington, assessed the current art scene for the retired president and noted that "a Young artist, Tho[mas] Sully, is certainly the first on the list of our portrait painters."[5] By the time Sully reached Monticello ten years later, his talents were being equated with those of Gilbert Stuart and Rembrandt Peale. The artist was a slight five feet, eight inches tall and possessed a demeanor that would later be described as a "general gentleness of character" that apparently appealed to Jefferson.[6] William Dunlap—artist, writer, and close acquaintance of Sully—wrote of the artist's experience in taking a bust portrait from life in preparation for the full-length portrait for West Point: "For this purpose he visited the sage at Monticello, and in his house made a painting, head size, of the venerable ex-president. The painter was an inmate of Monticello twelve days, and left the place with the greatest reluctance."[7]

Sully and Jefferson had a brief, formal correspondence when Jefferson was elected an honorary member of the newly formed Society of Artists of the United States, of which Sully was acting secretary, on December 11, 1811. The stated purpose of the new society echoed closely what Jefferson had expressed so many years before on the importance of the arts to the developing United States: "To improve the taste of my countrymen, to increase their reputation, to reconcile to them the respect of the world and procure them it's praise."[8] Sully's letter proposed in a similar patriotic tone that the society would have "a tendency to form a correct taste in this Country" and that "by calling into Action Native genius, many prejudices will be removed with respect to foreign productions."[9]

Jefferson's response to the society was positive, and he had just sent his letter of thanks for the offer of honorary membership and had expressed his good wishes when he received a second letter from Sully announcing that he had been elected president of the organization. Sully's letter was candid in the hope that the infant society might benefit from its association with Jefferson's name. Jefferson graciously declined the appointment, expressing "uneasiness of unmerited distinction." He was still trying to convince the American Philosophical Society that he should be replaced as president of that organization, arguing that the distance between Philadelphia and Monticello was far too great for the leadership that he had at one time provided.[10] Apparently, he did not choose to engage another titular office, even though it was an organization with goals that he fully approved. However, as the society included architecture alongside painting, sculpture, and engraving, Jefferson's excuse of "unmerited distinction" was not totally valid, even though it would be several years before his finest public buildings for the University of Virginia would be realized.[11] These positions, though strictly honorary, reflected a continued respect for his support of the arts and of scientific inquiry and spoke to the reputation he still carried, even in retirement, with some segments of American society.

Thomas Sully had personal knowledge of Jefferson's earliest public architectural work, as he had visited the Virginia state capitol building in Richmond. He agreed that there were problems in the execution of Jefferson's design, which was based on a standing Roman building, the Maison Carrée in Nîmes, France. Late in life, when Sully wrote "Recollections of an Old Painter," he remembered admiring Jefferson's model, on view in the capitol's library, but he found many faults in the execution of the building itself. Even so, he maintained that "Mr. Jefferson was a very good judge of architecture."[12]

What seemed most import to Jefferson was the opportunity to introduce the forms and proportions of classical architecture into the United States as a means of educating the citizenry and ultimately gaining artistic credibility with the Old World. In a letter to James Madison he emphasized that his proposed design for the Virginia capitol was based on classical models that would provide "an object and proof of national good taste." He expanded on this idea by speculating that such architecture would demonstrate to European visitors "a morsel of taste in our infancy promising much for our mature age."[13] Yet upon seeing the completed building following his return to the United States, his impression was much like that of Sully. He admitted in his memoir that his plans were executed with "some variations, not for the better," but he optimistically saw opportunity for "future correction."[14]

Despite these variations, Jefferson's Roman-modeled statehouse signified a major change from other American statehouses of the time. Architectural historian Richard Guy Wilson describes most state buildings that held over from the colonial era into the early republic as enlarged houses with modifications. Jefferson's designs for the campus of the University of Virginia continued his pursuit of classical models that would set a new standard in American architecture. Perhaps this ambition contributed to his eagerness to have Sully view the buildings under construction in the neighboring village of Charlottesville. Jefferson arranged for the artist to tour the site but did not accompany him due to the unusually cold weather. Instead he sent a note stating, "The bearer, Mr. Sully, a celebrated Portrait painter of Philadelphia calls to see the University, and as he is a judge, and will be questioned about it on his return, I will request you to shew it to him advantageously."[15] Although his wish for artist John Trumbull to tour the site never materialized, here was another skilled artist who could perhaps lend an astute eye to his designs.

Obviously Jefferson valued Sully's opinion, and conversations about architecture must have ensued. Sully recommended and promised to send his host a book by J. N. L. Durand contrasting ancient and modern architecture: *Recueil et parallèles des édifices de tout genre, anciens et moderns.* But upon Sully's return to Baltimore, where he maintained a studio, he was unable to locate a copy and was forced to send his apologies. Jefferson assured Sully not to worry; he would add this title to a book order that he was preparing to send to Paris. He must have approved of Sully's recommendation, for he included Durand's study in his list of books for the library at the University of Virginia.[16]

Given their mutual interest in the development of the arts in the United States and their respect for each other's work, it is reasonable to speculate that artist and subject worked closely in creating the portrait for West Point. Sully's task was to capture a truthful likeness that suggested an elevated character, a gentleman of virtue who capably played a role as founder of the nation and founder of the military academy. Jefferson likely participated in the process with recommendations as the artist considered the appropriate pose, choice of props and clothing, and the background that would surround the figure. The reputation of each man was invested in the portrait's success.[17]

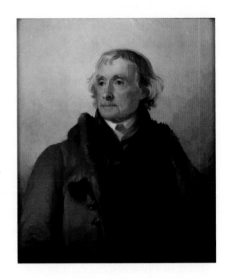

FIGURE 45. Thomas Jefferson by Thomas
Sully, 1821–30. Oil on canvas, 37½ in. ×
32½ in.

This bust portrait was taken from life by Sully
at Monticello. He made several copies before
selling the original to Jefferson's protégé
William Short, who donated it to the American Philosophical Society in Philadelphia
following Jefferson's death.

The collaboration between Sully and Jefferson resulted in a half-length portrait taken on site during Sully's stay at Monticello (fig. 45). This be-came the basis for the full-length portrait that was finalized the following year (in May 1822) and that completed Sully's commission for the military academy (fig. 46). He painted replicas from his original life portrait before completing and selling the original taken at Monticello to Jefferson protégé William Short, who donated it to the American Philosophical Society in June 1830. It hangs today very appropriately in Benjamin Franklin Hall at the American Philosophical Society in Philadelphia.[18] The half-length life portrait shows Jefferson in a black coat and waistcoat; a very small area of red at his neck appears to be the collar of an underwaistcoat. A fur-lined greatcoat covers the black suit-coat. The full-length portrait follows the original very closely.

A public portrait such as Sully created for West Point was intended to mark a specific time and event, which in this case was the establishment of the military academy in 1802. But overriding the specific temporal moment, this portrait would also stand as a lasting reminder of an even larger historic contribution, the founding of the American republic. The suit and shoes that Sully depicts in his portrait connect Jefferson stylistically to his years as president. The figure wears a black three-piece suit that with Sully's skillful rendering appears to be made of velvet. The front of the suit-coat has long, sloping sides angling away from the Center Front, a cut fashionable late in the eighteenth century that had carried over into the early nineteenth. This

FIGURE 46. Thomas Jefferson by Thomas Sully, 1821–22. Oil on canvas, 102¼ in. × 66 in.

This full-length image of the seventy-eight-year-old Jefferson was his last painted portrait. Sully spent approximately ten days at Monticello in March 1821 taking a bust portrait and beginning his study for the United States Military Academy commission.

FIGURE 47. Marie-Joseph Paul Yves Roch Gilbert du Motier, marquis de Lafayette by Thomas Sully, 1825–26.

The marquis de Lafayette made a hero's tour of the United States in 1824–25. Sully was commissioned to paint this full-length portrait, which offers an example of the latest in men's fashions as opposed to the early nineteenth-century clothing depicted in Sully's Jefferson portrait for West Point.

earlier style is reinforced by the wide V-shape of the front of the waistcoat, and coat and waistcoat are paired with knee-breeches instead of the more fashionable pantaloons.[19]

Just a few years after the West Point commission, Sully painted another important portrait that better illustrates fashionable men's dress of the 1820s and highlights how Jefferson's clothing in the academy portrait dates to his years as president. Sully was commissioned to paint the Revolutionary War hero the marquis de Lafayette during Lafayette's celebratory return visit to the United States in 1824–25 (fig. 47). He detailed Lafayette in a dark suit with a high, rolled collar and slightly rounded, almost horizontal waistline that opened the front of the coat. Lafayette's waistcoat, visible just below the waistline of the coat, follows the horizontal line as well and contrasts with the longer V-shape of Jefferson's. In addition, Lafayette wears pantaloons rather than knee breeches.

As previously noted, visitors to Monticello in Jefferson's retirement years mentioned that he still wore what they referred to as the old "Quaker" style, but none ever referred to him wearing black velvet.[20] For the purpose of the portrait, Jefferson may have pulled out a suit that actually dated to his presidential years, as he appears in Sully's work much as he was described at his second inauguration, "dressed in black and even in black silk stockings."[21] The cut of the suit in Sully's full-length portrait was fashionable when Jefferson was signing into law the establishment of the military academy in 1802. If he had packed away such a suit, this would have been the moment to bring it forward.

The shoes that Jefferson wears in the portrait visually connect to his years at the forefront of republican politics, as they look exactly like the low bootees first illustrated in "The Providential Detection" to suggest his radical French leanings, and which are seen again in the engravings made by Edwin and Tiebout. Apparently Jefferson continued to favor the laced, ankle-high boots in retirement, whether in deference to old political connotations or simply for practicality and comfort; Congressman Daniel Webster described Jefferson wearing "shoes of the kind that bear his name" during his 1824 visit to Monticello.[22] The bootees worked with the suit to relate the figure in Sully's portrait to Jefferson as president.

The most notable garment in the portrait is the long, fur-lined greatcoat worn over the black suit. Presumably the coat came from Jefferson's wardrobe, or at least it was a part of the original study, as Sully preferred to sketch his subjects in drapery at the first sitting. He advised beginning painters, "If it is a large picture where more of the person is seen, the drapery must be painted from an exact study made from the person."[23] Jefferson had such a coat, according to family members, and interestingly enough this was another fur linked to Revolutionary War hero Thaddeus Kosciuszko.

A second Kosciuszko fur came into Jefferson's possession when he inventoried the items that Kosciuszko left behind on his return to Europe. Jefferson listed among them "a pelisse of fine fur." Due to its value, he decided to store it at his own apartments rather than placing it in the warehouse with the remainder of his friend's property. He reported to Kosciuszko that his "fur was valued by an honest furrier here at 25 Doll. according to the price of Martins here."[24] The marten, the North American equivalent of the Russian sable, was considered a very fine fur, and thus Jefferson thought that the pelisse should be sold privately rather than at public auction. No additional information about this marten/sable-skin pelisse appears in the known Kosciuszko-Jefferson correspondence, but a family record reveals that it remained with Jefferson.

"The splendid 'Golden Sables' over coat, very large & long, which 'Kosiosko' wore during his 'Russian Campaign,'" appeared in an inventory of items that had remained within the Jefferson family. A list of "Monticello relics" was compiled in May 1907 by one of Jefferson's great-granddaughters. She was knowledgeable of the fate of this fine garment and stated that it was cut up into *"Muffs & Tippets."*[25] This suggests that the sable-lined pelisse left behind by Kosciuszko remained with Jefferson, and its tradition was known in the family.

Certainly Sully's rendering of the coat in the West Point commission implies a fur such as marten or sable, and its use in the portrait could have invoked recollections of Kosciuszko's fortification of the Hudson River stronghold during the American Revolution. Kosciuszko remains a legend at the Point, and early in the nineteenth century the Corps of Cadets raised money towards a monument that stands today in a prominent position on academy grounds.[26] A small garden that bears his name is located on the cliff side above the Hudson River and is well maintained. Margaret Bayard Smith mentions this garden in her reminiscence "The Fur Cloak." She writes, "There on the high & roky banks of the Hudson, he amused his leisure moments in the cultivating of flowers" and describes how he planted and cared for his garden.[27] Sully might not have been interested in replicating the fur used in Rembrandt Peale's presidential portrait, especially as the painting was still on display in the Peale galleries; however, if Jefferson owned a second garment with a Kosciuszko connection, including it in the West Point commission could have been a logical consideration.

The sable-lined coat is far more elegant in line and texture than the wolf-skin cape used in Rembrandt's work, and it adds dignity to the figure. The wolf skin had served its purpose when Jefferson posed for Rembrandt's portrait as the democratic man of the people, but for a memorial to his legacy he would prefer something that could define him as a gentleman and statesman of the world. The fur lining and frog closures pictured in the original half-length suggested an eastern European origin, but Sully changed the frog closures to round buttons in the final full-length, even though they were impractical for this fur-lined garment. The artist's brush strokes show that the fur continued to the hem, which is visible in the portion of the skirt behind Jefferson's left leg. Sully even included the wear to the edge of the fur collar, giving visual evidence that the fur was not new. Such fashionable, fur-lined garments that exceeded simple practicality were attached stylistically to the hussars of Eastern Europe, especially Poland.[28] On the eve of another crisis, the War of 1812, Jefferson contemplated the hard lesson that Poland provided: it was "a lesson which all our countrymen should study; the example of a country erased from the map of the world by the dissensions of its own citizens."[29]

The fur-lined greatcoat may have been encouraged by the artist, not so much for its provenance but for what it adds compositionally, as it echoes the long line of the column and makes the figure far more substantial than it would appear otherwise. Sully's Jefferson stands erect, confident, and composed. In the figure's pose the artist demonstrates elements of the traditional grand manner: the head is turned to the right; the gaze is directed into the distance and away from the viewer; and the stance adheres to the requirement that the weight of the body rests on the right foot with the left foot slightly advanced. But rather than portray the right hand extended in an oratorical gesture, Sully leaves Jefferson's arms at his sides.[30] The rolled document in the left hand serves as the only prop within the painting. As such it becomes notable, especially with Sully's subtle placement of light along the leading edge of the paper. A close examination of the document gives no clue as to its identity, and the absence of writing opens the possibilities of the many documents linked to Jefferson's name. Of course, it could represent the bill he signed in 1802 establishing the military academy.[31]

Sully skillfully guides the eye through the painting with his use of light and shadow. The effect in his portrait of Jefferson is quite dramatic and perhaps reflects Sully's upbringing in a theatrical family. (Both of his parents were actors.) He creates an environment within the painting that gives the impression that Jefferson has just stepped before his audience, the viewer.[32] Light calls attention to the document in Jefferson's hand, but his face is the focus for the most pronounced area of light. It is illuminated as though by a theatrical spotlight, and the slight dash of red provided by the collar of the underwaistcoat draws further focus to the face. Sully followed his own advice offered in *Hints to Young Painters:* "In a portrait every part may be exactly rendered, but should be kept subordinate in regard to the face."[33]

The setting of the figure, just as the pose, borrows elements of the grand manner. Jefferson stands by an impressive column backed by a swag of red drapery, but to this tradition, which is often found in European state portraits, Sully adds detail that makes the setting specific to the United States.

FIGURE 48. Detail from the full-length portrait of Jefferson by Thomas Sully.

The water-leaf design on the base supporting a column that appears to be breccia marble identifies the setting as the House chamber.

Through his placement of light, Sully guides the eye downward from Jefferson's face, tips the rolled document in his hand, but then strongly illuminates the lower shaft of the column to the right in the painting. The shaft and base of the column catch almost as much light as the face and become a secondary area of focus. Sully's careful rendering of the base's carved water-leaf design and his painterly indication that the shaft is breccia marble (fig. 48), distinct from the marble of the base, identify the column as belonging in the rebuilt Hall of Representatives (known after 1857 as National Statuary Hall). When Capitol architect Benjamin Henry Latrobe redesigned the House chamber after the Capitol was burned by British forces during the War of 1812, he replaced the sandstone columns with the breccia marble. As the unpredictable nature of breccia made it problematic to attempt a cincture at the bottom of the shaft, Latrobe devised the water-leaf pattern to compensate for the lack of a cincture, resulting in the unique and identifiable base. He designed a very grand room that would be completed in 1819 by his successor, architect Charles Bullfinch. It became the pride of the country at the time, but one that Jefferson would never see.[34]

Sully had probably informed Jefferson of the reconstruction of the Capitol and the President's House that was underway in Washington. Prior to his trip to Monticello he had been working in Baltimore, putting him closer to Washington than he was from his home and studio in Philadelphia.[35]

The new Hall of Representatives had been in use for a year and had opened to the first session of the Sixteenth Congress in December 1819.[36] During Jefferson's years in the national government, especially during his presidency, he had been quite involved in the creation of the national buildings. In *History of the United States Capitol* William Allen states, "Few people had such an enduring influence on the Capitol's early history as Thomas Jefferson. . . . Until his retirement in 1809, Jefferson managed affairs at the Capitol with the same care and attention he lavished on his beloved Monticello, and later on the University of Virginia."[37] Although Jefferson never revisited Washington after leaving in March 1809, he had confidently sent his much-prized library there, anticipating the rebuilding that would take place. He knew through Trumbull that the Capitol building was to be enlarged and decorated with his scenes from the revolution. If Sully had any news of or descriptions of what was taking place, it could have been a welcome conversational topic, especially as Jefferson demonstrated his confidence in Sully's architectural judgement by seeking his opinion on the buildings going up at the University of Virginia.

The architectural setting and the sparseness of that setting in the full-length portrait make Sully's Jefferson distinctive. This is apparent when it is compared with two other full-length portraits that would eventually hang alongside that of Jefferson. Sully's earlier 1815 portrait of Jonathan Williams is an obvious comparison, as Jared Mansfield mentioned it when he contacted Jefferson about the painting commission (fig. 49). Behind the seated figure of Williams, who is dressed in his officer's uniform, is a view of Castle Williams, constructed as a part of his fortifications for New York Harbor. Including this fort in the background pays tribute to Williams's position as the ranking engineer in the army and serves as a reminder of its importance to the defense of New York during the War of 1812. Sully adds a dark, turbulent sky, a feature often found in British military portraits and notable in portraits of officers by Joshua Reynolds and Thomas Lawrence, whose work and opinions Sully admired.[38]

In 1829 the military academy commissioned Sully to take another full-length portrait of a former US president who had been very supportive of the academy, that of James Monroe (fig. 50). Sully called on Monroe at his home, Oak Hill.[39] The resulting portrait places Monroe in an interior scene, and he is dressed in clothing that would recall his presidency; the dark dress coat, pale knee breeches, and white stockings are also reminiscent of the official dress that Monroe had prescribed for the US diplomatic corps in 1813,

FIGURE 49. Jonathan Williams by Thomas Sully, 1815. Oil on canvas, 78 in. × 57½ in.

Williams was appointed by President Jefferson as the first superintendent of West Point. The academy commissioned a portrait of Williams from Sully that was completed in 1815.

and thus would recall his own diplomatic service to his country as well.[40] Perhaps of more interest at West Point, however, was his military service during the Revolutionary War and his positions as secretary of war and secretary of state during the War of 1812. This martial history is suggested by the cape, hat, and sword that lie before him. Monroe's figure rests against a large sculptural piece that appears to be swathed in classical drapery. More specific is the fasces held by the figure that was an accepted symbol for republican power and values. The interior scene is not specific, and the view through an open doorway reveals only an idealized pastoral scene. Perhaps the bucolic landscape was a visual metaphor for the phrase "Era of Good Feelings" that had been applied to Monroe's first term in office when all seemed right with the country and political polarization had diminished.

The Williams portrait was painted six years before Jefferson's, Monroe's eight years after; thus the simplicity Sully gave his Jefferson was not an evolution of artistic style but a statement specific to this particular portrait. A small, loose study made in oil on paper indicates that at some point Sully had considered placing Jefferson in a very different setting that was far more complex (fig. 51). This study is not recorded in Sully's register of paintings, yet the figure of Jefferson is recognizable in this loose sketch and

FIGURE 50. James Monroe by Thomas Sully, 1832. Oil on canvas, 108 in. × 60 in.

Sully's portrait of James Monroe, a commission for West Point, shows him dressed in the blue coat and white breeches that could reflect either his military career or his work in the diplomatic corps.

comparable to the final West Point version. The pose is similar, and the long coat, although closed, is essentially the same. Here a sheaf of papers replaces the rolled document, and they are moved from the left to the right hand, leaving the left hand free to gesture towards a crowd of people. Men stand behind Jefferson, and a crowd is gathered in front of what appears to be an outdoor terrace with a large column and steps leading downward from the spot where the Jefferson figure stands. The original half-length made from life at Monticello has a very atmospheric background, as though Sully initially may have been contemplating an outdoor scene. Yet the idea did not move forward—whether the small study was made at Monticello or later in his studio—and Sully chose instead a setting in the chamber of the House of Representatives.

The loose sketch shows an intriguing step in the artist's development of the final painting. The outdoor setting of the small study cannot be conclusively identified, yet Sully gave it characteristics quite similar to the north entrance of the President's House in Washington during Jefferson's

FIGURE 51. Thomas Jefferson by Thomas Sully, c. 1821–22. Oil on paper, 9¾ in. × 7 in.

This small study in oil on paper suggests one consideration by Sully for the West Point commission. The crowd in the background hints at an idea that he would later use for his portrait of Lafayette.

administration. Adams had used the south entrance, but Jefferson chose to make the north entrance the main public entry. When he first occupied the executive mansion in 1801, this entrance was accessed by temporary wooden steps leading to a wooden platform. Jefferson and architect Latrobe enhanced the north entrance by adding a shallow terrace to the four-columned frontispiece that was a part of the original design, then extended broad stone steps from the terrace to ground level. This configuration continued in use until the north and south porticos were added in 1824 and 1829.[41]

Sully's study makes it appear that other figures are following Jefferson onto a narrow terrace through a dark doorway opening slightly behind the column. Steps are visible descending from the terrace. This does suggest the north entrance to the President's House as completed by Jefferson and Latrobe, which was still in use when Sully was completing his painting in 1821–22. Sully's rendering is not completely accurate, however, as the façade of the house should have continued in the same plane as the columns, as they were a frontispiece and not free-standing. Still, was Sully's first impulse to place Jefferson at the executive mansion addressing the people? Even though the President's House was his residence, the House chamber represented the most direct link with the people. Perhaps with further thought, Sully chose this setting as more appropriate for his painting of Jefferson.

In the final portrait Sully gives the figure of Jefferson a stronger focus. The crowd is gone; Jefferson stands alone and quietly holds a single document. It gives the impression that he has just stepped onstage, and there is an anticipation of action.[42] The column alongside him stands as a universal symbol of the Western classical world, but on closer inspection, its water-leaf cincture identifies it as a space particularly American.

Sully left no indication as to what prompted him to place the Jefferson figure in the House chamber; however, he could have been influenced by the work of another artist. At the time Sully was completing his portrait of Jefferson in 1822, fellow artist Samuel F. B. Morse was at work on a large and complex painting that depicted a night session of the House of Representatives that included miniature but recognizable portraits of many of the congressmen (fig. 52). Morse had been given studio space in the Capitol itself and wrote to his wife in January 1822 that "I find the picture becoming the subject of much conversation, and every day gives me greater encouragement to believe that it will be more popular than any picture heretofore

FIGURE 52. *The House of Representatives* by Samuel F. B. Morse, 1822, probably reworked 1823. Oil on canvas, 86⅞ in. × 130⅝ in.

Samuel Morse's large painting of the House chamber gives a full view of the setting that Sully ultimately chose for his Jefferson.

exhibited." A few weeks later, Samuel Harrison Smith's *National Intelligence* described Morse's rendering of the chamber interior "mathematically correct."[43]

Sully's obvious familiarity with the detail and placement of the columns and the drapery of the room suggests that the site was known to him. The very deep red of the drapery worked well for his theory that "in large pictures very sober colours may be employed to produce the richness of effect."[44] The final portrait, with its simplified composition and classical yet specifically American setting, becomes a much stronger work than the oil sketch with a crowd. The focus rests completely on Jefferson and allows a strength and dignity of character that was diluted when surrounded by the busyness of many people.

Jefferson never saw the completed full-length portrait. Sully finished the West Point commission in May 1822, but the earliest known engraving was not produced until 1834. Would it have fulfilled Jefferson's hopes for an appropriate and enduring likeness? He never mentioned the portrait, but his granddaughter Ellen Randolph expressed her views of the original half-length in a letter to her cousin shortly after Sully left Monticello. She believed that he had "succeeded admirably." The area around Jefferson's mouth and chin constituted the only shortcoming, "but the painter seems to be aware of this defect and will endeavor to correct it." She predicted that the finished full-length portrait "will probably be the best representation existing of one to whom future ages must look back with gratitude and admiration."[45]

Approximately 120 people paid to see the completed full-length portrait during the ten days that Sully displayed it in his Philadelphia gallery. In his journal he noted that he made about thirty dollars from the showing, and as the usual price of admission to the gallery was twenty-five cents per person, over one hundred Philadelphians must have had the means and the desire to see the portrait of the former president. Sully's matter-of-fact records give no indication whether he considered the showing successful, but on May 20, 1822, he packaged the portrait and frame for shipment to West Point.[46] The portrait gained favorable notice after its installation in West Point's library. This was where American writer James Fenimore Cooper viewed the portrait and reassessed his opinion of Thomas Jefferson.

"I would have gone twice as far to see the picture of almost any other man," Cooper remarked upon learning that the newly installed portrait at West Point, which he was told he really must see, was of former president Thomas Jefferson.[47] The portrait had been installed in the academy library in the summer of 1822, and by the time of Cooper's trip up the Hudson River the following year, it was obviously drawing some notice. Cooper was a tough and articulate critic who admitted to being trained to view Jefferson as a political heretic. He stated, "I was brought up in that school where his image seldom appeared unless it was clad in red breeches, and where it was always associated with the idea of infidelity and political heresy."[48] The son of Judge William Cooper, at one time a prominent New York Federalist, James Fenimore had been raised in an active political environment decidedly opposed to Jefferson and the republican faction.[49] Judge Cooper had worked his way upward to wealth and power primarily through land speculation. He aspired to gentility but failed in completely removing the rougher side of his nature. He held hopes, however, that his children would rise to an unquestionable position among the better sort. Despite his humble beginnings, Judge Cooper aligned politically with the Federalists and tried to ensure that his sons stayed clear of any democratic notions.[50] This accounts for his son's grumbled response to the prospect of viewing the portrait and his reference to always thinking of Jefferson clad in the red breeches. Obviously he had not forgotten this symbol of political heresy despite the fourteen years since Jefferson left the presidency.[51]

Sully's portrait could be counted a success and a boon to the Jefferson legacy in at least this one instance, especially with Cooper's professed change of sentiment: "It has really shaken my opinion of Jefferson as a man, if not as a politician. I saw nothing but Jefferson, standing before me, not in red breeches and slovenly attire, but a gentleman, appearing in all republican simplicity, with a grace and ease on the canvas, that to me seemed unrivalled. And when his image occurs to me now, it is in the simple robes of Sully, sans red breeches, or even without any of the repulsive accompaniments of a political 'sans culotte.'"[52] Sully had succeeded. While looking at the portrait, Cooper was able to put aside the old issues relating to the political Jefferson, and in that moment he could admit to a Jefferson positioned for posterity—"appearing in all republican simplicity."

Cooper assessed Jefferson's portrait in a letter to Charles Kitchell Gardner. He may have written his review with the assumption that it would be read by more than just the recipient, and indeed, Gardner used the story as an essay on the fine arts in his newly established paper, *American Patriot*.[53] Cooper felt the critical judgement of his traveling companion, British actor Charles Matthews, superior to his own, and included in his review that Matthews "pronounced it one of the finest portraits he had ever beheld." The encouragement Cooper received to view the portrait while at West Point suggests Sully's painting was popular. Whether Jefferson saw the letter as published by Gardner is uncertain, but no doubt he would have been pleased and reassured by Cooper's remarks.

Early in their retirement correspondence, Jefferson cavalierly stated to Adams, "I leave others to judge of what I have done, and to give me exactly that place which they shall think I have occupied." He speculated that the libels written by John Marshall in his *Life of Washington* would be countered by a republican author and added that "the world will shift both, and separate the truth as well as they can."[54] This was written several years before Sully painted his portrait for West Point and before Trumbull had thoughts of mounting his scenes from the revolution in the Capitol rotunda. When Jefferson wrote Adams he counted on a written history and could hardly have anticipated that his role in the revolution and the nation's founding would be preserved in the work of two artists. His legacy became visual.

EPILOGUE

On his own Monticello Mountain Jefferson left two monuments to his final image and legacy—his house and his gravestone. A visitor reaching the top of the mountain from the east would first encounter the house that Jefferson had designed and redesigned over a forty-year period (fig. 53). In many ways this house stands as a metaphor for the man himself and his grounding in Enlightenment thought. It also suggests the controversial Jefferson, as the visitor might find that this mountaintop villa is not exactly what it seems at first glance and requires a closer study in order to understand the design. How many times throughout his long public career had political adversaries claimed the same about Jefferson? Hamilton and others had warned of his deliberate deception; Charles Carroll was concerned with his trickery.

Deception does not appear to have been Jefferson's goal, yet he did not always take the conventional approach in either politics or architecture. Benjamin Henry Latrobe, referenced in previous chapters, continued to observe Jefferson's eccentricities. Latrobe admitted, "He thinks, writes, and acts differently from others; and who ever does that must submit to abuse." But overall he supported Jefferson, writing, "As a man, I neer knew his superior in candor, kindness, and universal information;—as a political character he has not his equal anywhere in patriotism, right intentions, and uniform perserverance in the system he has conceived to be the most beneficial for his country."[1] Latrobe had worked closely with Jefferson and admired the man and his abilities, but he was able to recognize the seeming contradictions perceived by those who did not know him well or who disagreed with his politics. Latrobe could accept his oddities, but to some Jefferson remained perplexing and even frightening.

Similarly, Jefferson created a house that is not what it might seem at first glance. When approaching the east front, the public entrance, visitors must look closely to see that what appears to be a single-story house in

FIGURE 53. East front of Monticello.

This photograph of Monticello illustrates how Jefferson designed his house to appear as a single story on approach.

actuality has multilevels, from the basement to the dome room. Jefferson never intended it to be imposing, but the house is rich in a design unique for the time that features an abundance of light. Benjamin Rush reflected on Jefferson, "The whole of Mr. Jefferson's conversation on all subjects is instructing: He is wise without formality, and maintains a consequence without pomp or distance."[2] Jefferson's twenty-one room house could be described much like its architect-owner. It allows formality in its division and use of space, but it is not nearly so grand as its counterparts in Britain or Europe.[3] And Jefferson intended the house to instruct. In its design and content, Monticello, like Jefferson, could stand for Enlightenment thought.

Borrowing from the distant past, Jefferson employed motifs and architectural elements from classical models to create a house that for its day was very modern in its use of glass, which thereby allows an abundance of natural light. Standing in the center of the entrance hall, one can look through the house to the out-of-doors in four directions, as glass is used for both exterior and interior doors. Light becomes an element of the design. The classical blends with nature as the exterior glass doors open onto wide porticos and terraces. Triple-sashed windows lift to the height of a doorway to become secondary connections to the outside. The house reflects the Enlightenment belief that the empirical study of nature is the truer way to an understanding of the world. Natural light gives a feeling of openness to the interior space that suggests breadth of thought.

Stepping inside, the visitor further experiences the tangible influence of the Enlightenment. During Jefferson's lifetime, the entrance hall received guests amid his varied collection of fine art, Native American artifacts, maps, and natural history specimens. More than one visitor referred to this hall as a museum. Those invited further into the house might step into the parlor and view even more art, including Jefferson's collection of worthies that he began assembling in Paris and that served to tell the history of the American republic. Then there was the dining room, where the late afternoon meal was still important, even if it did not carry the political overtones of the dinners at some of Jefferson's former dining spaces. Yet when visitors were in attendance, as they so often were, politics past and present could still enter the conversation. The dining table remained a part of Jefferson's image, and when Daniel Webster visited in 1824, he commented on the food at Monticello's table that reflected Jefferson's continued preference for things French. Webster observed, "Dinner was served in half Virginian, half French style, in good taste and abundance."[4]

Monticello reflected Jefferson—his taste and the image of himself he wished remembered.[5] When Attorney General Richard Rush visited in 1816, he pronounced that "Monticello is a curiosity! Artificial to a high degree; in many respects superb." A visitor in 1827, the year following Jefferson's death, first stopped at the University of Virginia and recognized Jefferson's talents and influence in accomplishing such an educational institution. Then he called at Monticello and remarked, "Indeed on all hands you are struck with the marks of Mr. Jefferson's attention to science."[6] These remarks could also describe Jefferson the man—a curiosity to many people, and thus to some artificial to a high degree, but still superb in his intellect and its application towards the notion of an independent republic based on democratic principles. This ideal was teamed with his belief that knowledge through education and scientific inquiry was the means of moving society forward.

Jefferson never retreated from the words he wrote to Edward Rutledge in 1796: "I know no safe depository of the ultimate powers of the society but the people themselves: and if we think them not enlightened enough to exercise their control with a wholesome discretion, the remedy is not to take it from them, but to inform their discretion by education."[7] He believed raising the standards of the general populace through education to be the safeguard of the republic. After the revolution, as he worked on revising the laws for the state of Virginia, he proposed the Bill for the More General Diffusion of Knowledge.[8] Jefferson included all free children in his bill; even girls would have reading, writing, and basic arithmetic for three years. He did not include slaves in his education plans, but they would be gradually emancipated and living under their own government, in perhaps Libya, Haiti, or another part of the world—or so he wanted to believe. But his education bill did not pass the Virginia legislature, and slaves were not gradually emancipated. His consoled himself with the view from his north terrace, where he could see the buildings for the University of Virginia as they were constructed.

Even the architecture at the University of Virginia was designed to educate and inform. He was very proud of his plan for separate pavilions for each professor, all connected by the student dormitories. Arranged along three sides of a square, the buildings opened onto a large lawn, and so just as his house, the buildings at his university offered an immediate connection with nature. He wrote to Latrobe and requested of his friend a few sketches, "no more than a minute apiece," that could assist with the architectural orders for each of the pavilions. Each building was to represent a different architectural order and be used as a teaching tool. Jefferson explained to Latrobe that they "should be models of taste and correct architecture, and of a variety of appearance, no two alike, so as to serve as specimens of [the] orders for the architectural lectures."[9] At the closed end of the square stood the rotunda, the domed building modeled after the Pantheon in Rome that would house the library. This was an example of spherical architecture, just as the Maison Carrée he had used as a model for the Virginia capitol represented perfect cubical architecture.[10] His designs for the university worked towards his goal set so many years earlier with the choice of the Maison Carrée. He wished his country to have examples of the purist classical architecture that aimed at improving the taste of Americans and thus raising their respect in the Western world. He never stopped pushing against their reputation as provincials.

Jefferson's final creation of a lasting image to shape his legacy was a rough stone obelisk that he designed to mark his gravesite. The family cemetery was on the southwest side of Monticello Mountain, about a half mile from the house. He would be buried there on July 5, 1826, the day after he and

John Adams so famously died just hours apart on the fiftieth anniversary of the adoption of the Declaration of Independence.

He was very specific in the design of and epitaph for his grave marker (fig. 54). The base of the marker was to be "a plain die or cube of 3.f. without any mouldings." This was to be "surmounted by an obelisk of 6.f. height." He requested a coarse stone be used so that no one would be tempted to destroy it for its materials. (He did not foresee it being chipped away by visitors wishing a souvenir.) The cube as a geometric form had attracted him to the Maison Carrée when he was looking for a classical model for the Virginia capitol. He experimented with this shape himself in his design for the dining room in the center of his retreat house, Poplar Forest, where he created a twenty-foot cubical space. The obelisk dates to antiquity; some of the finest examples were found in Egypt and transported to Europe to satisfy the curiosity and interest of western Europeans. During his time in Europe Jefferson saw many examples, and he even had a mantel clock made in Paris with the clock face supported by two obelisks. On his tour of English country houses with John Adams during the spring 1786, Jefferson made notes of obelisks used in the gardens. At Cheswick, he felt the obelisk

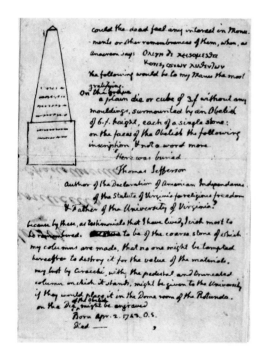

FIGURE 54. Drawing of obelisk gravestone with his epitaph by Thomas Jefferson. Ink on paper, 12¼ in. × 9³⁄₁₀ in.

Jefferson designed his gravestone and carefully wrote out instructions for his epitaph. His sketch was found by a family member after his death.

"of very ill effect." The obelisk at Twickenham was inscribed with Latin and used as a grave monument, and it may have offered an idea for his own gravesite.[11] However, what he proposed for his epitaph incorporated very American institutions that were not conducive to Latin, and he certainly wanted all to be able to read his memorial.

He knew exactly what he wanted inscribed on the stone and "not a single word more."

Here was buried
Thomas Jefferson
Author of the Declaration of American Independence
of the Statute of Virginia for religious freedom
& Father of the University of Virginia.

Many observers have noted that there is no mention of the political offices and appointments that he held: president, vice president, secretary of state, minister plenipotentiary, governor. Others could hold these offices and had, both before and after him. The accomplishments that he desired listed were unique to him. They reflected the Enlightenment thought that underlay his ideology: political freedom, religious freedom, and the freedom offered by knowledge. Another word more was not needed and would have diluted the significance of these three accomplishments. He stated his reasons: "Because by these, as testimonials that I have lived, I wish most to be remembered."[12] This was his final effort at shaping a lasting public image. The simple, timeless shapes of cube and obelisk and the plain stone texture spoke to a part of the image he had cultivated in his lifetime. This simplicity had been the alternate side of his cosmopolitan image, the other side of the Janus face.

Jefferson's image remained controversial, even in death. Newspapers reported the passing of the two patriots on the important anniversary of the declaration. Some writers commented on how remarkable it was that these two men who "glowed with the same patriotic fervor" should be united in death. In reporting Jefferson's death, some commentators resurrected the controversy that had surrounded him as a public figure. His contributions to the revolution and the declaration were not questioned: "An unanimity, most honorable to his name, must always prevail with regard to the excellence of his revolutionary labors." But, the obituary maintained, "a wide diversity of opinion may long continue respecting the quality of his public career after the establishment of our present constitution." As was not uncommon during his active years in public office, the obituary recognized "the pre-eminence of his talents, the variety and dignity of his acquirements, the suavity and refinement of his manners." A final acknowledgement was added for "the mild lustre of his last years and final pursuits." These comments appeared in New England newspapers, where his legacy was modified with long-held reservations, especially when compared with Adams's. The Virginia newspapers were far more uniform in approval, although diversity of opinion still plagued his final legacy.[13]

Jefferson could never let go his concern that the political gains made by his Democratic-Republican Party might not last. What if the moribund Federalist Party could still exert enough influence to swing the government towards their preference for control by a small, elite group? It might not be based on the old class distinctions of heredity aristocracies, but there was still the danger of an oligarchy based on wealth and privilege. In one of his many exit letters written to various Democratic-Republican groups upon his retirement from the presidency in 1809, he reminded the Democratic-Republican delegates of Washington County, Pennsylvania, that unlike the degrading and oppressive practices of Europe, "it is our happiness that honourable distinctions flow only from public approbation; & that finds no object in titled dignitaries and pageants." He had worked against claims to titles and against state-sponsored pageantry; still he warned that they must keep "a watchful eye over the disaffection of wealth & ambition to the republican principles of our constitution."[14]

In his retirement the Sage—simply dressed, often in homespun—greeted the many visitors who called upon him. His final creation of image, his gravestone, was equally simple in form. The obelisk with his epitaph pushed into the future his ambitions for how he wished to be remembered. He could advise vigilance against tyranny, but with his epitaph, his final image, he offered direction and a formula for nation building. In a letter composed early in his retirement he had admitted that his vision for the American republic might be a dream, but in true Enlightenment fashion he remained forever optimistic: "Mine, after all, may be an Utopian dream; but being innocent, I have thought I might indulge in it till I go to the land of dreams, and sleep there with the dreamers of all past and future times."[15]

NOTES

ABBREVIATIONS

AFC   *Adams Family Correspondence*

AHN   America's Historical Newspapers (subscription site, www.readex.com/content /americas-historical-newspapers)

JMB   *Jefferson's Memorandum Books*

LC   Library of Congress

PTJ   *The Papers of Thomas Jefferson*

PTJ:RS   *The Papers of Thomas Jefferson: Retirement Series*

TJW   *Thomas Jefferson: Writings*

INTRODUCTION

1. Augustus John Foster, *Jeffersonian America: Notes on the United States of America Collected in the Years 1805-6-7 and 11–12 by Sir Augustus John Foster, Bart.*, ed. Richard Beale Davis (San Marino, CA: Huntington Library, 1954), 10, 50, 146, 157.

2. Benjamin Henry Latrobe to John Lenthall, May 11, 1805, Benjamin Henry Latrobe papers, LC. The original spelling from all historic documents is retained unless it might cause misunderstanding for the reader.

3. For discussions of the American gentleman, see Richard L. Bushman, *The Refinement of America: Persons, Houses, Cities* (New York: Vintage Press, 1993), 3–203; and Michal J. Rozbicki, *The Complete Colonial Gentleman: Cultural Legitimacy in Plantation America* (Charlottesville: University of Virginia Press, 1998).

4. Philip Dormer Stanhope, 4th Earl of Chesterfield, July 30, O.S. 1747, reprinted in *Letters to His Son on the Art of Becoming a Man of the World and a Gentleman, 1746–47* c. 1774 (San Bernardino, CA: n.p., 2013), 25.

5. Bushman, *Refinement of America*, 36.

6. This book is indebted to the work of Alfred Bush, *The Life Portraits of Thomas Jefferson* (Charlottesville, VA: Thomas Jefferson Memorial Foundation, 1987); and that of Noble E. Cunningham Jr., *The Image of Thomas Jefferson in the Public Eye: Portraits for the People, 1800–1809* (Charlottesville: University of Virginia Press, 1981). It is supported and inspired by many other art historians and especially the work of Ellen Miles and her many works on American eighteenth-century portraiture.

7. *TJW*, 663.

8. Rozbicki, *Complete Colonial Gentleman*, chapter 3, "The Curse of Provincialism," 76–126.

9. Kenneth Clark, *Moments of Vision* (London: John Murray,1981), 52–53. Bernard Bailyn references this same comment by Clark on provincialism in *To Begin the World Anew: The Genius and Ambiguities of the American Founders* (New York: Random House, 2004), 7–8. See also Gordon Wood, *Revolutionary Characters: What Made the Founders Different* (New York: Penguin, 2006), 20–21, for a comparison of the Americans and the Scots, both on the periphery of England.

10. Philipp Ziesche, "American Exceptionalism: Cosmopolitanism by Another Name?," in *Cosmopolitanism and Nationhood in the Age of Jefferson*, eds. Peter Nicholaisen and Hannah Spahn (Heidelberg: Universitätsverlag Winter, 2014), 225–34.

11. Merrill D. Peterson, *The Jefferson Image in the American Mind* (Charlottesville: University of Virginia Press, 1998) xiii, 9. Peterson's acclaimed work looks at Jefferson's legacy from his death until 1943 and the opening of the Jefferson Memorial. In *Thomas Jefferson: Reputation and Legacy* (Charlottesville: University of Virginia Press, 2006), Francis D. Cogliano builds on Peterson's work, including addressing issues of Jefferson and slavery. *Jefferson on Display* acknowledges these excellent works but differs in that it focuses on the Jefferson image during his life and career. It holds more in common with Robert M. S. McDonald's *Confounding Father: Thomas Jefferson's Image in His Own Time* (Charlottesville: University of Virginia Press, 2016) and looks at similar sources, but I differ in relying more heavily on art and material culture.

12. Susan Kern, *The Jeffersons at Shadwell* (New Haven, CT: Yale University Press, 2010), 14–22. Kern begins her book with a synopsis of Jefferson's parents and the milieu into which he was born. She argues that the Jeffersons maintained a genteel lifestyle on the edge of the frontier.

13. TJ, "Autobiography," as reprinted in *TJW*, 3.

14. Sarah N. Randolph, *The Domestic Life of Thomas Jefferson* (Charlottesville: University of Virginia Press, 1978), 23.

15. Jefferson was born under the "old style" Julian calendar, in which his birthday fell on April 2; however, when the "new style" Georgian calendar was introduced, his birthday fell on April 13, which is the date celebrated today.

16. TJ, "Autobiography," *TJW*, 4.

17. TJ to Louis Girardin, January 15, 1815, *PTJ:RS*, 8:200; for Jefferson as a musician in Williamsburg, see Helen Cripe, *Thomas Jefferson and Music*, rev. ed. (Charlottesville, VA: Thomas Jefferson Foundation, 2009), 17–19.

18. Latrobe to Mary Elizabeth Latrobe, November 24, 1802, *The Papers of Benjamin Henry Latrobe* (New Haven, CT: Yale University Press, 1977–94), 1:232.

19. TJ to John Page, May 25, 1766, *PTJ*, 1:19; Jefferson's tour is discussed in Dumas Malone, *Jefferson and His Times* (Boston: Little, Brown, 1948–81), 1:98–99.

20. *TJW*, 46.

21. These figures are taken from the calculations by Malone, *Jefferson and His Times*, appendix 2:B, 1:430–46.

22. Summary of TJ's journey to and stay in Philadelphia, June–August 1775, *JMB*, 1:396–412; and May–September 1776, 1:417–15.

23. Nora Waugh, *Cut of Men's Clothes, 1600–1900* (London: Faber and Faber, 1964), 52–53.

24. Linda Baumgarten, *What Clothes Reveal: The Language of Clothing in Colonial and Federal America* (New Haven, CT: Yale University Press, 2002), 76–105. This chapter, "Homespun and Silk," provides an excellent discussion of and examples of fabrics available to the Americans, including homespun or Virginia cloth.

25. Martha Wayles Jefferson, "Household Accounts," facsimile copy, Jefferson Library, Thomas Jefferson Foundation, Special Collections, Charlottesville, VA.

26. Stephen Hawtrey to Edward Hawtrey, London, March 26, 1765, Alumni File, College Archives, Earl Gregg Swem Library, College of William and Mary, Williamsburg, VA. I want to thank Dr. Martin Clagett for supplying me with a full copy of this letter. A portion of the letter is referenced in Linda Baumgarten, *Eighteenth-Century Clothing at Williamsburg* (Williamsburg, VA: Colonial Williamsburg Foundation, 1993), 13.

27. Discussed in Geoffrey Squire, *Dress and Society, 1560–1970* (New York: Viking, 1974), 128–29.

28. Ann Buck, *Dress in Eighteenth-Century England* (London: B. T. Batsford, 1979), 207.

29. For a very complete discussion, see "Revisal of the Laws, 1776–1786; Editorial Notes," in *PTJ*, 2:305–24.

30. Malone, *Jefferson and His Times*, appendix 1, 1:434.

31. Hamilton W. Pierson, "The Private Life of Thomas Jefferson," in *Jefferson at Monticello: Memoirs of a Monticello Slave*, ed. James A. Bear Jr. (Charlottesville: University of Virginia Press, 1967), 100.

32. See especially Lucia Stanton, *"Those Who Labor for My Happiness": Slavery at Thomas Jefferson's Monticello* (Charlottesville: University of Virginia Press, 2012); and Annette Gordon-Reed, *The Hemingses of Monticello: An American Family* (New York: Norton, 2008), and *Thomas Jefferson and Sally Hemings: An American Controversy* (Charlottesville: University of Virginia Press, 1997). Gordon-Reed's most recent work, coauthored with Peter Onuf, *"Most Blessed of the Patriarchs": Thomas Jefferson and the Empire of the Imagination* (New York: Liveright Publishing, 2016), includes insights into Jefferson's relationship with Sally Hemings.

33. Francois Jean Chastellux, *Travels in North America in the Years 1780, 1781, and 1782*, trans. An English Gentleman (London: G. G. J. and J. Robinson, 1787), 2:177.

34. Ibid., 2:42–44.

35. Ibid., 2:204.

36. John Barrell, *The Political Theory of Painting from Reynolds to Hazlitt: "The Body of the Public"* (New Haven, CT: Yale University Press, 1986), 3–4.

37. David Solkin, *Painting for Money: The Visual Arts and the Public Sphere in Eighteenth-Century England* (New Haven, CT: Yale University Press, 1993), 12.

38. *TJW*, 46.

39. *JMB* contains many of the important dates in Jefferson's life. For a narrative account of Jefferson's assignment to, travel to, and arrival in France, see Malone, *Jefferson and His Times*, 1:245–46, and 2:3–8.

40. TJ to Franklin, August 13, 1777, *PTJ*, 2:26.

41. TJ to Chastellux, November 26, 1782, *PTJ*, 6:203.

1. AT THE FRENCH COURT AND AMONG THE LITERATI

1. Jefferson to Charles Bellini, September 30, 1785, *PTJ*, 8:568–70.

2. The invoice from the *emballieur*, Grevin, who packed Jefferson's books, art, and household goods in Paris, lists crates 1–15 as "books," from transcription in *PTJ*, 18:35.

3. TJ to Charles Bellini, September 30, 1785, *PTJ*, 8:568–70, quote at 569.

4. TJ to Geismar, September 6, 1785, *PTJ*, 8:499–500; TJ, "Hints to Americans Travelling in Europe," *PTJ*, 13:269–70; TJ to James Monroe, November 11, 1784, *PTJ*, 7:512.

5. This discussion is based on points made by Norbert Elias throughout *The Court Society,* trans. Edmund Jephcott (New York: Pantheon, 1983). The relationship of appearance and rank is discussed also in Daniel Roche, *The Culture of Clothing: Dress and Fashion in the Ancien Regime,* trans. Jean Birrell (Cambridge, UK: Cambridge University Press, 1994), 184–87; and in Philip Mansel, *Dressed to Rule: Royal and Court Costume from Louis XIV to Elizabeth II* (New Haven, CT: Yale University Press, 2005), 1–54.

6. JA, *Diary and Autobiography of John Adams,* ed. L. H. Butterfield (Cambridge, MA: Belknap Press of Harvard University Press, 1961), 4:131–32.

7. Elias, *The Court Society,* 64.

8. Benjamin Franklin to JA, September 26, 1778, *Papers of John Adams,* ed. Robert J. Taylor, et al. (Cambridge, MA: Belknap Press of Harvard University Press, 1977–2010), 7:79; Benjamin Franklin, *Benjamin Franklin's Autobiographical Writings,* ed. Carl Van Doren (New York: Viking, 1945), 454.

9. JA, *Diary and Autobiography,* 3:37.

10. Mansel, *Dressed to Rule,* 8–9; Aileen Ribeiro, "Fashion in the Eighteenth Century: Some Anglo-French Comparisons," in *Fabrics and Fashions: Studies in the Economic and Social History of Dress,* ed. N. B. Harte (London: Pasold Research Fund, 1985), 329–30.

11. Mansel, *Dressed to Rule;* Waugh, *Cut of Men's Clothes,* 53–54.

12. Abigail Adams to Mary Smith Cranch, September 5, 1784, *AFC,* 5:443; Abigail Adams II, *Journal and Correspondence of Miss Adams, Daughter of John Adams,* ed. Her Daughter (New York: Wiley and Putnam, 1841), 14; Martha Jefferson to Eliza House Trist, after August 24, 1785, *PTJ,* 8:437.

13. Aileen Ribeiro, *Dress in Eighteenth-Century Europe, 1715–1789* (New Haven, CT: Yale University Press, 2002), 29–32. Ribeiro identifies the dress sword as "a necessary mark of gentility in France" but notes that it gave way to the cane in England earlier in the eighteenth century.

14. *JMB,* 1:557–60.

15. *Journal de Paris,* September 3, 1784, no. 247; electronic facsimile viewed. The prince is identified as Charles Auguste Frederic, Prince Héréditaire De Deux Ponts. He was the son of Charles II, Duke of Zweibrücken. See also *AFC,* 5:444n.7.

16. Abigail Adams to Mary Smith Cranch, September 5, 1784; and to Cotton Tufts, September 8, 1784, *AFC,* 5:443, 458. Abigail's letter to her sister must have extended over several days, as Jefferson and Humphreys would have been at the Adamses on Tuesday, September 7, as indicated in her letter to Cotton Tufts.

17. Abigail Adams to Cotton Tufts, *AFC,* 5:458.

18. *JMB,* 1:563.

19. *JMB,* 1:562.

20. John Adams to Richard Cranach, April 27, 1785, *AFC,* 6:109–11.

21. Abigail Adams to TJ, June 6, 1785, *AFC,* 8:178. For the friendship between Abigail Adams and TJ, see Cassandra Good, *Founding Friendships: Friendships between Men and Women in the Early American Republic* (New York: Oxford University Press, 2016), 13–18.

22. Gordon S. Wood, *The Americanization of Benjamin Franklin* (New York: Penguin, 2004), 172.

23. Elisabeth Vigée-Lebrun, *Memoirs of Elisabeth Vigée-Lebrun,* trans. Siàn Evans (London: Camden Press, 1989), 318–19.

24. Wood, *Americanization*, 61–66; St. John de Crevecoeur to TJ, July 15, 1784, *PTJ*, 7:376. The letter mentions the use of lightning rods in France and their benefits.

25. Franklin to Mrs. Emma Tompson, February 8, 1777, Franklin, *Autobiographical Writings*, 427–28.

26. Charles Coleman Sellers, *Benjamin Franklin in Portraiture* (New Haven, CT: Yale University Press, 1962), 228–29.

27. TJ to William Smith, February 19, 1791, *PTJ*, 19:113.

28. Howard C. Rice, *Thomas Jefferson's Paris* (Princeton, NJ: Princeton University Press, 1976), 37, 51.

29. Elias, *Court Society*, 54.

30. TJ to Abigail Adams, September 4, 1785, *PTJ*, 8:473.

31. TJ to John Jay, June 17, 1785, *PTJ*, 8:226.

32. Jean-Nicolas Dufort, *Mémoires Du Comte Dufort de Cheverny*, 3rd ed. (Paris, 1909), 1:82–84; this is cited in English translation in Marie Kimball, *Jefferson: The Scene of Europe, 1784–1789* (New York: Coward-McCann, 1950), 36–37.

33. David Humphreys to George Washington, July 17, 1785, *The Papers of George Washington*, vol. 3, *Confederation Series*, eds. W. W. Abbott and Dorothy Twohig (Charlottesville: University of Virginia Press, 1992–97), 132–33.

34. TJ to Barré, January 13, 1786, *PTJ*, 9:179.

35. Quotes from and descriptions of Shippen's presentation are from Thomas Lee Shippen to William Shippen Jr., February 14–March 26, 1788, LC, Shippen Family papers; transcribed in *PTJ*, 12:502–4.

36. *PTJ*, 12:502–4.

37. Mansel, *Dressed to Rule*, 4–5; Roche, *Culture of Clothing*, 184–88.

38. This summary of the king's *lever* is taken from Elias, *Court Society*, 82–86; Mansel, *Dressed to Rule*, 3–5; and Ribeiro, *Dress in Eighteenth-Century Europe*, 183.

39. Count de Montmorin had replaced the Count de Vergennes following Vergennes's death in 1787, as discussed in Rice, *Jefferson's Paris*, 100.

40. Thomas Lee Shippen to William Shippen Jr., February 14–March 26, 1788, *PTJ*, 12:504.

41. These knightly orders are referenced in many clothing histories, such as Aileen Ribeiro's *Fashion in the French Revolution*, (London: B. T. Batsford, 1988), 40; for Nabby's reference, see Abigail Adams II, *Journal and Correspondence*, 77.

42. TJ to George Washington, April 16, 1784, *PTJ*, 7:105–10.

43. William Doyle, *Aristocracy and Its Enemies in the Age of Revolution* (Oxford: Oxford University Press, 2009), 99–100. Doyle's full discussion of the Cincinnati provides background as to its formation in American as well as its reception in France, 86–137.

44. TJ to Washington, November 14, 1786, *PTJ*, 10:532.

45. JA, *Diary and Autobiography*, 4:130–31.

46. Abigail Adams II, *Journal and Correspondence*, 38–39.

47. JA, *Diary and Autobiography*, 4:130–31. For the circumstances of Adams's portrait by Copley, see Jane Kamensky, *A Revolution in Color: The World of John Singleton Copley* (New York: Norton, 2016), 313–14.

48. Abigail Adams to Mary Smith Cranch, December 9, 1784, *AFC*, 6:17.

49. *JMB*, 1:605, 649, 690, 723.

50. TJ to Geismer, September 6, 1785, *PTJ*, 8:500; and TJ to Bellini, September 30, 1785, *PTJ*, 8:568–70.

51. TJ to David Humphreys, August 14, 1787, *PTJ*, 12:32.

52. Jefferson was correct that court dress for men would be slow to change. Coat, waistcoat, and knee breeches persisted at many European courts, rivaled only by elaborately trimmed uniforms. See Nigel Arch and Joanna Marschner, *Spendour at Court: Dressing for Royal Occasions since 1700* (London: Unwin Hyman, 1987), 70–73; Mansel, *Dressed to Rule*, 77–102.

53. For the origin of the term "frock," see the *Oxford English Dictionary*, 2nd ed. A standard source for the development of the frock coat is C. Willett Cunnington and Phillis Cunnington, *Handbook of English Costume in the Eighteenth Century*, 2nd ed. (London: Faber and Faber, 1972), 16–20, 193–203; and Waugh, *Cut of Men's Clothes*, 53–54.

54. Arthur Murphy, *The Grey's-Inn Journal*, 1752, quoted in Waugh, *Cut of Men's Clothes*, 105; Squire, *Dress and Society*, 125.

55. Waugh, *Cut of Men's Clothes*, 110; Squire, *Dress and Society*, 125.

56. Louis-Philippe de Ségur, *Memoirs*, quoted in Ribeiro, *Fashion in the French Revolution*, 39; Abigail Adams II, *Journal and Correspondence*, 63; TJ to Humphreys August 14, 1787, *PTJ*, 12:32.

57. Portions of this discussion of the Mather Brown portraits were first published in the journal of the Costume Society of America: see Gaye Wilson and Elizabeth V. Chew, "Fashioning an American Diplomat," *Dress* 29 (2002): 19–24. A revised and expanded version appeared as Gaye Wilson, "Thomas Jefferson and Creating an American Image Abroad," in *Old World, New World: America and Europe in the Age of Jefferson*, eds. Leonard Sadosky et al. (Charlottesville: University of Virginia Press, 2010), 155–78.

58. JA, *Diary and Autobiography*, 3:182–83n.2; for Jefferson's purchases while in London, see *JMB*, 1:613–23; "Notes of a Tour of English Gardens," *PTJ*, 9:369–75; a summary of Jefferson's trip to London is found in Malone, *Jefferson and His Times*, 2:50–63.

59. Abigail Adams II to John Quincy Adams, July 4–August 11, 1785, *AFC*, 6:2215–16.

60. Dorinda Evans, *Mather Brown: Early American Artist in England* (Middletown, CT: Wesleyan, 1982), 26, 42–46, 62–63.

61. Madeleine Delpierre, *Dress in France in the Eighteenth Century*, trans. Carolie Beamish (New Haven, CT: Yale University Press, 1997), 165. Delpierre identifies the French *frac* as fashioned after the English garment but more often without buttons or pockets. See also Jacques Ruppert, *Le Costume Époques Louis XVI et Directoire* (Paris: Flammarion, 1990), 9; per Ruppert, "Il y a des fracs sans boutons."

62. Cunnington and Cunnington, *Handbook of English Costume*, 197–200.

63. Robert Cannon invoices, March 14, 1786, and April 24, 1786, Thomas Jefferson papers, Special Collections, University of Virginia, Charlottesville. Jefferson's records show payments to three different Parisian tailors between the dates of his arrival in Paris in August 1784 and his London visit in March and April 1786; however, only one is itemized and lists a coat. Payment to "Lonpry, the tailor," for a coat at seventy-two francs, *JMB* 1:563–606.

64. Abigail Adams to Cotton Tufts, September 8, 1784, *AFC*, 5:458.

65. *JMB*, 1:560, 563.

66. David Hackett Fischer, *Liberty and Freedom: A Visual History of America's Founding Ideas* (Oxford, UK: Oxford University Press, 2005), 6, 41–42, 97–103; Yvonne Korshak, "The Liberty Cap as a Revolutionary Symbol in America and France," *Smithsonian Studies in American Art* 1

(Fall 1987): 53–69; Jennifer Harris, "The Red Cap of Liberty: A Study of Dress Worn by French Revolutionary Partisans, 1789–94," *Eighteenth-Century Studies* 14, no. 3 (1981): 283–312.

67. TJ to William Stephens Smith, February 19, 1781, *PTJ*, 11:169; TJ to Smith, December 31, 1787, *PTJ*, 12:484; remark by William Short regarding the portraits is from Bush, *Life Portraits of Thomas Jefferson*, 4; portraits received, TJ to John Trumbull, September 10, 1788, *PTJ*, 13:597.

68. TJ to William Stephens Smith, October 22, 1786, *PTJ*, 10:479.

69. Jefferson used this term more than once. Two examples are TJ to William Short, April 6, 1790, *PTJ*, 16:318, and TJ to Joseph Delaplaine, May 3, 1814, *PTJ:RS*, 7:340–41.

70. Brandon Brame Fortune, "Portraits of Virtue and Genius: Pantheons of Worthies and Public Portraiture in the Early American Republic, 1780–1820," PhD diss., University of North Carolina at Chapel Hill, 1987, 1–34; Barrell, *Political Theory of Painting*, 18–23; Doris Devine Fanelli and Karie Diethorn, *History of the Portrait Collection, Independence National Historical Park* (Philadelphia: American Philosophical Society, 2001), 8.

71. Jonathan Richardson, *The Works of Jonathan Richardson* (London, 1792), 10, 13.

72. *JMB*, 1:550, entry under May 28 (see also note 40); Francis Hopkinson to TJ, May 30, 1784, *PTJ*, 7:295; TJ to Francis Hopkinson, July 6, 1785, *PTJ*, 8:262; Monroe H. Fabian, *Joseph Wright: American Artist, 1756–1793* (Washington, DC: Smithsonian Institution Press, 1985), 101–6.

73. "Payment to Valade for picture," September 10, 1786, *JMB*, 1:638 (see also note 62).

74. TJ to John Trumbull, January 12, 1789, *PTJ*, 14:440; for the commissions from the Uffizi, see TJ to Philip Mazzei, October 17, 1787, *PTJ*, 12:245.

75. TJ to William Stephens Smith, October 22, 1786, *PTJ*, 10:479.

76. For Jefferson's commission of the Raleigh portrait, see TJ to William Stephens Smith, October 22, 1786, *PTJ*, 10:478–79; Jefferson's quote, "portraits of its first discovers," is in TJ to Joseph Delaplaine, May 3, 1814, *PTJ:RS*, 7:340.

77. TJ to Trumbull, February 15, 1789, *PTJ*, 14:561.

78. TJ to Washington, December 10, 1784, *PTJ*, 7:567.

79. Anne L. Poulet, *Jean-Antoine Houdon: Sculptor of the Enlightenment* (Chicago: University of Chicago Press, 2003), 263.

80. Ibid., 271.

81. TJ to James Madison, October 18, 1825, *Writings of Thomas Jefferson*, ed. Albert Ellery Bergh (Washington, DC, 1907), 19:287.

82. The Jefferson image on medals and coins created during his presidency will be discussed further in chapter 5. In *Jean-Antoine Houdon*, cited above, Anne Poulet stated that Houdon was the source for the image on the Jefferson dollar minted in 1903 and for the obverse image of the American nickel, first minted in 1938. See also Noble Cunningham, *Image of Thomas Jefferson in the Public Eye: Portraits for the People, 1800–1809* (Charlottesville: University of Virginia Press, 1981), 71–78.

2. REMEMBERING THE REVOLUTION

1. TJ to John Dickinson, March 6, 1801, *PTJ*, 33:196–97.

2. JA to Benjamin Rush, June 21, 1811, quoted in *The Spur of Fame*, eds. John A. Schutz and Douglass Adair (San Marino, CA: Liberty Fund, 1966), 197.

3. TJ to Robert Walsh, December 4, 1818, unpublished letters, *PTJ:RS* files.

4. TJ to Richard Henry Lee, July 8, 1776, and Lee's reply, July 21, 1776, *PTJ*, 1:455–56, 471; Edmund Pendleton to TJ, August 10, 1776, *PTJ*, 1:488.

5. Ezra Stiles, sermon delivered on May 8, 1783, Hartford, CT, and printed in Hartford by Thomas and Samuel Green, 1783, as viewed on America's Historical Imprints, Early American Imprints, series 1, no. 18198, www.readex.com/content/americas-historical-imprints.

6. E. Millicent Sowerby, comp., *Catalogue of the Library of Thomas Jefferson* (Charlottesville: University of Virginia Press, 1983), 2:141, entry 1576.

7. "A Fourth of July Tribute to Jefferson," Paris, July 4, 1789, *PTJ*, 15:239–40.

8. JA, *Diary and Autobiography*, 3:335–36.

9. Edmund Randolph, *History of Virginia*, ed. Arthur H. Shaffer (Charlottesville: University of Virginia Press, 1970), 182.

10. TJ on JA, as cited by Daniel Webster in *The Private Correspondence of Daniel Webster*, eds. F. Webster and E. D. Sanborn (Boston: Little, Brown, 1857), 1:370.

11. TJ, "A Summary View of the Rights of British Americans," originally printed in Williamsburg, VA, in 1774; reprinted in *TJW*, 105–22.

12. Samuel Ward to Henry Ward, June 22, 1775, cited in McDonald, *Confounding Father*, 14.

13. On more than one occasion Jefferson stated his high regard for Francis Bacon; for two primary examples see TJ to John Trumbull, January 18, 1789, *PTJ*, 14:467; and TJ to Benjamin Rush, January 16, 1811, *PTJ:RS*, 3:305.

14. John Trumbull, *Autobiography of Colonel John Trumbull, Patriot-Artist, 1756–1843*, ed. Theodore Sizer (New Haven, CT: Yale University Press, 1953), 60. Trumbull mentions that he was acquainted with Franklin and Adams during his first brief stay in Paris in 1780.

15. John Trumbull to Andrew Elliot, March 4, 1786, cited in Helen Cooper, *John Trumbull: The Hand and Spirit of a Painter* (New Haven, CT: Yale University Art Gallery, 1982), 31.

16. Trumbull, *Autobiography*, 380; Jules David Prown, *Art as Evidence: Writings on Art and Material Culture* (New Haven, CT: Yale University Press, 2001), 184–85.

17. Cooper, *Trumbull: Hand and Spirit*, 2–4; Irma B. Jaffe, *John Trumbull: Patriot-Artist of the American Revolution* (Boston: New York Graphic Society, 1975), 27–29.

18. Trumbull, *Autobiography*, 92–93.

19. Jules David Prown, "John Trumbull as History Painter," in Cooper, *Trumbull: Hand and Spirit*, 33.

20. Solkin, *Painting for Money*, 209–13.

21. John Trumbull to Jonathan Trumbull Jr., January 18, 1785, in Oswaldo Rodriguez Roque, "Trumbull's Portraits," in Cooper, *Trumbull: Hand and Spirit*, 98.

22. Trumbull, *Autobiography*, 90–92.

23. TJ to Francis Hopkinson, August 14, 1786, *PTJ*, 10:250. Jefferson would be referring to David Ramsay's *History of the Revolution in South Carolina*, published 1785; Ramsay's *History of the American Revolution* was not published until 1787. For a discussion, see Peter C. Messer, "From a Revolutionary History to a History of Revolution: David Ramsay and the American Revolution," *Journal of the Early Republic* 22, no. 2 (Summer 2002): 205–33.

24. TJ to Hilliard d'Auberteuil, February 20, 1786, *PTJ*, 9:290.

25. Theodore Sizer, *The Works of Colonel John Trumbull: Artist of the American Revolution*, rev. ed. (New Haven, CT: Yale University Press, 1967), fig. 157.

26. Trumbull to TJ, November 28, 1817, in Trumbull, *Autobiography*, 311.

27. Richardson, *Works*, 27.

28. TJ, "Autobiography," *TJW*, 17.

29. Trumbull, *Autobiography*, 146–47.

30. Ibid., 152.

31. Jaffe, *Trumbull: Patriot-Artist*, 115–18.

32. TJ to JA, September 4, 1823, in JA, *The Adams-Jefferson Letters: The Complete Correspondence between Thomas Jefferson and Abigail and John Adams*, ed. Lester J. Cappon (Chapel Hill: University of North Carolina Press, 1959; reprinted 1988 in 1 vol.), 597; TJ, "Autobiography," *TJW*, 9.

33. TJ to John Dickinson, December 19, 1801, *PTJ*, 36:165; TJ to Lafayette, May 14, 1817, *PTJ:RS*, 11:354.

34. For an account of the British invasion of Virginia and the surrender at Yorktown, see Andrew Jackson O'Shaughnessy, *The Men Who Lost America: British Leadership, the American Revolution, and the Fate of the Empire* (New Haven, CT: Yale University Press, 2013), 273–81; and Michael Kranish, *Flight from Monticello: Thomas Jefferson at War* (Oxford, UK: Oxford University Press, 2010), 252–311.

35. John Harvie to TJ, "Enclosing a Resolution to Inquire into the Conduct of the Executive," November 27, 1781, *PTJ*, 6:133; TJ to Isaac Zane, December 24, 1781, *PTJ*, 6:143; "Resolution of Thanks to Jefferson by the Virginia General Assembly," December 12, 1781, *PTJ*, 6:135.

36. "The Jeffersoniad—No. I," *Columbian Centinel*, as published in the *Providence Journal*, Providence, RI, July 9, 1800, AHN.

37. For an account of Jefferson as war-time governor, see Kranish, *Flight from Monticello*. For Jefferson's concerns about the effects on his legacy of accusations stemming from his role as governor, see Cogliano, *Jefferson: Reputation and Legacy*, esp. chapter 2, 44–73.

38. O'Shaughnessy, *Men Who Lost America*.

39. Trumbull to TJ, August 28, 1787, *PTJ*, 12:60; TJ to Trumbull, February 23, 1787, *PTJ*, 11:181; TJ to Trumbull, August 30, 1787, *PTJ*, 12:69.

40. Trumbull, *Autobiography*, 152.

41. Trumbull to TJ, August 28, 1787, *PTJ*, 12:60.

42. Stephen Lloyd and Kim Sloan, *The Intimate Portrait: Drawings, Miniatures, and Pastels from Ramsay to Lawrence* (Edinburgh: National Galleries of Scotland, 2009), 20–21; Cooper, *Trumbull: Hand and Spirit*, 125.

43. Carol Burnell, *Divided Affections: The Extraordinary Life of Maria Cosway* (Lausanne, Switzerland: Column House, 2007). On the Cosway-Jefferson meeting, see 147; for final correspondence, see 397. For discussion of Jefferson's well-known "Head and Heart" letter to Cosway and their Paris meeting, see Andrew Burstein, *The Inner Jefferson: Portrait of a Grieving Optimist* (Charlottesville: University of Virginia Press, 1995), 75–98.

44. Elizabeth Cometti, "Maria Cosway's Rediscovered Miniature of Jefferson," *William and Mary Quarterly* 9, no. 2 (April 1951): 152–55.

45. Cosway to TJ, March 6, 1788, *PTJ*, 12:645; Cosway to TJ, April 29, 1788, *PTJ*, 13:115–16.

46. See Lloyd and Sloan, *The Intimate Portrait*, 20–21, for a discussion of Cosway's display of her miniature portraits.

47. Cosway to TJ, August 19, 1788, *PTJ*, 13:525; Angelica Schuyler Church, July 21, 1788, *PTJ*, 13:391.

48. These observations were made from my close study of Trumbull's miniature of Jefferson in comparison with that of Thomas Paine *in situ* at Monticello.

49. The discussion of the Adams portrait is found in TJ to William Stephens Smith, December 31, 1787, *PTJ*, 12:485; Smith to TJ, January 16, 1788, *PTJ*, 12:517; and TJ to Smith, February 2, 1788, *PTJ*, 12:558.

50. TJ to Ezra Stiles, September 1, 1786, *PTJ*, 10:317.

51. Dorinda Evans, *Benjamin West and His American Students* (Washington, DC: Smithsonian Institution Press for the National Portrait Gallery, 1980), 86–87.

52. Trumbull to TJ, December 19, 1788, *PTJ*, 14:364.

53. The print of Paine taken from C. W. Peale's portrait by John Watson in 1783 may have been familiar to Trumbull; however, Trumbull's rendering of Paine is quite different.

54. Trumbull to TJ, December 19, 1788, *PTJ*, 14:365.

55. Susan R. Stein, *Worlds of Thomas Jefferson at Monticello* (New York: Harry N. Abrams, 1993), 126.

56. Jefferson to Trumbull, October 4, 1787, *PTJ*, 12:207. The term "kit-kat" was originated by Sir Godfrey Kellner and named for the many portraits created in this size for members of London's famous Kit Kat Club. The information on the kit-kat portrait is from Carolyn Kinder Carr and Ellen G. Miles, *A Brush with History: Paintings from the National Portrait Gallery* (Washington, DC: Smithsonian Institution Press, 2001), 32; and Fortune, "Portraits of Virtue," 17.

57. TJ to Trumbull, January 12, 1789, *PTJ*, 14:440.

58. For a discussion of contemporary portraits of Thomas Paine, see G. S. Wilson, "Thomas Jefferson's Portrait of Thomas Paine," in *Paine and Jefferson in the Age of Revolutions*, eds, Simon P. Newman and Peter Onuf (Charlottesville: University of Virginia Press, 2013), 229–51.

59. Keith Thomson, *Jefferson's Shadow: The Story of His Science* (New Haven, CT: Yale University Press, 2012), 145.

60. St. John de Crèvecoeur to TJ, July 15, 1784, *PTJ*, 7:376.

61. Philip Mazzei's Memorandum Regarding Persons and Affairs in Paris [c. July 1784], *PTJ*, 7:386–391.

62. TJ to Abigail Adams, June 21, 1785, *PTJ*, 8:241; Rice, *Thomas Jefferson's Paris*, 94; Kimball, *Jefferson: Scene of Europe*, 78–107.

63. Kimball, *Jefferson: Scene of Europe*, 105–6; Tessé to TJ, March 24, 1810, editor's translation from the French, *PTJ:RS*, 2:310–12.

64. Madame de Staël to TJ, January 6, 1816, *PTJ:RS*, 9:326–28.

65. Timothy Sweet, "Jefferson, Science, and the Enlightenment," in *Cambridge Companion to Thomas Jefferson*, ed. Frank Shuffelton (Cambridge, UK: Cambridge University Press, 2009), 107; see also TJ, *Notes on the State of Virginia*, Query VI, for his discussion of Buffon's theories.

66. TJ to Chastellux, June 7, 1785, *PTJ*, 8:185.

67. Thomson, *Jefferson's Shadow*, 11–13, 62–73.

68. TJ to Chastellux, June 7, 1785, *PTJ*, 8:184.

69. TJ to Francis Hopkinson, January 3, 1786, *PTJ*, 9:148.

70. Gordon Barker, "Unraveling the Strange History of Jefferson's 'Observations sur la Virginie,'" *Virginia Magazine of History and Biography* 112, no. 2 (2004): 13–77.

71. For an example of an ad for *Notes*, see the *St. James's Chronicle or the British Evening Post* (London), October 13, 1787–October 16, 1787, issue 4164; 17th and18th Century Burney Col-

lection Newspapers subscription database, www.gale.com/c/17th-and-18th-century-burney -newspapers-collection.

72. Joel Barlow to TJ, June 15, 1787, *PTJ*, 11:473.

73. *PTJ*, 10:603–4.

74. Gouverneur Morris, *The Diary and Letters of Gouverneur Morris*, ed. Anne Cary Morris (New York: Scribner's Sons, 1888), 1:315.

75. TJ, "Autobiography," *TJW*, 82–83.

76. Ibid., 85, 87; TJ to JM, January 12, 1789, *PTJ* 14:437, and editorial note, 15:231.

77. Lafayette to TJ, August 25, 1789, *PTJ*, 15:354; TJ, "Autobiography," *TJW*, 95–98, 62–63.

78. Lafayette to Washington, February 6, 1786, *Papers of George Washington: Confederation Series*, 3:545, and January 1, 1788, ibid., 6:6.

79. John Sinclair, *Correspondence of the Right Honourable Sir John Sinclair* (London, 1831), 2:39.

80. TJ to Benjamin Hawkins, August 4, 1787, *PTJ*, 11:683–84.

81. JA, *Diary and Autobiography*, 4:133.

3. RETURNING TO A NEW AMERICA

Portions of this chapter were published as "Thomas Jefferson and Creating an Image for a New Nation," in *Cosmopolitanism and Nationhood in the Age of Jefferson*, eds. Peter Nicolaisen and Hannah Spahn (Heidelberg: Universitätsverlag Winter, 2013), 138–55.

1. TJ to David Humphreys, March 18, 1789, *PTJ*, 14:679.

2. TJ to Maria Cosway, October 14, 1789, *PTJ*, 15:521.

3. *JMB*, 1:747.

4. Washington to TJ, October 13, 1789, *PTJ*, 15:519; TJ to Washington, December 15, 1789, *PTJ*, 16:34; TJ to JM, January 9, 1790, *PTJ*, 16:92.

5. JM to TJ, June 30, 1789, *PTJ*, 15:224; Washington to TJ, January 21, 1790, *PTJ*, 16:117.

6. Washington to TJ, *Papers of George Washington: Presidential Series*, 5:30; JM to TJ, January 24, 1790, *PTJ*, 16:126.

7. JM to TJ, June 30, 1789, *PTJ*, 15:224.

8. Washington to TJ, January 21, 1790, *PTJ*, 16:182.

9. Thomas Paine to Washington, *Papers of George Washington: Presidential Series*, 4:196; reference to "fervor" from TJ, "Anas," *TJW*, 665–66.

10. TJ to Maria Cosway, October 14, 1789, *PTJ*, 15:521.

11. TJ to Washington, December 15, 1789, *PTJ*, 16:34.

12. TJ to John Paradise, July 5, 1789, *PTJ*, 15:242.

13. Washington to TJ, January 21, 1790, *PTJ*, 16:116; TJ to JM, February 14, 1790, *PTJ*, 16:182.

14. In his *Memorandum Book*, Jefferson noted his daughter's marriage on February 23, his departure from Monticello on March 1, and his arrival in New York on March 23; see *JMB*, 1:750, 754. The wedding made the national newspapers, even though the date was a day off: "On Monday the 22d of February, at Monticello, in Albemarle county, Virginia, *Thomas Randolph*, jun. Esq. to Miss *Patsy Jefferson*, eldest daughter of his Excellency Thomas Jefferson, Esquire." *Pennsylvania Mercury*, Philadelphia, March 13, 1790, AHN.

15. "Alexandria, March 18," as reprinted in the *Daily Advertiser* (New York), March 29, 1790, AHN. The mayor's speech and Jefferson's reply have been reprinted in *PTJ*, 16:224–25.

16. *PTJ*, 16:224–25.

17. Abigail Adams to Mary Smith Cranch, April 3, 1790, *AFC*, 9:40.

18. TJ, "Anas" *TJW*, 666.

19. Joanne B. Freeman, *Affairs of Honor: National Politics in the New Republic* (New Haven, CT: Yale University Press, 2002), 16–18.

20. William Maclay, *Journal of William Maclay, United States Senator from Pennsylvania*, ed. Edgar S. Maclay (New York: D. Appleton, 1890), 272.

21. Ibid., 310.

22. *Daily Advertiser*, March 29, 1790, AHN.

23. The slim cut of the man's coat by 1790 is described in several sources: Cunnington and Cunnington, *Handbook of English Costume*, 186, 192–97; Squire, *Dress and Society*, 128.

24. *JMB*, 1:748. Presumably the coat was a personal purchase. Even though his slave James Hemings was traveling with him, he usually noted "servants" clothing if a garment intended for a slave or someone in his hire.

25. *JMB*, 1:760.

26. William Peden, "A Book Peddler Invades Monticello," *William and Mary Quarterly* 6 (1949): 634–35.

27. TJ to JM, March 18, 1785, *PTJ*, 8:40.

28. Benjamin Rush, "Common Place Book," March 17, 1790, as quoted in John P. Kaminski, ed., *The Quotable Jefferson* (Princeton, NJ: Princeton University Press, 2006), 454.

29. Upon landing in Norfolk, November 24, 1789, TJ paid a tailor $17.33 for a blue broadcloth coat, *JMB*, 748; in route to New York, on March 9, 1790, he purchased a cloak from a Mr. Fitzhugh in Fredericksburg, Virginia, for $50.00, *JMB*, 753.

30. David Waldstreicher, "Why Thomas Jefferson and African Americans Wore Their Politics on Their Sleeves," in *Beyond the Founders: New Approaches to the Political History of the Early American Republic*, eds. Jeffery L. Pasley, Andrew W. Robertson, and David Waldstreicher (Chapel Hill: University of North Carolina Press, 2004), 79–97.

31. TJ, *The Complete Anas of Thomas Jefferson*, ed. Franklin B. Sawvel (New York: Round Table Press, 1903), 96–97.

32. TJ to JM, March 15, 1789, *PTJ*, 14:661.

33. JM to TJ, May 9 and 23, 1789, *PTJ*, 15:115, 147.

34. *Journal of the Senate*, Thursday, April 23, 1789, vol. 1, p. 16; *Journal of the House*, Friday, April 24, 1789, p. 20; *Annals of Congress*, House of Representatives, "On Titles," May 11, 1789, p. 331–37; from electronic facsimiles on A Century of Lawmaking for a New Nation: U.S. Congressional Documents and Debates, http://memory.loc.gov.

35. JM to TJ, May 9, 1789, *PTJ*, 15:115.

36. William Roosen, "Modern Diplomatic Ceremonial: A Systems Approach," *Journal of Modern History* 52, no. 3 (September 1980): 452–76; see especially pp. 465, 473.

37. JA, *Diary and Autobiography*, 4:130–31; initially discussed in chapter 1.

38. Maclay, *Journal*, 6. Freeman uses Maclay's *Journal* as a basis of chapter 1 of *Affairs of Honor* and offers an excellent discussion of the issues of the first Congress. See also Gordon Wood, *Empire of Liberty: A History of the Early Republic, 1789–1815* (Oxford, UK: Oxford University Press, 2009), esp. 62–65.

39. Maclay, *Journal*, 12, 82.

40. Ibid., 15, 4, 7, 42.

41. Rufus Wilmot Griswold, *Republican Court; or, American Society in the Days of Washington* (1867, reprinted New York: Haskell House, 1971), 165.

42. Crèvecoeur to Short, c. July 15, 1790; DLC: Short Papers, as cited in *PTJ*, 16:278.

43. TJ to Thomas Willing, February 23, 1798, *PTJ*, 30:132.

44. TJ to Martha Jefferson Randolph, April 4, 1790, *PTJ*, 16:300.

45. "Jefferson's Instructions for Procuring Household Goods," *PTJ*, 16:322; Trumbull to TJ, January 18, 1789, *PTJ*, 14:468; for a description of the "Crane Neck Chariot," see invoice from John Kemp to TJ, *PTJ*, 14:469–72.

46. Edward Thornton to James Burges, June 11, 1792, reprinted in S. W. Jackman, "A Young Englishman Reports on the New Nation: Edward Thornton to James Bland Burgess, 1791–1793," *William and Mary Quarterly* 3rd series, vol. 18, no. 1 (January 1961): 85–121; quote on 111; and Abigail Adams to Mary Smith Cranch, August 9, 1789, *AFC*, 8:399–400.

47. Abigail Adams to Cotton Tufts, January 17, 1790, *AFC*, 9:5.

48. *JMB*, 1:770.

49. TJ to Short, *PTJ*, 16:319.

50. Short to TJ, November 7, 1790, *PTJ*, 18:33–34; for a partial list of goods, see 35–39.

51. *JMB*, 2:815n.33. The advertisement appeared in Benjamin Franklin Bache's *General Advertiser* and ran January 7–February 2, 1791. On November 2, 1791, he hired John Mole, who remained in his employ only until January 15, 1792. Joseph, the French boy, joined him in March 1792.

52. C. W. Peale to Edmond Jennings, December 10, 1783, in Mrs. Burd Peale Collection, American Philosophical Society Library, B.P. 31.8b; David Ward, *Charles Willson Peale: Art and Selfhood in the Early Republic* (Berkeley: University of California Press, 2004), 83. For a discussion of Peale's collection, see Fanelli and Diethorn, *History of the Portrait Collection;* see also Fortune, "Portraits of Virtue."

53. C. W. Peale, "Address delivered by Charles W. Peale, to the Corporation and Citizens of Philadelphia," July 18, 1816, p. 17, America's Historical Imprints, series 2, no 38567, on subscription site www.readex.com.

54. C. W. Peale to President Reed of the Supreme Executive Council, as quoted in Charles Coleman Sellers, *Charles Willson Peale* (New York: Scribner's, 1969), 183–84.

55. Charles Willson Peale to TJ, undated, after December 3, 1791, *PTJ*, 22:372; and about December 13, 1791, *PTJ*, 22:400.

56. Fanelli and Diethorn, *History of the Portrait Collection,* 7.

57. Washington, "General Orders," June 18, 1780, *The Writings of George Washington,* ed. John C. Fitzpatrick (Washington, DC: United Sates Printing Office, 1931–44), 19:21–23.

58. Washington to James Mease, May 12, 1777, ibid., 8:55.

59. Nathaniel William Wraxall, *Historical Memoirs of My Own Time,* ed. Richard Askham (1815, reprinted London: Kegan Paul, 1904), 349.

60. Ibid., 338, 358.

61. TJ to Christian Baehr, August 14, 1791, and August 29, 1791, *PTJ*, 22:39.

62. *JMB*, 2:861.

63. Bush, *Life Portraits of Thomas Jefferson,* 20.

64. "The Exhibition of the Columbianum or American Academy of Painting, Sculpture, Architecture, Etc.," Philadelphia, 1795, in the American Antiquarian Society, AHN; referenced in Bush, *Life Portraits of Thomas Jefferson*, 20; and Cunningham, *Image of Thomas Jefferson*, 5.

65. Simon P. Newman, *Parades and the Politics of the Street: Festive Culture in the Early American Republic* (Philadelphia: University of Pennsylvania Press, 1997), 83–119.

66. Bush, *Life Portraits of Thomas Jefferson*, 15–17; "550 DL paiment for a marble bust of myself made by Ceracci," January 14, 1800, *JMB*, 1013.

67. Stein, *Worlds of Thomas Jefferson*, 219.

68. Sowerby, *Library of Thomas Jefferson*, 3:158.

69. TJ to James Monroe, July 10, 1791, *PTJ*, 20:297.

70. "Publicola No. 1," reprinted from the Boston *Columbian Centinel* in the New York *Journal & Patriotic Register*, July 6, 1791, vol. 45, issue 53, p. 210, AHN.

71. TJ to Benjamin Vaughan, May 11, 1791, *PTJ*, 20:391.

72. TJ to Edmund Pendleton, July 24, 1791, *PTJ*, 20:671.

73. TJ to Tom Paine, June 19, 1792, *PTJ*, 24:312.

74. Edward Thornton to James Burges, April 28, 1792, reprinted in Jackman, "Young Englishman Reports," 108.

75. Thornton to Burges, March 5, 1793, ibid., 121.

76. "Louis XVI & 3-21-1793," *Connecticut Gazette* (New London), March 21, 1793, AHN.

77. Merrill Peterson, *Thomas Jefferson and the New Nation: A Biography* (Oxford, UK: Oxford University Press, 1970), 479–81; Stanly Elkins and Eric McKitrick, *The Age of Federalism* (Oxford, UK: Oxford University Press, 1993), 308–12.

78. TJ to Benjamin Rush, January 16, 1811, *PTJ:RS*, 3:305.

79. Alexander Hamilton, "An American No. 1," in *Alexander Hamilton: Writings*, ed. Joanne B. Freeman (New York: Library of America, 2001), 755–59.

80. Alexander Hamilton "Cattalus No. III," *Gazette of the United States*, September 29, 1792, AHN.

81. *National Gazette* (Philadelphia), January 16, 1793, AHN.

82. Thornton to Burges, March 5, 1793, in Jackman, "Young Englishman Reports," 121.

83. Trumbull to TJ, November 26, 1789, *PTJ*, 15:561; "Letter of Introduction," enclosed in TJ to Trumbull, February 20, 1791, *PTJ*, 19:298; promoting Trumbull's engravings, TJ to Lafayette, November 21, 1791, *PTJ*, 22:313.

84. Trumbull to TJ, October 24, 1791, *PTJ*, 22:228.

85. TJ, "Catalogue of Paintings &c. at Monticello," c. 1809–15, Thomas Jefferson Papers, Special Collections, University of Virginia Library; transcribed in Stein, *Worlds of Thomas Jefferson*, appendix 2, p. 434.

86. Stein, *Worlds of Thomas Jefferson*, 173–75.

87. TJ to Edward Rutledge, June 24, 1797, *PTJ*, 29:456.

88. TJ to Francis Hopkinson, March 13, 1789, *PTJ*, 14:651.

89. TJ to Washington, September 9, 1792, *PTJ*, 24:358.

90. TJ, "Anas," *TJW*, 685.

91. Jackman, "Young Englishman Reports," 110.

92. TJ, "Anas," *TJW*, 685. For a discussion of political gossip, see Freeman, *Affairs of Honor*, 62–104.

93. Freeman, *Affairs of Honor*, 28. Freeman discusses the importance of reputation and gives examples of honor threatened among early national leaders.

94. JA to Abigail Adams, December 26, 1793, *AFC*, 9:484–85, 485n.3. Adams refers to *Histoire de Gil Blas de Santillane Par M. Le Sage*, 1769. There is a copy of this work in the Thomas Jefferson Foundation collection that is believed to have belonged to Martha Jefferson Randolph.

95. Hamilton, *Writings*, 846.

4. CAMPAIGNING FOR CHANGE

Portions of this chapter were published in "Thomas Jefferson and Creating an Image for a New Nation," in Nicolaisen and Spahn, *Cosmopolitanism and Nationhood in the Age of Jefferson*, 156–64.

1. *Gazette of the United States* (Philadelphia), March 3, 1797, AHN.

2. TJ to Elbidge Gerry, May 13, 1797, *PTJ*, 29:362.

3. See chronology in *JMB*, 1:li.

4. JM to James Monroe, February 26, 1796, *Papers of James Madison, Digital Edition*, ed. J. C. A. Stagg (Charlottesville: University of Virginia Rotunda Project, 2010), 16:233–34.

5. TJ to JM, April 27, 1795, *PTJ*, 28:338–39.

6. Ibid.

7. JM to James Monroe, September 29, 1796, *Papers of James Madison*, 16:403.

8. See a more detailed reference to this exchange in McDonald, *Confounding Father*, 47–49.

9. TJ to William Cocke, October 21, 1796, *PTJ*, 29:199.

10. TJ to JM, January 22, 1797; and TJ to Thomas Mann Randolph, January 22, 1797, *PTJ*, 29:271, 274.

11. *Gazette of the United States* (Philadelphia), March 3, 1797, AHN.

12. "Vales at Mr. Madison's," March 3, 1797, *JMB*, 2:954–55n.84; "Pd. Francis," March 13, 1797, *JMB*, 2:956.

13. Identified, *JMB*, 2:808n.7; first payment as vice president, July 2, 1797, *JMB*, 2:964.

14. His accounting records show only two payments to "Duffy, the taylor," on December 18, 1796, and April 17, 1797, *JMB*, 2:934, 958.

15. *Philadelphia Gazette*, March 6, 1797, AHN; for Adams's carriage, see JA to Abigail Adams, March 5, 1797, Founders Online, Adams Papers, https://founders.archives.gov/?q=%22John%20 Adams%22&s=1211311111&r=8904.

16. *JMB*, 976–1019.

17. TJ to Benjamin Rush, January 22, 1797, *PTJ*, 29:275.

18. On October 23, 1797, Jefferson recorded, "My daughter Maria married this day," *JMB*, 2:972.

19. Elkins and McKitrick, *Age of Federalism*, 498–512; Wood, *Empire of Liberty*, 205–6; John Keane, *Tom Paine: A Political Life* (New York: Little, Brown, 1995), 429–30.

20. Shipboard welcome, Gallatin to his wife, June 28, 1797, Malone, *Jefferson and His Times*, 3:324n.28; dinner for Monroe and toasts, *Philadelphia Gazette*, July 3, 1797, AHN.

21. TJ to Francis Hopkinson, March 13, 1789, *PTJ*, 14:651.

22. Linda Kerber, *Federalists in Dissent: Imagery and Ideology in Jeffersonian America* (Ithaca, NY: Cornell University Press, 1970), 8–9.

23. James Broussard, *The Southern Federalists, 1800–1816* (Baton Rouge: Louisiana State University Press, 1978), 74.

24. TJ to JM, September 21, 1795, *PTJ*, 28:475.

25. Hamilton to Edward Carrington, May 26, 1792, *The Papers of Alexander Hamilton, Digital Edition*, ed. Harold C. Syrett (Charlottesville: University of Virginia Rotunda Project, 2011), 11:439.

26. Hamilton to Lafayette, October 6, 1789, ibid., 5:425.

27. Hamilton to John Jay, November 26, 1775, ibid., 1:177.

28. "Phocion IV," *Gazette of the United States* (Philadelphia), October 19, 1796, AHN.

29. "To the Citizens of Maryland," *Federal Gazette* (Baltimore), October 25, 1796, AHN.

30. "Phocion IV," *Gazette of the United States* (Philadelphia), October 19, 1796, AHN.

31. Stein, *Worlds of Thomas Jefferson*, 267.

32. "Phocion I," *Gazette of the United States* (Charleston, SC), November 8, 1796, AHN.

33. "Phocion IV," *Gazette of the United States* (Philadelphia), October 19, 1796, AHN.

34. "Pretensions of Thomas Jefferson to the Presidency Examined," *Philadelphia Gazette*, August 30, 1800, AHN.

35. TJ, *Notes on the State of Virginia*, ed. William Peden (Chapel Hill: University of North Carolina Press, 1982), 159.

36. "Investigator for the Newport Mercury," *Newport Mercury* (Rhode Island), September 30, 1800, AHN.

37. "Phocion X," *Gazette of the United States* (Philadelphia), October 27, 1796, AHN.

38. "The Meddler," *Massachusetts Spy* (Boston), April 26, 1797; "The Jeffersoniad—No. III," *Columbian Centinel* (Boston), July 5, 1800, both in AHN.

39. *Philadelphia Gazette*, May 8, 1800, AHN.

40. "The Jeffersoniad—No. I," *Columbian Centinel* (Boston), July 9, 1800, AHN.

41. Steven Hess and Sandy Northrop, *Drawn and Quartered: The History of American Political Cartoons* (Montgomery, AL: Elliott & Clark Publishing, 1996), 38; Marcia Pointon, *Hanging the Head: Portraiture and Social Formation in Eighteenth-Century England"* (New Haven, CT: Yale University Press, 1993), 86, 94–95, 251n.35.

42. Diana Donald, *Age of Caricature: Satirical Prints in the Reign of George III* (New Haven, CT: Yale University Press, 1996), 19. Donald states that the actual extent of circulation of caricatures is hard to define.

43. "The Great Seal of the United States," US Department of State, Bureau of Public Affairs, Washington, DC, July 2003, www.state.gov/documents/organization/27807.pdf.

44. TJ to Mazzei, April 24, 1796, *PTJ*, 29:82.

45. "Editorial Note: Jefferson's Letter to Philip Mazzei," *PTJ*, 29:73–74.

46. TJ to JM, August 3, 1797, *PTJ*, 29:489.

47. John Marshall to Alexander Hamilton, January 1, 1801, cited in Kaminski, *Quotable Jefferson*, 467.

48. TJ to Bishop James Madison, January 31, 1800, *PTJ*, 31:350–51; Sowerby, *Library of Thomas Jefferson*, 3:24–25.

49. TJ to Thomas Law, June 13, 1814, *PTJ:RS*, 7:414–15; TJ library, Sowerby, *Library of Thomas Jefferson*, 2:4–5.

50. "Phocion X," *Gazette of the United States* (Philadelphia), October 27, 1796, AHN.

51. Discussed in Malone, *Jefferson and His Times*, 3:338–39.

52. "Extract from a publication in the *Connecticut Courant,* of the 24th inst. undersigned *Gustavus,"* reprinted in the *Albany Centinel* (New York), July 28, 1797, AHN.

53. Rozbicki, *Complete Colonial Gentleman,* 51–52.

54. TJ to David Rittenhouse, *PTJ,* 25:31.

55. Ibid., editor's note.

56. Maclay, *Journal,* 311, 397.

57. Ribeiro, *Fashion in the French Revolution,* 54, 67, citing Madame Trussand's *Memoirs and Reminiscences of France,* ed. F. Hervé (London, 1838), 177.

58. Wraxall, *Historical Memoirs,* 83–84.

59. Cunnington and Cunnington, *Handbook of English Costume,* 225.

60. *Greenleaf's New York Journal,* June 9, 1798, p. 3, AHN.

61. "Communication," *Daily Advertiser* (New York), March 27, 1800, AHN.

62. "Extract from a Publication in the *Connecticut Currant,"* reprinted in the *Albany Centinel,* July 28, 1797, AHN.

63. TJ to JA, November 13, 1787, *PTJ,* 12:350; JA to TJ, December 6, 1787, *PTJ,* 12:396.

64. TJ to Francis Hopkinson, March 13, 1789, *PTJ,* 14:650.

65. Hamilton, "An American No. 1," August 4, 1792, *Hamilton: Writings,* 755–59.

66. Hamilton, "Tully No. III," August 28, 1794, ibid., 830–32.

67. "A Gentleman at Newbarn, North Carolina," *City Gazette* (Charleston, SC), November 3, 1796, AHN.

68. Newman, *Parades and Politics,* 88–91.

69. David Waldstreicher, *In the Midst of Perpetual Fetes: The Making of American Nationalism, 1776–1820* (Chapel Hill: University of North Carolina Press, 1997), 206; David Armitage, *The Declaration of Independence: A Global History* (Cambridge, MA: Harvard University Press, 2007), 92.

70. Newman, *Parades and Politics,* 93; *Independent Chronicle* (Boston), May 26–29, 1800; *Constitutional Telegraph,* May 17, 1800, both on AHN.

71. Elijah Griffiths to TJ, July 8, 1800, *PTJ,* 32:45.

72. Newman, *Parades and Politics,* 112–13, citing the *Aurora* (Philadelphia), July 8, 1800.

73. See Bush, *Life Portraits of Thomas Jefferson.* I am grateful to Barbara Oberg, editor emeritus of *The Papers of Thomas Jefferson,* for calling to my attention that Jefferson sat for four artists during this period.

74. Cunningham, *Image of Thomas Jefferson,* 23.

75. Ellen G. Miles, "George Washington (The Lansdowne Portrait)," in Carrie Rebora Barratt and Ellen G. Miles, *Gilbert Stuart* (New Haven, CT: Yale University Press, 2005), 174.

76. Roche, *Culture of Clothing,* 283–85, and Roche citing Louis-Sébastien Mercier, *Tableau de Paris,* 285.

77. Baldesar Castiglione, *The Book of the Courtier* [1528], trans. George Bull (New York: Penguin, 1967), 134–35.

78. Anne Hollander, *Seeing through Clothes* (New York: Viking, 1978), 367–68, 375; Millia Davenport, *The Book of Costume* (New York: Crown Publishers, 1948), 609–30.

79. Arthur Young, *Travels in France during the Years 1787, 1788, 1789,* intro. M. Bethan-Edwards (London, 1889), 103–5.

80. Ribeiro, *Fashion in the French Revolution*, 45–46.

81. TJ to David Humphreys, Paris, March 18, 1789, *PTJ*, 14:677.

82. Viccy Coltman, *Fabricating the Antique: Neoclassicism in Britain, 1760–1800* (Chicago: University of Chicago Press, 2006), 1–16.

83. Ludmila Kybalová, Olga Herbenová, and Milena Lamarová, *Pictorial Encyclopedia of Fashion*, trans. Claudia Rosoux (London: Hamlyn, 1968), 324; Ribeiro, *Fashion in the French Revolution*, 68.

84. Ribeiro, *Fashion in the French Revolution*, 68.

85. Wraxall, *Historical Memoirs*, 83–84.

86. Bush, *Life Portraits of Thomas Jefferson*, 35–36.

87. Cunningham, *Image of Thomas Jefferson*, 11–21; Bush, *Life Portraits of Thomas Jefferson*, 35–36, 43–44.

88. TJ to Henry Dearborn, July 5, 1819, Thomas Jefferson Papers, LC.

89. Bush, *Life Portraits of Thomas Jefferson*, 45–47, 57. Bush agrees with the theory that Stuart sent the portrait to England to be engraved and it was lost. Other art historians question this theory. See a discussion of the lost portrait and of the final Stuart portrait of Jefferson in Barrett and Miles, *Gilbert Stuart*, 281–83.

90. *American Citizen* (New York), October 16, 1800, italics in original, AHN.

91. Congressman Daniel Webster visited Jefferson at Monticello in 1824 and described him wearing "shoes of the kind that bear his name" and "a common round hat." Webster, *Private Correspondence*, 364.

92. Valerie Cumming, C. Willitt Cunnington, and Phillis Cunnington, *The Dictionary of Fashion History* (reprinted, Oxford, UK: A&C Black, 1976), 176; Ribeiro, *Fashion in the French Revolution*, 122.

93. Charles Carroll to Hamilton, April 18, 1800, Alexander Hamilton papers, LC.

5. A NEW PRESIDENTIAL PROFILE

1. Manasseh Cutler, *Life, Journals and Correspondence of Rev. Manasseh Cutler,* ed. William P. Cutler and Julia Perkins Cutler (Cincinnati, OH: R. Clarke & Co., 1888; reprinted 2010), 2:43–64; direct quotes found on 43, 64. Emphasis on "new order of things" was Cutler's; TJ to James Monroe, April 13, 1800, *PTJ*, 31:499.

2. For an account of Washington City at the time of Jefferson's inauguration, see Catherine Allgor, *Parlor Politics: In Which the Ladies of Washington Help Build a City and a Government* (Charlottesville: University of Virginia Press, 2000), 4–17. A description of the inauguration appears in the *National Intelligencer* (Washington, DC), March 6, 1801; and the *Alexandria Times* (Virginia), March 6, 1801, AHN.

3. Edward Thornton had served in various posts within the British ministry since 1791. He was appointed chargé d'affaires in 1800 and held this post until the arrival of Anthony Merry. For further details of his appointments, see *PTJ*, 33:190.

4. Thornton to Lord Grenville, Foreign Secretary, March 4, 1801, as reprinted in Henry Adams, *History of the United States of America during the Administrations of Thomas Jefferson* [1889] (reprinted, New York: Library Classics, 1986), 134.

5. *National Intelligencer* (Washington, DC), March 6, 1801, AHN.

6. *Aurora* (Philadelphia), February 26 and 27, 1801, and February 23, 1801, both in Cunningham, *Image of Thomas Jefferson*, 56, 58.

7. For examples, see *Federal Gazette* (Philadelphia), April 21, 1790; *Cumberland Gazette* (Portland, ME), May 31, 1790; *General Advertiser* (Philadelphia), January 19, 1792. Reference to Jefferson as a "Man of the People," found in *Philadelphia Gazette*, March 3, 1797. All can be viewed on AHN.

8. Cunningham, *Image of Thomas Jefferson*, 56. This work has proved extremely thorough and exact in recording the sequence of advertising and publication dates and has been a valuable source of background data surrounding these two prints.

9. George Helmbold to TJ, April 3, 1801, *PTJ*, 33:529.

10. Cunningham, *Image of Thomas Jefferson*, 59.

11. *Aurora* (Philadelphia), February 23, 1801, cited in ibid., 57.

12. Mantle Fielding, "David Edwin, Engraver," *Pennsylvania Magazine of History and Biography* 29, no. 1 (1905): 82. Unfortunately, there is no mention of the Jefferson print in this article.

13. "First Inaugural Address," final version, *PTJ*, 33:150.

14. TJ to JM, September 20, 1785, *PTJ*, 8:534–36.

15. These elements as they relate to state and aristocratic portraiture are discussed in many sources: see, for example, Christopher Lloyd, "Portraits of Sovereigns and Heads of State," in *Citizens and Kings: Portraits in the Age of Revolution, 1760–1830*, exhibition catalogue, eds. Norman Rosenthal and Mary Anne Stevens (London: Royal Academy of Arts, 2007), 60–62; Desmond Shawe-Taylor, *The Georgians: Eighteenth-Century Portraiture and Society* (London: Barrie & Jenkins, 1990), 83; and Andrew Wilton, *The Swagger Portrait: Grand Manner Portraiture in Britain from Van Dyck to Augustus John, 1630–1930* (London: Tate Gallery Publications, 1992), 19–23.

16. For a detailed discussion of these two portraits, gifts from France to the United States, see T. Lawrence Larkin, "A 'Gift' Strategically Solicited and Magnanimously Conferred: The American Congress, the French Monarchy, and the State Portraits of Louis XVI and Marie-Antoinette," *Winterthur Portfolio* 44, no. 1 (Spring 2010): 31–76.

17. Larkin identifies the image in the background of the Louis XVI portrait (ibid., 52–53). The close similarities are obvious when one compares the Bervic engraving of Louis XVI with Edwin's *Jefferson*, and they are noted in Noble Cunningham, *Popular Images of the Presidency: From Washington to Lincoln* (Columbia: University of Missouri Press, 1991), 139.

18. There is an "electric machine" dated from c. 1775–1800 in the American Philosophical Society collection, catalogue #58.39. As its notations for "high" and "low" are in French, it is believed to be of French origin and could possibly have been owned by Franklin—or it could be the one presented to the APS in 1785 by M. Noel. An image and information on this machine can be accessed through http://amphilsoc.pastperfectonline.com. Cunningham, in *Image of Thomas Jefferson*, refers to this machine as a "static electrical machine" (67) and cites Day's advertisement (58).

19. "First Inaugural Address," *PTJ*, 33:149.

20. *Aurora*, September 8, 1800, in Cunningham, *Image of Thomas Jefferson*, 55. For a discussion of the print in America, see Margaretta Lovell, *Art in a Season of Revolution: Printers, Artisans, and Patrons in Early America* (Philadelphia: University of Pennsylvania Press, 2005), 15–21.

21. Barratt and Miles, *Gilbert Stuart*, 166–75.

22. Flügel, *Psychology of Clothes,* 34.

23. Abigail Adams to Mary Smith Cranch, August 9, 1789, *AFC,* 8:397–400.

24. TJ to Tadeusz Kosciuszko, April 2, 1802, *PTJ,* 37:168.

25. Barratt and Miles, *Gilbert Stuart,* 172.

26. The first quote is from Bernard Mayo, "A Peppercorn for Mr. Jefferson," *Virginia Quarterly Review* 19 (Spring 1943): 224. The second quote is from the *Commercial Advertiser* (New York), July 21, 1802, AHN.

27. John Minchin invoice, Henry E. Huntington Library, San Marino, CA, microfilm, "Jefferson Accounts 1797–1824"; John Minichin identified in *JMB,* 2:984n.59; payment to Minichin for shoestrings, *JMB,* 2:1059; payment to Minchin for boots, *JMB,* 2:1064.

28. Robert Troup to Rufus King, April 9, 1802, in Kaminski, *Quotable Jefferson,* 473.

29. William Plumer to Jeremiah Smith, December 9, 1802, "William Plumer's Letterbook," as cited in Lynn W. Turner, *William Plumer of New Hampshire* (Chapel Hill: University of North Carolina Press, 1962), 94–95.

30. As cited in Ribeiro, *The Art of Dress: Fashion in England and France, 1750–1820* (New Haven, CT: Yale University Press, 1995), 29.

31. Jackman, "Young Englishman Reports," 110.

32. Anthony Merry's account as it was recorded by Josiah Quincy and printed in Edmund Quincy, *Life of Josiah Quincy* (Boston, 1868), 92–93.

33. Samuel Taggart, "Letters of Samuel Taggart," in *Proceedings of the American Antiquarian Society* 33, part 1 (Worcester, MA: American Antiquarian Society, 1924), 113. All of Taggart's letters were to the Reverend John Taylor.

34. Rosalie Stier Calvert, *Mistress of Riversdale: The Plantation: Letters of Rosalie Stier Calvert, 1795–1821,* ed. Margaret Law Callcott (Baltimore: Johns Hopkins University Press, 1991), 72.

35. JM to James Monroe, January 19, 1804, *Papers of James Madison: Secretary of State Series,* ed. Robert J. Brugger et al. (Charlottesville: University of Virginia Press, 1986–), 6:361–66. See also Adams, *History of the United States,* 551–53; Malone, *Jefferson and His Times,* 4:378–81.

36. *TJW,* 705.

37. Stanley Lane-Poole, *Life of the Right Honourable Stratford Canning, Viscount Stratford de Redcliffe* (London, 1888), 1:315–16.

38. JM to Monroe, January 19, 1804, *Papers of James Madison, Digital Edition,* 6:362; Foster, *Jeffersonian America,* 54.

39. Diana de Marly, *Fashion for Men: An Illustrated History* (New York: Holmes & Meier, 1985), 65; and Brandon Brame Fortune with Deborah J. Warner, *Franklin and His Friends: Portraying the Man of Science in Eighteenth-Century America* (Washington, DC: Smithsonian Institution Press, 1999), 51–52.

40. For a biography of Anthony Merry, see Malcolm Lester, *Anthony Merry "Redivivus": A Reappraisal of the British Minister to the United States, 1803–6* (Charlottesville: University of Virginia Press, 1978). Lester has achieved a concise but detailed account of this British statesman about whom relatively little has been written.

41. "Memorandum of Conversation between Philemon Dickinson and George Hammond," *PTJ,* 23:345.

42. TJ to James Monroe, January 8, 1804, Thomas Jefferson papers, LC.

43. Ibid.

44. JM to James Monroe, February 16, 1804, *Papers of James Madison, Digital Edition*, 6:485.

45. James Monroe to JM, March 3, 1804, ibid., 6:538; and JM to TJ, March 15, 1804, Thomas Jefferson papers, LC.

46. *Papers of James Madison, Digital Edition*, 6:539.

47. This period in American diplomacy is discussed in Wood, *Empire of Liberty*, 620–58.

48. Thomas Moore to "His Mother," June 13, 1804, in Moore, *Memoirs, Journal, and Correspondence of Thomas Moore*, ed. John Russell (London, 1853), 1:162.

49. Foster, *Jeffersonian America*, 9–10; bio, ix–x.

50. Ibid., 10.

51. Ibid., 8–10.

52. Ibid., 10, 50, 146.

53. Ibid., 6–7, 9–12, 50.

54. William Plumer, *William Plumer's Memorandum and Proceedings in the United States Senate, 1803–1807*, ed. Everett Somerville Brown (New York: Macmillan, 1923), 179, 193.

55. William Dunlap, *Diary of William Dunlap*, ed. Dorothy C. Barch (New York: New York Historical Society, 1930), 2:388.

56. C. W. Peale, "Diary 20, Part 3: A Journey to Baltimore and Washington, D.C., 27 December 1804–3 February 1805," entry for January 9, *Selected Papers of Charles Willson Peale and His Family*, ed. Lillian B. Miller et al. (New Haven, CT: Yale University Press, 1983–2000), 2: part 2, 785; Jefferson's Presidential Dinner Lists, original, Massachusetts Historical Society, Boston; facsimile copy in Jefferson Library, Thomas Jefferson Foundation, Special Collections.

57. C. W. Peale, *Selected Papers*, 2: part 2, 786.

58. C. W. Peale to Raphaelle, Rubens, and Sophonisba Peale, January 19 and 30, 1805, ibid., 793–94, 797.

59. C. W. Peale to Rubens and Sophonisba Peale, January 19, 1805, ibid., 785, 794.

60. TJ to William Dunbar, January 12, 1801, *PTJ*, 32:448.

61. See Fanelli and Diethorn, *History of the Portrait Collection*, for a reconstruction and catalogue of portraits known to have been part of the Peale gallery, later the Philadelphia Museum. Most subjects in the portraits wear uniforms or suits, but none appear in fur. This is not a totally comprehensive reconstruction of Peale's collection; however, it is believed representative.

62. Margaret Bayard Smith, "The Fur Cloak," Margaret Bayard Smith papers, LC, container 5, reel 2.

63. *Federal Gazette* (Baltimore), April 8, 1797. This same story appeared in newspapers from New York, New Jersey, New Hampshire, Rhode Island, and elsewhere. AHN.

64. Kosciuszko to TJ, before May 5, 1798, *PTJ*, 30:331.

65. Smith, "The Fur Cloak," Margaret Bayard Smith papers, LC, container 5, reel 2.

66. TJ to Martha Jefferson Randolph, December 27, 1798, *PTJ*, 30:605; TJ to Martha Jefferson Randolph, November 4, 1815, in Edwin M. Betts and James A. Bear, eds., *The Family Letters of Thomas Jefferson* (Charlottesville: University of Virginia Press, 1986), 411.

67. Jane Hollins Randolph to Thomas Jefferson Randolph, January 1837, Edgehill-Randolph Collection, University of Virginia Library, Special Collections.

68. Donald Jackson, ed., *Letters of the Lewis and Clark Expedition, with Related Documents, 1783–1854* (Urbana: University of Illinois Press, 1978), 1:253–54.

69. Ibid.

70. For complete discussion of the Duplessis portrait of Franklin in the fur collar and its copies, see Charles Coleman Sellers, *Franklin in Portraiture*, 247–64. Neil Harris references the popularity of the portrait and its support of the American cause in France in *The Artist in American Society: The Formative Years, 1790–1860* (New York: George Braziller, 1966), 18.

71. George Ticknor, as cited in Merril D. Peterson, ed., *Visitors to Monticello* (Charlottesville: University of Virginia Press, 1989), 62.

72. TJ to Ferdinand Grand, April 23, 1790, *PTJ*, 16:369. Jefferson used similar words when referring to Franklin in 1798; see TJ to Samuel Smith, August 22, 1798, *PTJ*, 30:484.

73. "Confabulation between a Federalist & a Democrat" appeared in the *Alexandria Expositor* (Virginia), February 16, 1804. *Spirit of the Press* (Philadelphia), December 8, 1806, printed an attack on newly elected republican representative Alexander Ogle and offered to send him a pair of red breeches and enough red cloth to "furnish him with a pair of *rosy organs*." Both on AHN.

74. "Reminiscences of New York," *The Talisman* (New York: 1828–1830), 3:340.

75. George Tucker, *The Life of Thomas Jefferson* (Philadelphia: Carey, Lea & Blanchard, 1837), 2:506.

76. Thomas Jefferson Randolph, "Memoirs of Thomas Jefferson Randolph," University of Virginia Library, Special Collections, MS 5454-c.

77. TJ to Christian Baehr, November 14, 1792, *PTJ*, 24:617.

78. *New York Evening Post*, March 4, 1809, AHN.

79. James Kelly and B. S. Lovell, "Thomas Jefferson: His Friends and Foes," in "'In the Modest Garb of Pure Republicanism': Thomas Jefferson as Reformer and Architect," special issue, *Virginia Magazine of History and Biography* 101, no. 1 (January 1993): 133–57. The reference to "Philosophical Cock" is on page 149.

80. Michael Durey, *With the Hammer of Truth: James Thomson Callender and America's Early National Heroes* (Charlottesville: University of Virginia Press, 1990), 126–27, 142–46, 157–59.

81. John Moore, *A Journal during a residence in France from the beginning of August to the middle of December 1792* (London, 1793), 2:429–30; and *A View of the Causes and Progress of the French Revolution* (London, 1795), 1:150.

82. Flügel, *Psychology of Clothes*, 111–12.

83. For discussion of issues surrounding proposed parliamentary changes and the unrest following the American war and the war with France, see Linda Colley, *Britons: Forging the Nation 1707–1837* (New Haven, CT: Yale University Press, 1992), esp. 149–55.

84. Wraxall, *Historical Memoirs*, 1:99.

85. TJ to Monroe, May 4, 1806, Thomas Jefferson papers, LC.

86. Lester, *Anthony Merry*, 116.

87. For Fox as a "Man of the People," see Colley, *Britons*, 246. For Fox as foreign secretary and regarding "the Ministry of All the Talents," see John Drinkwater, *Charles James Fox* (New York: Ernest Benn, 1928), 362–66.

88. Bush, *Life Portraits of Thomas Jefferson*, 40, 55–56.

6. BUT ALWAYS THE COSMOPOLITAN GENTLEMAN

1. Foster, *Jeffersonian America*, 15.

2. Mahlon Dickerson to Silas Dickerson, April 21, 1802, in Jackson, *Letters of the Lewis and Clark Expedition*, 2:677.

3. TJ to Benjamin Rush, January 16, 1811, *PTJ:RS*, 3:304; TJ uses term "safe depository" in letters to John Vanmetre, September 4, 1800, *PTJ*, 32:126, and to James Bowdoin, March 8, 1801, *PTJ*, 33:213. This book follows the guidelines established by *The Papers of Thomas Jefferson* and *The Papers of Thomas Jefferson: Retirement Series* in adhering to Jefferson's idiosyncrasies. In most cases he did not capitalize the beginnings of sentences, and he consistently used "it's" rather than "its."

4. Plumer, *Proceedings in the US Senate*, 205, 193.

5. Ibid., 211–12.

6. Ibid., italics are Plumer's emphasis.

7. Merry Ellen Scofield, "'The Fatigues of His Table: The Politics of Presidential Dining during the Jefferson Administration," *Journal of the Early Republic* 26, no. 3 (Fall 2006): 453, 457, 468.

8. Margaret Bayard Smith, *First Forty Years of Washington Society in the Family Letters of Margaret Bayard Smith*, ed. Gaillard Hunt (New York: Scribner's Sons, 1906), 389, 391. This edition can be viewed electronically at http://memory.loc.gov/ammem/index.html.

9. TJ to David R Williams, January 31, 1806, quoted in Charles T. Cullen, "Jefferson's White House Dinner Guests," *White House History* 17 (Winter 2006): 29. Cullen's essay is an excellent resource on Jefferson's presidential dinners. See also Scofield, "Fatigues of His Table."

10. Plumer, *Proceedings in the US Senate*, 212; Taggart, "Letters," 140.

11. Louisa Catherine Adams, "Autobiographical Sketches," quoted in Malone, *Jefferson and His Times*, 4:375.

12. Smith, *Washington Society*, 391–92. Jefferson's Washington household is discussed in Lucia Stanton, "'A Well-Ordered Household': Domestic Servants in Jefferson's White House," *White House History* 17 (Winter 2006): 5–23.

13. TJ to Martha Jefferson Randolph, October 7, 1804, in Betts and Bear, *Family Letters*, 262.

14. See Cullen, "Jefferson's Dinner Guests," and Scofield, "Fatigues of His Table," for discussions of the number and variety of dinner guests.

15. Smith, *Washington Society*, 397–98.

16. Plumer, *Proceedings in the US Senate*, 363–64.

17. Foster, *Jeffersonian America*, 22, 23.

18. Plumer, *Proceedings in the US Senate*, 550–51.

19. Foster, *Jeffersonian America*, 9.

20. Smith, *Washington Society*, 392.

21. Margaret Bayard Smith, "Mr. Jefferson's Last Visit," October 12 [1808], *Commonplace Book*, on microfilm, Jefferson Library, Thomas Jefferson Foundation, Special Collections, Charlottesville, VA.

22. "Letter I to Thomas Jefferson, Vice President of the United States," July 5, 1800, *Gazette of the United States* (Philadelphia), AHN.

23. "A Subscriber: General Assemble of Virginia," October 21, 1796, ibid.

24. "Death Threat," December 6, 1804, Thomas Jefferson papers, LC.

25. "Conrad Hanse's Account," for chariot and harness, *PTJ*, 35:181–82.

26. TJ to John Wayles Eppes, April 25, 1801, *PTJ*, 33:641.

27. TJ to Samuel H. Smith, August 15, 1813, *PTJ:RS*, 6:399.

28. Smith, *Washington Society*, 393.

29. Per dates in Betts and Bear, *Family Letters*, 284n.1; and *JMB*, 2:1084n.90, 1166n.98.

30. Thomas Jefferson Randolph, "Memoirs of Thomas Jefferson Randolph," University of Virginia Library, Special Collections, MS 5454-c.

31. Taggert to John Taylor, January 13, 1804, "Letters," 125.

32. For an account of the Hamilton-Burr duel, see Freeman, *Affairs of Honor*, chapter 4.

33. Taggart to John Taylor, November 17, 1804, "Letters," 134.

34. *JMB*, 2:1067–68n.48.

35. Plumer, *Proceedings of the US Senate*, 200.

36. James Bowdoin to TJ, February 24, 1801, *PTJ*, 33:55.

37. Identification of Bowdoin as a "republican" in Levi Lincoln to TJ, April 16, 1801, *PTJ*, 33:596.

38. For a discussion of the dispute over East and West Florida, see Wood, *Empire of Liberty*, 374–75.

39. James Bowdoin to Henry Dearborn, March 25, 1805, cited in Marvin Sadik, *Colonial and Federal Portraits at Bowdoin College* (Brunswick, ME: Bowdoin College, 1966), 155; and Barratt and Miles, *Gilbert Stuart*, 273.

40. Stuart's career is well documented in Barratt and Miles, *Gilbert Stuart*; Dorinda Evans, *The Genius of Gilbert Stuart* (Princeton, NJ: Princeton University Press, 1999); and Richard McLanathan, *Gilbert Stuart* (New York: Harry N. Abrams, 1986).

41. Richard H. Saunders and Ellen G. Miles, *American Colonial Portraits, 1700–1776* (Washington, DC: Smithsonian Institution Press, 1987), 20–21.

42. These portraits were mentioned by Edward Thornton; see Jackman, "Young Englishman Reports," 121.

43. Thomas Jefferson's Presidential Dinner Lists, December 5, 1804–March 6, 1809, Thomas Jefferson Papers, LC; facsimile copy in Jefferson Library, Thomas Jefferson Foundation, Special Collections, Charlottesville, VA.

44. *JMB*, 2:1018.

45. TJ to Henry Dearborn, July 5, 1819, Thomas Jefferson Papers, LC; facsimile copy Jefferson Library, Thomas Jefferson Foundation, Special Collections, Charlottesville, VA.

46. Dearborn to Thomas Winthrop, June 27, 1805, cited in Sadik, *Portraits at Bowdoin College*, 135.

47. Barratt and Miles, *Gilbert Stuart*, 166–75.

48. Rosenthal and Stevens, *Citizens and Kings*, 60.

49. Barratt and Miles, *Gilbert Stuart*, 240.

50. Katherine Watson, ed., *Legacy of James Bowdoin III* (Brunswick, ME: Bowdoin College, 1994), 68. This work provides an excellent overview of Bowdoin's life, career, and art collection.

51. Bush, *Life Portraits of Thomas Jefferson*, 59.

52. Cunningham, *Image of Thomas Jefferson*, 88.

53. Ibid., 87; Bush, *Life Portraits of Thomas Jefferson*, 59.

54. Bush, *Life Portraits of Thomas Jefferson*, 55–56.

55. *JMB*, 2:1156; TJ to Gilbert Stuart, June 18, 1805, cited in Charles H. Hart, "Life Portraits of Thomas Jefferson," *McClure's Magazine* 11 (1898): 48.

56. TJ to Henry Dearborn, July 5, 1819, Thomas Jefferson Papers, LC; "deemed the best," TJ to Horatio Spafford, February 21, 1815, *PTJ:RS*, 8:281.

57. Report from Orland Campbell to James A. Bear Jr., curator, Thomas Jefferson Foundation, December 16, 1956, Thomas Jefferson Foundation, Special Collections, Charlottesville, VA.

58. C. W. Peale to Raphaelle, Rubens, and Sophonisba Peale, January 19 and 30, 1805, *Select Papers of Charles Willson Peale*, 2: part 2, 793–94.

59. Lloyd and Sloan, *The Intimate Portrait*, 165.

60. Desmond Shawe-Taylor, *Genial Company: The Theme of Genius in Eighteenth-Century British Portraiture* (Nottingham, UK: University Art Gallery, 1987) 53.

61. Pointon, *Hanging the Head*, 95.

62. For a full discussion of Jefferson medals, see Cunningham, *Image of Thomas Jefferson*, 71–78.

63. TJ to Mary Jefferson Eppes, March 29, 1802, in Betts and Bear, *Family Letters*, 220–21; and TJ to Martha Jefferson Randolph, April 3, 1802, ibid.

64. Cunningham, *Image of Thomas Jefferson*, 71–73.

65. For a discussion of the development of the profile portrait in the United States, see Ellen G. Miles, *Saint-Mémin and the Neoclassical Profile Portrait in America* (Washington, DC: Smithsonian Institution Press, 1994), 47–56.

66. Ann Uhry Abrams, *The Valiant Hero: Benjamin West and Grand-Style History Painting* (Washington, DC: Smithsonian Institution Press, 1985), 170–80; Eleanor Davidson Berman, *Thomas Jefferson among the Arts: An Essay in Early American Esthetics* (New York: Philosophical Library, 1947), 84; Solkin, *Painting for Money*, 3–13. Solkin uses as an example the Closterman portrait *The 3rd Earl of Shaftesbury and the Hon. Maurice Ashley-Cooper*, in which they are depicted in classical dress.

67. Plumer, *Proceedings in the US Senate*, 193.

68. General James Wilkinson, 1801, as quoted in Miles, *Saint-Mémin*, 86.

69. Miles, *Saint-Mémin*, 130.

70. John Barnes to TJ, September 7, 1801, *PTJ*, 35:225; Barnes to TJ, September 14, 1801, *PTJ*, 35:282; Barnes to TJ, September 21, 1801, *PTJ*, 35:329.

71. William Russell Birch, "Autobiography," typescript copy in Jefferson Library, Special Collections, Thomas Jefferson Foundation at Monticello.

72. Henry Pickering, quoting Stuart, 1817, cited in Barratt and Miles, *Gilbert Stuart*, 280.

73. Noble Cunningham, "The Diary of Frances Few 1808–1809," *Journal of Southern History* 29, no. 3 (August 1963): 350–51.

74. TJ to James Bowdoin, March 8, 1801, *PTJ*, 33:213.

75. Foster, *Jeffersonian America*, 9, 156.

7. CONTEMPLATING LEGACY

1. JA to TJ, *Adams-Jefferson Letters*, 284–85.

2. JA to TJ, *PTJ:RS*, 6:297.

3. *PTJ:RS*, 6:297.

4. *PTJ:RS*, 6:50–52; John Marshall, *The Life of George Washington*, ed. Robert Faulkner and Paul Cerrese (Indianapolis, IN: Liberty Fund, 2000), xii, xv, 366. TJ to JA, August 10, 1815, *PTJ:RS*, 8:656–58, quote at 657.

5. Cogliano, *Jefferson: Reputation and Legacy*, 50–52, 62–65; Kranish, *Flight from Monticello*.

6. Cogliano, *Jefferson: Reputation and Legacy*, 50–65; Sam W. Haynes, *Unfinished Revolution: The Early American Republic in a British World* (Charlottesville: University of Virginia Press, 2010), 106–12.

7. Cogliano, *Jefferson: Reputation and Legacy,* 26, 36, 49.

8. For an excellent study of Jefferson at Monticello and among his family, see Gordon-Reed and Onuf, *"Most Blessed of the Patriarchs."*

9. Trumbull to TJ, December 26, 1816, *PTJ:RS,* 10:615.

10. Trumbull, *Autobiography,* 255; Jaffe, *Trumbull: Patriot-Artist,* 234–35. In his autobiography, Trumbull makes no mention of writing Jefferson and simply states that he dealt with Congress, with the choice of subjects left to President Madison. *Autobiography,* 257.

11. Gore to Rufus King, *Life and Correspondence of Rufus King,* 6:47–48, cited in Jaffe, *Trumbull: Patriot-Artist,* 235.

12. Trumbull's break with Jefferson is discussed in chapter 3.

13. Trumbull to TJ, *PTJ:RS,* 10:615–16.

14. TJ to Trumbull, January 10, 1817, *PTJ:RS,* 10:654–55; TJ to James Monroe, January 10, 1817, *PTJ:RS,* 10:653–54.

15. Harris, *Artist in American Society,* especially chapter 2, "Perils of Vision: Art, Luxury and Republicanism," which includes a thorough discussion of these issues in the American republic.

16. JA to Trumbull, July 1, 1817, quoted in Trumbull, *Autobiography,* 310–11.

17. Jaffe, *Trumbull: Patriot-Artist,* 236.

18. Trumbull to TJ, March 3, 1817, *PTJ:RS,* 11:166–67; Jaffe, *Trumbull: Patriot-Artist,* 237.

19. Trumbull to TJ, October 23, 1818, *PTJ:RS,* 13:328.

20. Jaffe, *Trumbull: Patriot-Artist,* 246–48.

21. Ibid., 241–45; visit from Adams, Trumbull, *Autobiography,* 314.

22. JA to TJ, December 8, 1818, *PTJ:RS,* 13:471–72.

23. John Quincy Adams, *Memoirs of John Quincy Adams,* ed. Charles Francis Adams (Philadelphia: J. B. Lippincott, 1874–77), 4:4, cited in Trumbull, *Autobiography,* 313.

24. Jaffe, *Trumbull: Patriot-Artist,* 238.

25. Ibid., 238–39.

26. TJ to Benjamin Harrison, December 24, 1783, *PTJ,* 6:419.

27. Trumbull to TJ, June 28, 1823, Thomas Jefferson papers, LC.

28. Trumbull to JM, October 1, 1823, cited in Cooper, *Trumbull: Hand and Spirit,* 89.

29. James Monroe, *Papers of James Monroe,* ed. Daniel Preston (Westport, CT: Greenwood Press, 2003–9), 1:124, 128, 444; J. Q. Adams, *Memoirs,* 5:317. Monroe was inaugurated for a second term on Monday, March 5, 1821, rather than the traditional March 4. It could be argued that Andrew Jackson was a participant in the American Revolution, as at age thirteen he did join in irregular fighting against the British and was captured; however, his public reputation was linked to the next war with Britain, the War of 1812; see Sean Wilentz, *The Rise of American Democracy: Jefferson to Lincoln* (New York: Norton, 2005), 168–70.

30. Richard Rush to Charles Jared Ingersoll, October 9, 1816, reprinted in Peterson, *Visitors to Monticello,* 73.

31. Martha Jefferson Randolph to Ellen Coolidge, September 18, 1825; and Cornelia Randolph to Ellen Coolidge, August 3, 1825, files of *PTJ:RS,* unpublished letters.

32. Kate Haulman, *The Politics of Fashion in Eighteenth-Century America* (Chapel Hill: University of North Carolina Press, 2011), 105–16.

33. Waldstreicher, "Why Thomas Jefferson," 85.

34. William Pope to TJ, May 30, 1808, transcribed from microfilm in the Jefferson Library at Monticello.

35. TJ to Thomas Jefferson Randolph, December 19, 1808, in Betts and Bear, *Family Letters,* 372.

36. Webster, "Memorandum of Conversations with Mr. Jefferson," in *Private Correspondence,* 1:364.

37. Josephus B. Stuart, "Account of a Visit to Monticello, December 24–25, 1816," MS, MiU-C Stuart Papers; extract from diaries 4–5.

38. Francis C. Gray, "Account of a Visit to Monticello," February 4–7, 1815, *PJR:RS,* 8:232–37.

39. George Flower, *History of the Settlement in Edwards County, Illinois: Founded in 1817* (Chicago, 1882), 43.

40. Webster, *Private Correspondence,* 1:364.

41. Ellen Randolph Coolidge to Henry S. Randall, 1856, reprinted in Henry S. Randall, *The Life of Thomas Jefferson* (New York: Derby & Jackson, 1858), 3:330.

42. *American Citizen,* published as *American Citizen and General Advertiser* (New York), October 16, 1800, AHN.

43. "George Ticknor's Account of a Visit to Monticello," February 4–7, 1815, *PTJ:RS,* 8:239.

44. Alan Taylor, *Civil War of 1812: American Citizens, British Subjects, Irish Rebels, and Indian Allies* (New York: Knopf, 2010), 214–17.

45. TJ to JM, September 24, 1814, *PTJ:RS,* 7:692.

46. *Boston Gazette,* July 10, 1815, AHN.

47. TJ to Samuel H. Smith, September 21, 1814, *PTJ:RS,* 7:681. Jefferson sent his proposal with cover letter to Smith for delivery to the chair of the congressional library committee. For a discussion of Jefferson's proposal and sale, see "Editor's Note," in *PTJ:RS,* 7:679–81.

48. *Alexandria Gazette* (Virginia), October 15, 1814, AHN.

49. *Salem Gazette* (Massachusetts), October 21, 1814, AHN.

50. *Alexandria Gazette* (Virginia), October 22, 1814, AHN.

51. *Petersburg Daily Courier* (Virginia), October 22, 1814, AHN.

52. For details of the sale, see "Editor's Note," in *PTJ:RS,* 7:679–81.

53. Sowerby, *Library of Thomas Jefferson,* 1:181–82.

54. TJ to Mdm. Tessé, December 8, 1813, *PTJ:RS,* 7:33.

55. "Ticknor's Visit to Monticello," *PTJ:RS,* 8:239.

56. Taylor, *Civil War of 1812,* 417–21.

57. *Rhode-Island American* (Providence), April 21, 1815, AHN.

58. TJ to Martha Jefferson Randolph, January 5, 1808, in Betts and Bear, *Family Letters,* 319.

59. Jefferson's debts are fully discussed in Herbert Sloan, *Principle and Interest: Thomas Jefferson and the Problem of Debt* (Charlottesville: University of Virginia Press, 1995). Discussion of debt among Virginia planters and their issues with British merchants is found in T. H. Breen, *Tobacco Culture: The Mentality of the Great Tidewater Planters on the Eve of Revolution* (Princeton, NJ: Princeton University Press, 1985); and David Hancock, *Citizens of the World: London Merchants and the Integration of the British Atlantic Community, 1735–1785* (Cambridge, UK: Cambridge University Press, 1995).

60. Sloan, *Principle and Interest,* 219–20.

61. Bushman, *Refinement of America,* 193–97; Rozbicki, *Complete Colonial Gentleman,* 127–36.

62. Elias, *Court Society*, 64.

63. TJ to Abbé Correa de Serra, October 24, 1820, Thomas Jefferson papers, LC.

64. TJ to M. Jullien, July 23, 1818, *PTJ:RS*, 13:153–54.

65. TJ, "A Bill for the More General Diffusion of Knowledge," *PTJ*, 2:526–35.

66. Richard Guy Wilson, "Thomas Jefferson's Classical Architecture: An American Agenda," in *Thomas Jefferson, the Classical World, and Early America*, eds. Peter S. Onuf and Nicholas P. Cole (Charlottesville: University of Virginia Press, 2011), 109–10, 118–20.

67. TJ to JA, August 15, 1820, in JA, *Adams-Jefferson Letters*, 565.

68. TJ to Trumbull, July 15, 1823, working transcription from files of *PTJ:RS*.

69. Jaffe, *Trumbull: Patriot-Artist*, 241.

70. Reverend Henry C. Thweatt, manuscript diary (before 1826), cited in Stein, *Worlds of Thomas Jefferson*, 162.

71. Jaffe, *Trumbull: Patriot-Artist*, 241.

72. Robert M. S. McDonald, "West Point's Lost Founder," in *Thomas Jefferson's Military Academy*, ed. Robert M. S. McDonald (Charlottesville: University of Virginia Press, 2004), 199–201.

8. A FINAL IMAGE

Portions of this chapter were first published in "Recording History: The Thomas Sully Portrait of Thomas Jefferson," in *Light and Liberty: Thomas Jefferson and the Power of Knowledge*, ed. Robert M. S. McDonald (Charlottesville: University of Virginia Press, 2012), 187–206.

1. Jared Mansfield to TJ, January 26, 1821, transcription from original document in the USMA Library, West Point, Special Collections, MS 1047. This letter confirms that the academy had a portrait of Washington; however, the West Point Museum does not know which image of Washington originally hung there.

2. Ibid. The congressional bill establishing the United States Military Academy can be found on the LC website, "A Century of Lawmaking," Statues at Large, "Public Acts of the Seventh Congress, Session I; March 16, 1802, Statue I, Military Peace Establishment."

3. TJ to Mansfield, February 13, 1821, Thomas Jefferson Papers, LC.

4. Fortune, "Portraits of Virtue," 15.

5. Latrobe to TJ, May 19, 1811, *PTJ:RS*, 3:625.

6. William H. Gerdts, "Natural Aristocrats in a Democracy, 1818–1870," in *American Portraiture in the Grand Manner: 1720–1920*, ed. Michael Quick (Los Angeles: Los Angeles County Museum of Art, 1981), 33; Monroe H. Fabian, *Mr. Sully, Portrait Painter: The Works of Thomas Sully* (Washington, DC: Smithsonian Institution Press, 1983), 10–22; "gentleness of character" quoted in "Recollections of Jonathan Mason, Jr.," Joseph Downs Collection of Manuscripts and Printed Ephemera, vol. 3, doc. 30, Winterthur Research Library, Winterthur, DE.

7. William Dunlap, *A History of the Rise and Progress of the Arts of Design in the United States* (1834; reprinted New York: Dover Publications, 1969), 2:135.

8. TJ to JM, September 20, 1785, *PTJ*, 8:535.

9. Thomas Sully (for the Society of Artists of the US) to TJ, December 22, 1811, *PTJ:RS*, 4:355–56.

10. "Manuscript Minutes," published in the *Early Proceedings of the American Philosophical Society* (Philadelphia, 1884), reflect that Jefferson submitted letters of resignation on January 2,

1801, November 30, 1808, and November 23, 1814. This final letter was accepted at the meeting of January 20, 1815. (See entries according to date, Jefferson Library, Thomas Jefferson Foundation, Special Collections.)

11. TJ to Sully, January 8, 1812, *PTJ:RS,* 4:407; Sully to TJ, January 6, 1812, *PTJ:RS,* 4:398–400; TJ to Sully, January 25, 1812, *PTJ:RS,* 4:459–60.

12. Thomas Sully, "Recollections of an Old Painter," *Hours at Home: A Popular Monthly of Instruction and Recreation* 10 (November 1869): 69–74.

13. TJ to JM, September 20, 1785, *PTJ,* 8:534–35.

14. TJ, "*Anas,*" as reprinted in Fiske Kimball, *The Capitol of Virginia: A Landmark of American Architecture,* rev. ed. (Richmond: Library of Virginia, 2002), 5.

15. JT to Arthur Brockenbrough, March 28, 1821, Thomas Jefferson papers, University of Virginia Library, Special Collections.

16. Sully to TJ, April 6, 1821, Thomas Jefferson papers, LC; TJ to Sully, April 17, 1821, ibid.; William B. O'Neal, *Jefferson's Fine Arts Library for the University of Virginia* (Charlottesville: University of Virginia Press, 1976), 106–8.

17. The importance of an image of civility and virtue is discussed in Wood, *Revolutionary Characters,* 13–14.

18. Bush, *Life Portraits of Thomas Jefferson,* 77. I was allowed to study this portrait during my fellowship with the APS; it hangs behind the lectern in Benjamin Franklin Hall.

19. According to Jefferson's granddaughter Ellen, he did not adopt the newer fashion of pantaloons until much later in life. Ellen Randolph Coolidge to biographer W. H. Randall, c. 1856, Ellen Wayles Randolph Coolidge correspondence, MSS 9090, University of Virginia Library, Special Collections. Knee breeches continued to be worn fashionably for very formal occasions, although the practice was more common in Europe than America.

20. See visitors' accounts of TJ in the old "Quaker" style as discussed in chapter 7.

21. Foster, *Jeffersonian America,* 15.

22. Webster, "Memorandum of Mr. Jefferson's Conversations" in *Private Correspondence,* 1:364–66, reprinted in Peterson, *Visitors to Monticello,* 97–99.

23. Thomas Sully, *Hints to Young Painters,* 1873 (reprinted, New York: Reinhold Publishing, 1965), 15. In a study of Sully's portraits, both originals and printed reproductions, I have never found another coat exactly like this one, nor does his register of paintings list a "mauve coat with fur collar." I do not believe this to have been a studio piece belonging to or borrowed by Sully.

24. TJ to Kosciuszko, February 21, 1799, *PTJ,* 31:52. In this letter Jefferson listed those items that Kosciuszko left behind that he was turning over to John Barnes, Kosciuszko's American accountant. They would be stored until Barnes heard from Kosciuszko. Jefferson did not turn over the fur coat and decided to store it at his own residence due to its value.

25. Martha Trist Burke, "List of Monticello Relics, 1907–08," Trist-Burke Family papers, 1825–1936, University of Virginia Library, Special Collections, MSS 6696.

26. Samuel J. Watson, "Developing 'Republican Machines,'" in *Thomas Jefferson's Military Academy,* ed. Robert M. S. McDonald (Charlottesville: University of Virginia Press, 2004), 170.

27. Margaret B. Smith, "The Fur Cloak," Margaret Bayard Smith papers, LC, container 5, reel 2.

28. Ribeiro, *Art of Dress,* 229–30.

29. TJ to William Duane, July 25, 1811, *PTJ:RS,* 4:56.

30. F. Nivelon, "Rudiments of Genteel Behavior" (1737), quoted in Robin Simon, *The Portrait in Britain and America: With a Biographical Dictionary of Portrait Painters, 1680–1915* (Oxford, UK: Phaidon, 1978), 76.

31. I was allowed to study this painting very closely in October 2007, prior to its being glazed and hung in its current location in the Jefferson Library at the USMA. I noted no indication of writing on the document in the figure's left hand.

32. William K. Rudolph and Carol E. Soltis, *Thomas Sully: Painted Performance* (New Haven, CT: Yale University Press, 2014), 9–15.

33. Sully, *Hints to Young Painters*, 31.

34. Verification of the column as being from the Hall of the House of Representatives was obtained from personal correspondence with Architect of the Capitol William Allen, July 5, 2006. For further discussion of Latrobe's design of the Capitol, see William C. Allen, *History of the United States Capitol: A Chronicle of Design, Construction, and Politics* (Washington, DC: Government Printing Office, 2001); electronic version at www.gpo.gov/fdsys/pkg/GPO-CDOC-106sdoc29/content-detail.html.

35. Sully, "Thomas Sully's Journal," from typescript copy at the New York Public Library; copy viewed at Winterthur Research Library, Winterthur, DE. According to a journal entry of November 20, 1820, he spent the winter and summer painting in Baltimore.

36. Allen, *History of the United States Capitol*, 140.

37. Ibid., 49.

38. For discussion of British military portraits, see Shawe-Taylor, *The Georgians*, chapter 3. In his *Hints to Young Painters*, Sully recommended the study of Reynolds's *Discourses*; he studied under Lawrence while in London, 1809–10.

39. Hart, *Register of Portraits Painted by Sully*, 121.

40. Robert Ralph Davis, "Diplomatic Plumage: American Court Dress in the Early National Period," *American Quarterly* 20, no. 2, part 1 (Summer 1968): 169, 217.

41. William Seale, *The White House: The History of an American Idea* (Washington, DC: American Institute of Architects Press, 1992), 39, 47, 61.

42. Rudolph and Soltis, *Thomas Sully*. See especially chapter 1, "Thomas Sully: The Theatre of His World," for a discussion of the influence of theatre on Sully and his painting.

43. Samuel F. B. Morse to Lucretia Pickering Walker Morse, January 5, 1822, Samuel F. B. Morse papers, LC, bound vol.: January 24, 1821–December 8, 1823, 129–31; *National Intelligencer*, February 16, 1822, quoted in William Kloss, *Samuel F. B. Morse* (New York: Harry N. Abrams, 1988), 69–70.

44. Thomas Sully, "Notes on Pictures and Painting," reprinted in Dunlap, *Arts of Design in the United States*, 2:137.

45. Ellen Wayles Randolph to Francis Eppes, April 5, 1821, Papers of the Eppes Family, University of Virginia Library, Special Collections, MSS 7109.

46. Thomas Sully, "Journal," microfilm copy of transcription held at the New York Public Library, viewed at Winterthur Research Library, Winterthur, DE.

47. James Fenimore Cooper to Charles Kitchel Gardner, between April 24–June 17, 1823, *Letters and Journals of James Fenimore Cooper*, ed. James Franklin Beard (Cambridge, MA: Belknap Press of Harvard University Press, 1960–68), 1:95–97.

48. Ibid.

49. Alan Taylor, *William Cooper's Town: Power and Persuasion on the Frontier of the Early American Republic* (New York: Knopf, 1995), 6–7.

50. Ibid., 5–6, 13–14, 297.

51. Cooper to Kitchel, April 24–June 17, 1823, *Letters and Journals*, 1:95–97.

52. Ibid.

53. Wayne Franklin, *James Fenimore Cooper: The Early Years* (New Haven, CT: Yale University Press, 2007), 382.

54. TJ to JA, June 15, 1813, *PTJ:RS*, 6:193–95.

EPILOGUE

1. Latrobe to John Lenthall, May 11, 1805, Benjamin Henry Latrobe papers, LC.

2. Benjamin Rush, *Commonplace Book*, 1793, quoted in Kaminski, *Quotable Jefferson*, 460.

3. For a comparison of American and British country houses, see Bailyn, *To Begin the World Anew*, 9–17.

4. Webster, "Memorandum of Mr. Jefferson's Correspondence," in Webster, *Private Correspondence*, 1:365.

5. For a discussion of Monticello up to more recent times, see Cogliano, *Jefferson: Reputation and Legacy*, chapter 4, 106–29.

6. Richard Rush to Charles Jared Ingersoll, October 9, 1816, reprinted in Peterson, *Visitors to Monticello*, 72; Henry D. Gilpin, "A Tour of Virginia in 1827," ed. Ralph D. Gray, *Virginia Magazine of History and Biography* 76, no. 4 (October 1968): 444–71, quote at 466.

7. TJ to Edward Rutledge, December 27, 1796, *PTJ*, 29:231–33.

8. TJ, "79. Bill for the More General Diffusion of Knowledge," *PTJ*, 2:528.

9. TJ to Latrobe, June 12, 1816, *PTJ:RS*, 11:432.

10. Richard Guy Wilson, "Thomas Jefferson's Classical Architecture," 122.

11. TJ, "Notes of a Tour of English Gardens," *PTJ*, 9:369.

12. One page, undated document in Jefferson's hand, held in Thomas Jefferson papers, LC. An expanded discussion of Jefferson's epitaph and gravestone is found in Cogliano, *Jefferson: Reputation and Legacy*, chapter 5, 137–61.

13. "Jefferson and Adams are no more," *New-Hampshire Gazette* (Portsmouth), July 11, 1826. This appears to be a compilation from various newspapers: Jefferson's death from the *Philadelphia National Gazette*; Adams's death from the *Boston Gazette*. Both can be found at AHN.

14. TJ to the Democratic-Republican Delegate of Washington County, PA, March 31, 1809, *PTJ:RS*, 1:99–100.

15. TJ to José Correa da Serra, November 25, 1817, *PTJ:RS*, 12:202.

BIBLIOGRAPHY

UNPUBLISHED PRIMARY SOURCES
American Philosophical Society Library, Philadelphia
   Mrs. Burd Peale Collection
   Charles Willson Peale, Diary No. 1
   Charles Willson Peale, lectures
   Rembrandt Peale Papers, 1808–33. MSS Film, 1081.
Jefferson Library, Thomas Jefferson Foundation, Special Collections, Charlottesville, VA
   William Russell Birch. "Autobiography." Typescript copy.
   Martha Wayles Jefferson. "Household Accounts."
   "Manuscript Minutes." American Philosophical Society, 1884.
Library of Congress, Washington, DC
   Alexander Hamilton papers
   Thomas Jefferson papers
   Benjamin Henry Latrobe papers
   Samuel F. B. Morse papers
   Shippen Family papers
   Margaret Bayard Smith papers
University of Virginia Library, Special Collections, Charlottesville
   Edgehill-Randolph Collection. MSS 1397.
   Ellen Wayles Randolph Coolidge correspondence. MSS 9090.
   Papers of the Eppes Family. MSS 7109.
   Thomas Jefferson papers
   Trist-Burke Family papers, 1825–1936. MSS 6696.
United States Military Academy Library, Special Collections, West Point, NY
   Thomas Jefferson files
   Jared Mansfield files
United States Military Academy Museum, West Point, NY
   Thomas Jefferson files
   James Monroe files
   Thomas Sully's paintings on display and in storage
Winterthur Research Library, Winterthur, DE
   Joseph Downs Collection of Manuscripts and Printed Ephemera
   Thomas Sully, "Journal," from typescript copy at the New York Public Library

PUBLISHED PRIMARY SOURCES

Adams, Abigail, II. *Correspondence of Miss Adams, Daughter of John Adams.* Edited by her daughter. New York: Wiley and Putnam, 1842.

———. *Journal and Correspondence of Miss Adams, Daughter of John Adams.* Edited by her daughter. New York: Wiley and Putnam, 1841.

Adams, John. *Adams Family Correspondence.* Edited by L. H. Butterfield et al. 12 vols. to date. Cambridge, MA: Belknap Press of Harvard University Press, 1963–.

———. *The Adams-Jefferson Letters: The Complete Correspondence between Thomas Jefferson and Abigail and John Adams.* Edited by Lester J. Cappon. 2 vols. Chapel Hill: University of North Carolina Press, 1959; reprinted in one vol., Chapel Hill: University of North Carolina Press, 1988.

———. *Diary and Autobiography of John Adams.* Edited by L. H. Butterfield. 4 vols. Cambridge, MA: Belknap Press of Harvard University Press, 1961.

———. *Papers of John Adams.* Edited by Robert J. Taylor et al. 15 vols. Cambridge, MA: Belknap Press of Harvard University Press, 1977–2010.

Adams, John Quincy. *Diary of John Quincy Adams.* Edited by Marc Friedlaender and Robert J. Taylor. 2 vols. Cambridge, MA: Belknap Press of Harvard University Press, 1981.

———. *Memoirs of John Quincy Adams.* Edited by Charles Francis Adams. 12 vols. Philadelphia: J. B. Lippincott, 1874–77.

Annals of Congress, 1789. Electronic facsimiles on "A Century of Lawmaking for a New Nation: U.S. Congressional Documents and Debates." http://memory.loc.gov.ammem/amlaw /lawhome.html.

Betts, Edwin Morris, and James Adam Bear Jr., eds. *The Family Letters of Thomas Jefferson.* Rev. ed. Charlottesville: University of Virginia Press, 1986.

Calvert, Rosalie Stier. *Mistress of Riversdale: The Plantation Letters of Rosalie Stier Calvert, 1795–1821.* Edited and translated by Margaret Law Callcott. Baltimore: Johns Hopkins University Press, 1991.

Chastellux, François Jean. *Travels in North America in the Years 1780, 1781, and 1782.* Translated and with an introduction by Howard C. Rice. 2 vols. Chapel Hill: University of North Carolina Press, 1963.

Cooper, James Fenimore. *Letters and Journals of James Fenimore Cooper.* Edited by James Franklin Beard. 6 vols. Cambridge, MA: Belknap Press of Harvard University Press, 1960–68.

Cutler, Manasseh. *Life, Journals and Correspondence of Rev. Manasseh Cutler.* Edited by William P. Cutler and Julia Perkins Cutler. 2. vols. Cincinnati, OH: R. Clarke & Co., 1888; reprinted 2010.

Dunlap, William. *Diary of William Dunlap.* Edited by Dorothy C. Barch. 3 vols. New York: New York Historical Society, 1930.

———. *History of the Rise and Progress of the Arts of Design in the United States.* 2 vols. New York: George C. Scott and Co., 1834.

Foster, Augustus John. *Jeffersonian America: Notes on the United States of America Collected in the Years 1805-6-7 and 11–12 by Sir Augustus John Foster, Bart.* Edited by Richard Beale Davis. San Marino, CA: Huntington Library, 1954.

Franklin, Benjamin. *Benjamin Franklin's Autobiographical Writings.* Edited by Carl Van Doren. New York: Viking, 1945.

Gilpin, Henry D. "A Tour of Virginia in 1827." Edited by Ralph D. Gray. *Virginia Magazine of History and Biography* 76, no. 4 (October 1968): 444–71.

Hamilton, Alexander. *Alexander Hamilton: Writings*. Edited by Joanne B. Freeman. New York: Library of America, 2001.

———. *The Papers of Alexander Hamilton, Digital Edition*. Edited by Harold C. Syrett. Charlottesville: University of Virginia Rotunda Project, 2011.

Jarratt, Devereaux. *Life of Devereaux Jarratt, Rector of Bath Parish, Dinwiddie County, Virginia: In a Series of Letters to John Coleman*. 1806. Reprint, Bedford, MA: Applewood Books, 2009.

Jefferson, Thomas. *The Complete Anas of Thomas Jefferson*. Edited by Franklin B. Sawvel. New York: Round Table Press, 1903.

———. *Jefferson's Memorandum Books: Accounts, with Legal Records and Miscellany, 1767–1826*. Edited by James A. Bear Jr. and Lucia C. Stanton. 2 vols. Princeton, NJ: Princeton University Press, 1997.

———. *Notes on the State of Virginia*. 1785. Edited by William Peden. Chapel Hill: University of North Carolina Press, 1982.

———. *The Papers of Thomas Jefferson*. Edited by Julian P. Boyd, et al. 42 vols. to date. Princeton, NJ: Princeton University Press, 1950–.

———. *The Papers of Thomas Jefferson: Retirement Series*. Edited by J. Jefferson Looney. 13 vols. to date. Princeton, NJ: Princeton University Press, 2004–.

———. *Thomas Jefferson: Writings*. Edited by Merrill D. Peterson. New York: Library of America, 1984.

———. *Writings of Thomas Jefferson*. Edited by Albert Ellery Bergh. 20 vols. Washington, DC, 1907.

Latrobe, Benjamin Henry. *The Papers of Benjamin Henry Latrobe*. 9 vols. New Haven, CT: Yale University Press, 1977–94.

Maclay, William. *The Diary of William Maclay and Other Notes on Senate Debates*. Edited by Kenneth R. Bowling and Helen E. Veit. Baltimore: Johns Hopkins University Press, 1988.

———. *Journal of William Maclay, United States Senator from Pennsylvania*. Edited by Edgar S. Maclay. New York: D. Appleton, 1890.

Madison, James. *The Papers of James Madison, Digital Edition*. Edited by J. C. A. Stagg. Charlottesville: University of Virginia Rotunda Project, 2010.

———. *The Papers of James Madison, Secretary of State Series*. Edited by Robert J. Brugger et al. 9 vols. Charlottesville: University of Virginia Press, 1986–.

Monroe, James. *The Papers of James Monroe*. Edited by Daniel Preston. 3 vols. to date. Westport, CT: Greenwood Press, 2003–09.

Moore, John. *A Journal during a residence in France from the beginning of August to the middle of December 1792*. 2 vols. London, 1793.

———. *A View of the Causes and Progress of the French Revolution*. 2 vols. London, 1795.

Moore, Thomas. *Memoirs, Journal, and Correspondence of Thomas Moore*. Edited by John Russell. 8 vols. London, 1853.

Morris, Gouverneur. *The Diary and Letters of Gouverneur Morris*. Edited by Anne Cary Morris. 2 vols. New York: Scribner's Sons, 1888.

Nicolaisen, Peter, and Hannah Spahn, eds. *Cosmopolitanism and Nationhood in the Age of Jefferson*. Universitätsverlag Winter: Heidelberg, Germany, 2014.

Peale, Charles Willson. *An Historical Catalogue of Peale's Collection of Paintings*. Philadelphia, 1795.

———. *The Selected Papers of Charles Willson Peale and His Family*. Edited by Lillian B. Miller et al. 5 vols. bound in 6. New Haven, CT: Yale University Press, 1983–2000.

Plumer, William. *William Plumer's Memorandum of Proceedings in the United States Senate, 1803–1807*. Edited by Everett Somerville Brown. New York: Macmillan, 1923.

Reynolds, Joshua. *Sir Joshua Reynolds' Discourses*. Edited and introduction by Helen Zimmern. London: Walter Scott, 1887.

Richardson, Jonathan. *The Works of Jonathan Richardson: Containing I. The Theory of Painting; II. Essay on the Art of Criticism; III. The Science of a Connoisseur*. London, 1792.

Rush, Benjamin. *Information to Europeans Who Are Disposed to Migrate to the United States*. Philadelphia: Carey, Stewart, & Company, 1789.

Sinclair, John. *Correspondence of the Right Honourable Sir John Sinclair*. 2 vols. London, 1831.

Smith, Margaret Bayard. *First Forty Years of Washington Society in the Family Letters of Margaret Bayard Smith*. Edited by Gaillard Hunt. New York: C. Scribner's Sons, 1906.

Sowerby, E. Millicent, compiler. *Catalogue of the Library of Thomas Jefferson*. 5 vols. Charlottesville: University of Virginia Press, 1983.

Stanhope, Philip Dormer. *Letters to His Son on the Art of Becoming a Man of the World and a Gentleman, 1746–47*. c. 1774. San Bernardino, CA: n.p., 2013.

Sully, Thomas. *Hints to Young Painters*. 1873. Reprinted, New York: Reinhold Publishing, 1965.

———. "Recollections of an Old Painter." *Hours at Home: A Popular Monthly of Instruction and Recreation* 10 (November 1869): 69–74.

———. *A Register of Portraits Painted by Thomas Sully*. Edited, introduction, and notes by Charles Henry Hart. Philadelphia, 1909.

Taggart, Samuel. "Letters of Samuel Taggart." In *Proceedings of the American Antiquarian Society* 33, part 1. Worcester, MA: American Antiquarian Society, 1924.

Trumbull, John. *The Autobiography of Colonel John Trumbull, Patriot-Artist, 1756–1843*. Edited by Theodore Sizer. New Haven, CT: Yale University Press, 1953.

———. *Autobiography, Reminiscences and Letters of John Trumbull from 1756 to 1841*. New York, 1841.

Vigée-Lebrun, Elisabeth. *Memoirs of Elisabeth Vigée-Lebrun*. Translated by Siân Evans. London: Camden Press, 1989.

Washington, George. *The Papers of George Washington*. Vol. 3, *Confederation Series*. Edited by W. W. Abbott and Dorothy Twohig. Charlottesville: University of Virginia Press, 1992–97.

———. *The Writings of George Washington*. Edited by John C. Fitzpatrick. 39 vols. Washington, DC: United States Printing Office, 1931–44.

Webster, Daniel. *The Private Correspondence of Daniel Webster*. Edited by F. Webster and E. D. Sanborn. 2 vols. Little, Brown, 1857.

Wraxall, Nathaniel William. *Historical Memoirs of My Own Time*. 1815. Edited by Richard Askham. London: Kegan Paul, Trench Trubner, 1904.

Young, Arthur. *Travels in France during the Years 1787, 1788, 1789*. Introduction by M. Bethan-Edwards. London, 1889.

SECONDARY SOURCES

Abrams, Ann Uhry. *The Valiant Hero: Benjamin West and Grand-Style History Painting.* Washington, DC: Smithsonian Institution Press, 1985.

Adams, Henry. *History of the United States during the Administrations of Thomas Jefferson.* 1889. Reprinted, New York: Library Classics, 1986.

Allen, William C. *History of the United Stated Capitol: A Chronicle of Design, Construction and Politics.* Washington, DC: Government Printing Office, 2001.

Allgor, Catherine. *Parlor Politics: In Which the Ladies of Washington Help Build a City and a Government.* Charlottesville: University of Virginia Press, 2000.

Appleby, Joyce. "Thomas Jefferson and the Psychology of Democracy." In *The Revolution of 1800,* edited by James Horn, Jan Ellen Lewis, and Peter S. Onuf. Charlottesville: University of Virginia Press, 2002.

Arch, Nigel, and Joanna Marschner. *Splendour at Court: Dressing for Royal Occasions since 1700.* London: Unwin Hyman, 1987.

Armitage, David. *The Declaration of Independence: A Global History.* Cambridge, MA: Harvard University Press, 2007.

Bailyn, Bernard. *To Begin the World Anew: The Genius and Ambiguities of the American Founders.* New York: Random House, 2004.

Barker, Gordon. "Unraveling the Strange History of Jefferson's 'Observations sur la Virginie.'" *Virginia Magazine of History and Biography* 112, no. 2 (2004): 13–77.

Barratt, Carrie Rebora, and Ellen G. Miles. *Gilbert Stuart.* New Haven, CT: Yale University Press, 2005.

Barrell, John. *The Political Theory of Painting from Reynolds to Hazlitt: "The Body of the Public."* New Haven, CT: Yale University Press, 1986.

Barthes, Roland. *The Language of Fashion.* Translated by Andy Stafford, edited by Andy Stafford and Michael Carter. Oxford, UK: Berg, 2006.

Baudelaire, Charles. *Baudelaire: Selected Writings on Art and Artists.* Translated by P. E. Charvet. Cambridge, UK: Cambridge University Press, 1972.

Baumgarten, Linda. *Eighteenth-Century Clothing at Williamsburg.* Williamsburg, VA: Colonial Williamsburg Foundation, 1993.

———. *What Clothes Reveal: The Language of Clothing in Colonial and Federal America.* New Haven, CT: Yale University Press, 2002.

Bear, James A., Jr., et al. *Jefferson at Monticello: Memoirs of a Monticello Slave as Dictated to Charles Campbell.* Charlottesville: University of Virginia Press, 1967.

Bellion, Wendy. "Patience Wright's Transatlantic Bodies." In *Shaping the Body Politic: Art and Political Formation in Early America,* edited by Maurie D. McInnis and Louis P. Nelson, 15–46. Charlottesville: University of Virginia Press, 2011.

Berman, Eleanor Davidson. *Thomas Jefferson among the Arts: An Essay in Early American Esthetics.* New York: Philosophical Library, 1947.

Betts, Edwin M., and James A. Bear, eds. *The Family Letters of Thomas Jefferson.* Charlottesville: University of Virginia Press, 1986.

Breen, T. H. *George Washington's Journey: The President Forges a Nation.* New York: Simon & Schuster, 2016.

————. *The Market Place of Revolution: How Consumer Politics Shaped American Independence.* New York: Oxford University Press, 2005.

————. *Tobacco Culture: The Mentality of the Great Tidewater Planters on the Eve of Revolution.* Princeton, NJ: Princeton University Press, 1985.

Brigham, David R. *Public Culture in the Early Republic: Peale's Museum and Its Audience.* Washington, DC: Smithsonian Institution Press, 1995.

Broussard, James. *The Southern Federalists, 1800–1816* (Baton Rouge: Louisiana State University Press, 1978.

Buck, Anne. *Dress in Eighteenth-Century England.* London: B. T. Batsford, 1979.

Burnell, Carol. *Divided Affections: The Extraordinary Life of Maria Cosway.* Lausanne, Switzerland: Column House, 2007.

Burstein, Andrew. *Democracy's Muse: How Thomas Jefferson Became an FDR Liberal, a Regan Republican, and a Tea Party Fanatic, All the While Being Dead.* Charlottesville: University of Virginia Press, 2015.

————. *The Inner Jefferson: Portrait of a Grieving Optimist.* Charlottesville: University of Virginia Press, 1995.

Bush, Alfred L. *The Life Portraits of Thomas Jefferson.* Charlottesville, VA: Thomas Jefferson Memorial Foundation, 1987.

Bushman, Richard L. *The Refinement of America: Persons, Houses, Cities.* New York: Vintage Books, 1993.

Carr, Carolyn Kinder, and Ellen G. Miles. *A Brush with History: Paintings from the National Portrait Gallery.* Washington, DC: Smithsonian Institution Press, 2001.

Castiglione, Baldesar. *The Book of the Courtier.* 1528. Translated and introduction by George Bull. London: Penguin, 1967.

Christman, Margaret C. S. *The First Federal Congress, 1789–1791.* Washington, DC: Smithsonian Institution Press, 1989.

————. *The Spirit of Party: Hamilton and Jefferson at Odds.* Washington, DC: Smithsonian Institution Press, 1992.

Clark, Kenneth. *Moments of Vision.* London: John Murray, 1981.

Cogliano, Francis D. *Thomas Jefferson: Reputation and Legacy.* Charlottesville: University of Virginia Press, 2006.

Colley, Linda. *Britons: Forging the Nation, 1707–1837.* New Haven, CT: Yale University Press, 1992.

Coltman, Viccy. *Fabricating the Antique: Neoclassicism in Britain, 1760–1800.* Chicago: University of Chicago Press, 2006.

Cometti, Elizabeth. "Maria Cosway's Rediscovered Miniature of Jefferson." *William and Mary Quarterly* 9, no. 2 (April 1951): 152–55.

Cooper, Helen A. *John Trumbull: The Hand and Spirit of a Painter.* New Haven, CT: Yale University Art Gallery, 1982.

Craven, Avery O. *Soil Exhaustion as a Factor in the Agricultural History of Virginia and Maryland, 1606–1860.* Rev. ed. Columbia: University of South Carolina Press, 2006.

Craven, Wayne. *Colonial American Portraiture.* Cambridge, UK: Cambridge University Press, 1986.

————. "The Grand Manner in Early Nineteenth-Century American Painting: Borrowings from Antiquity, the Renaissance, and the Baroque." *American Art Journal* 11, no. 2 (April 1979): 4–43.

Cripe, Helen. *Thomas Jefferson and Music.* Rev. ed. Charlottesville, VA: Thomas Jefferson Foundation, 2009.

Cullen, Charles T. "Jefferson's White House Dinner Guests." *White House History* 17 (Winter 2006): 25–43.

Cumming, Valerie, C. Willett Cunnington, and Phillis Cunnington. *The Dictionary of Fashion History.* Reprinted, Oxford, UK: A&C Black, 1976.

Cunningham, Noble E., Jr. "The Diary of Frances Few, 1808–1809." *Journal of Southern History* 29, no. 3 (August 1962): 345–61.

———. *The Image of Thomas Jefferson in the Public Eye: Portraits for the People, 1800–1809.* Charlottesville: University of Virginia Press, 1981.

———. *The Inaugural Addresses of President Thomas Jefferson, 1801 and 1805.* Columbia: University of Missouri Press, 2001.

———. *Popular Images of the Presidency: From Washington to Lincoln.* Columbia: University of Missouri Press, 1991.

Cunnington, C. Willett, and Phillis Cunnington. *Handbook of English Costume in the Eighteenth Century.* 2nd ed. London: Faber and Faber, 1972.

Davenport, Millia. *The Book of Costume.* New York: Crown Publishers, 1948.

Davis, Robert Ralph, Jr. "Diplomatic Plumage: American Court Dress in the Early National Period." *American Quarterly* 20, no. 2, part 1 (Summer 1968): 164–79.

Delpierre, Madeleine. *Dress in France in the Eighteenth Century.* Translated by Caroline Beamish. New Haven, CT: Yale University Press, 1997.

de Marly, Diana. *Fashion for Men: An Illustrated History.* New York: Holmes & Meier, 1985.

Docherty, Linda. "Original Copies: Gilbert Stuart's Companion Portraits of Thomas Jefferson and James Madison." *American Art* 22, no. 2 (2008): 85–97.

Donald, Diana. *The Age of Caricature: Satirical Prints in the Reign of George III.* New Haven, CT: Yale University Press, 1996.

Doyle, William. *Aristocracy and Its Enemies in the Age of Revolution.* Oxford, UK: Oxford University Press, 2009.

Drinkwater, John. *Charles James Fox.* New York: Ernest Benn, 1928.

Dull, Jonathan R. *A Diplomatic History of the American Revolution.* New Haven, CT: Yale University Press, 1985.

Dunbar, Louise Burnham. *A Study of "Monarchical" Tendencies in the United States from 1776 to 1801.* Urbana: University of Illinois, 1922.

Dunlap, William. *A History of the Rise and Progress of the Arts of Design in the United States.* 1834. Reprinted, 2 vols. bound in 3, New York: Dover Publications, 1969.

Dupre, Daniel S. "Panic of 1819 and the Political Economy of Sectionalism." In *Economy of Early America,* edited by Cathy Matson, 263–93. University Park: Pennsylvania State University Press, 2006.

Durey, Michael. *With the Hammer of Truth: James Thomson Callender and America's Early National Heroes.* Charlottesville: University of Virginia Press, 1990.

Elias, Norbert. *The Court Society.* Translated by Edmund Jephcott. New York: Pantheon, 1983.

Elkins, Stanley, and Eric McKitrick. *The Age of Federalism*. Oxford, UK: Oxford University Press, 1993.

Evans, Dorinda. *Benjamin West and His American Students*. Washington, DC: Smithsonian Institution Press for the National Portrait Gallery, 1980.

———. *The Genius of Gilbert Stuart*. Princeton, NJ: Princeton University Press, 1999.

———. *Mather Brown: Early American Artist in England*. Middletown, CT: Wesleyan, 1982.

Fabian, Monroe H. *Joseph Wright: American Artist,1756–1793*. Washington, DC: Smithsonian Institution Press, 1985.

———. *Mr. Sully, Portrait Painter: The Works of Thomas Sully, 1783–1872*. Washington, DC: Smithsonian Institution Press, 1983.

Fanelli, Doris Devine, and Karie Diethorn. *History of the Portrait Collection, Independence National Historical Park*. Philadelphia: American Philosophical Society, 2001.

Feigenbaum, Gail. *Jefferson's America and Napoleon's France*. Edited by Victoria Cooke. Seattle: University of Washington Press, 2003.

Fielding, Mantle. "David Edwin, Engraver." *Pennsylvania Magazine of History and Biography* 29, no. 1 (1905): 82.

Fischer, David Hackett. *Liberty and Freedom: A Visual History of America's Founding Ideas*. Oxford, UK: Oxford University Press, 2005.

Flower, George. *History of the Settlement in Edwards County, Illinois: Founded in 1817*. Chicago, 1882.

Flügel, J. C. *The Psychology of Clothes*. London: John Murray, 1981.

Fortune, Brandon Brame. "Portraits of Virtue and Genius: Pantheons of Worthies and Public Portraiture in the Early American Republic, 1780–1820." PhD diss., University of North Carolina at Chapel Hill, 1987.

Fortune, Brandon Brame, with Deborah J. Warner. *Franklin and His Friends: Portraying the Man of Science in Eighteenth-Century America*. Washington, DC: Smithsonian Institution Press, 1999.

Franklin, Wayne. *James Fenimore Cooper: The Early Years*. New Haven, CT: Yale University Press, 2007.

Freeman, Joanne B. *Affairs of Honor: National Politics in the New Republic*. New Haven, CT: Yale University Press, 2002.

Goethe, Johann Wolfgang von. *Die Leiden des jungen Werther*, 1774.

———. *The Sorrows of Young Werther*. Translated and introduced by Michael Hulse. London: Penguin Classics, 1989.

Good, Cassandra. *Founding Friendships: Friendships between Men and Women in the Early American Republic*. New York: Oxford University Press, 2016.

Gordon-Reed, Annette. *The Hemingses of Monticello: An American Family*. New York: Norton, 2008.

———. *Thomas Jefferson and Sally Hemings: An American Controversy*. Charlottesville: University of Virginia Press,1998.

Gordon-Reed, Annette, and Peter Onuf. *"Most Blessed of the Patriarchs": Thomas Jefferson and the Empire of the Imagination*. New York: Liveright Publishing, 2016.

Griswold, Rufus Wilmot. *The Republican Court; or, Society in the Days of Washington*. 1867. Facsimile of the first edition, New York: Haskell House, 1971.

Hancock, David. *Citizens of the World: London Merchants and the Integration of the British Atlantic Community.* Cambridge, UK: Cambridge University Press, 1995.

Harris, Jennifer. "The Red Cap of Liberty: A Study of Dress Worn by French Revolutionary Partisans, 1789–94." *Eighteenth-Century Studies* 14, no. 3 (1981): 283–312.

Harris, Neil. *The Artist in American Society: The Formative Years, 1790–1860.* New York: George Braziller, 1966.

Hart, Charles H. "Life Portraits of Thomas Jefferson." *McClure's Magazine* 11 (1898): 47–55.

Harvey, John. *Men in Black.* Chicago: University of Chicago Press, 1995.

Haulman, Clyde. "Virginia Commodity Prices during the Panic of 1819." *Journal of the Early American Republic* 22, no. 4 (Winter 2002): 675–88.

Haulman, Kate. *The Politics of Fashion in Eighteenth-Century America.* Chapel Hill: University of North Carolina Press, 2011.

Haynes, Sam W. *Unfinished Revolution: The Early American Republic in a British World.* Charlottesville: University of Virginia Press, 2010.

Hess, Steven, and Sandy Northrop. *Drawn and Quartered: The History of American Political Cartoons.* Montgomery, AL: Elliott & Clark Publishing, 1996.

Hollander, Anne. *Seeing through Clothes.* New York: Viking, 1978.

Hoock, Holger. *The King's Artists: The Royal Academy of Arts and the Politics of British Culture 1760–1840.* Oxford, UK: Oxford University Press, 2003.

Hood, Graham. "Soul or Style? Questions about Early American Portraits." In *The Portrait in Eighteenth-Century America,* edited by Ellen G. Miles, 84–88. Newark: University of Delaware Press, 1993.

Hunt, Lynn. *Politics, Culture, and Class in the French Revolution.* Berkeley: University of California Press, 1984.

Isaac, Rhys. *The Transformation of Virginia, 1740–1790.* Chapel Hill: University of North Carolina, 1982.

Jackman, S. W. "A Young Englishman Reports on the New Nation: Edward Thornton to James Bland Burgess, 1791–1793." *William and Mary Quarterly* 18, no. 1 (January 1961): 85–121.

Jackson, Donald, ed. *Letters of the Lewis and Clark Expedition, with Related Documents, 1783–1854.* 2 vols. Urbana: University of Illinois Press, 1978.

Jaffe, Irma B. *John Trumbull: Patriot-Artist of the American Revolution.* Boston: New York Graphic Society, 1975.

Jarrett, Derek. *Britain, 1688–1815.* New York: St. Martin's Press, 1965.

Kamensky, Jane. *A Revolution in Color: The World of John Singleton Copley.* New York: Norton, 2016.

Kaminski, John P., ed. *The Quotable Jefferson.* Princeton, NJ: Princeton University Press, 2006.

Kaplan, Lawrence. *Thomas Jefferson, Westward the Course of Empire.* Wilmington, DE: Scholarly Resources, 1999.

Keane, John. *Tom Paine: A Political Life.* New York: Little, Brown, 1995.

Kelly, James, and B. S. Lovell. "Thomas Jefferson: His Friends and Foes." *Virginia Magazine of History and Biography* 101, no. 1 (January 1993): 133–57.

Kerber, Linda. *Federalists in Dissent: Imagery and Ideology in Jeffersonian America.* Ithaca, NY: Cornell University Press, 1970.

Kern, Susan. *The Jeffersons at Shadwell.* New Haven, CT: Yale University Press, 2010.

Kimball, Fiske. *The Capitol of Virginia: A Landmark of American Architecture*. Rev. ed. Richmond: Library of Virginia, 2002.

————. *Life Portraits of Thomas Jefferson and Their Replicas*. Philadelphia: American Philosophical Society, 1944.

Kimball, Marie. *Jefferson: The Scene of Europe, 1784–1789*. New York: Coward-McCann, 1950.

Kloss, William. *Samuel F. B. Morse*. New York: Harry N. Abrams, 1988.

Korshak, Yvonne. "The Liberty Cap as a Revolutionary Symbol in America and France." *Smithsonian Studies in American Art* 1 (Fall 1987): 53–69.

Kranish, Michael. *Flight from Monticello: Thomas Jefferson at War*. Oxford: Oxford University Press, 2010.

Kybalová, Ludmila, Olga Herbenová, and Milena Lamarová. *Pictorial Encyclopedia of Fashion*. Translated by Claudia Rosoux. London: Hamlyn, 1968.

Lane-Poole, Stanley. *Life of the Right Honourable Stratford Canning, Viscount Stratford de Redcliffe*. 2 vols. London, 1888.

Larkin, T. Lawrence. "A 'Gift' Strategically Solicited and Magnanimously Conferred: The American Congress, the French Monarchy, and the State Portraits of Louis XVI and Marie-Antoinette." *Winterthur Portfolio* 44, no. 1 (Spring 2010): 31–76.

Lester, Malcolm. *Anthony Merry "Redivivus": A Reappraisal of the British Minister to the United States, 1803–1806*. Charlottesville: University of Virginia Press, 1978.

Lloyd, Christopher. "Portraits of Sovereigns and Heads of State." In *Citizens and Kings: Portraits in the Age of Revolution*, edited by Norman Rosenthal and Mary Anne Stevens, 58–79. London: Royal Academy of Arts, 2007.

Lloyd, Stephen, and Kim Sloan. *The Intimate Portrait: Drawings, Miniatures, and Pastels from Ramsay to Lawrence*. Edinburgh: National Galleries of Scotland, 2009.

Lovell, Margaretta M. *Art in a Season of Revolution: Printers, Artisans, and Patrons in Early America*. Philadelphia: University of Pennsylvania Press, 2005.

Malone, Dumas. *Jefferson and His Time*. 6 vols. Boston: Little, Brown, 1948–81.

Mannings, David. *Sir Joshua Reynolds: A Complete Catalogue of His Paintings*. New Haven, CT: Yale University Press, 2000.

Mansel, Philip. *Dressed to Rule: Royal and Court Costume from Louis XIV to Elizabeth II*. New Haven, CT: Yale University Press, 2005.

Marshall, John. *The Life of George Washington*. Edited by Robert Faulkner and Paul Cerrese. Indianapolis, IN: Liberty Fund, 2000.

Mayo, Bernard. "A Peppercorn for Mr. Jefferson." *Virginia Quarterly Review* 19 (Spring 1943): 222–35.

McDonald, Robert M. S. *Confounding Father: Thomas Jefferson's Image in His Own Time*. Charlottesville: University of Virginia Press, 2016.

————. "The Hamiltonian Invention of Thomas Jefferson." In *The Many Faces of Alexander Hamilton: The Life and Legacy of America's Most Elusive Founding Father*, edited by Douglas Ambrose and Robert W. T. Martin, 54–76. New York: New York University Press, 2006.

————, ed. *Light and Liberty: Thomas Jefferson and the Power of Knowledge*. Charlottesville: University of Virginia Press, 2012.

————, ed. *Thomas Jefferson's Military Academy: Founding West Point*. Charlottesville: University of Virginia Press, 2004.

———. "West Point's Lost Founder." In McDonald, ed., *Thomas Jefferson's Military Academy*.

McLanathan, Richard. *Gilbert Stuart*. New York: Harry N. Abrams, 1986.

Mease, James. *A Picture of Philadelphia*. Carlisle, MA, 1811.

Meschutt, David. "William Byrd and His Portrait Collection." *Journal of Early Southern Decorative Arts* 14, no. 2 (May 1988): 19–46.

Messer, Peter C. "From a Revolutionary History to a History of Revolution: David Ramsay and the American Revolution." *Journal of the Early Republic* 22, no. 2 (Summer 2002): 205–33.

Miles, Ellen G., ed. *Portrait in Eighteenth-Century America*. Newark: University of Delaware Press, 1993.

———. "Portraits of the Heroes of Louisbourg, 1745–1751." *American Art Journal* 15, no. 2 (Winter 1983): 48–66.

———. *Saint-Mémin and the Neoclassical Profile Portrait in America*. Washington, DC: Smithsonian Institution Press, 1994.

Miller, Lillian B. *In Pursuit of Fame: Rembrandt Peale, 1778–1860*. Washington, DC: Smithsonian Institution, 1992.

———. *Patrons and Patriotism: The Encouragement of the Fine Arts in the United States, 1790–1860*. Chicago: University of Chicago Press, 1966.

Miller, Lillian B., and David Ward, eds. *New Perspectives on Charles Willson Peale*. Pittsburgh, PA: University of Pittsburgh Press, 1991.

Montgomery, Florence. *Textiles in America, 1650–1870*. New York: Winterthur Books, 1984.

Neil, J. Meredith. *Toward a National Taste: America's Quest for Aesthetic Independence*. Honolulu: University Press of Hawaii, 1975.

Nenadic, Stana. "The Enlightenment in Scotland and the Popular Passion for Portraits." *British Journal for Eighteenth Studies* 21 (1998): 175–92.

Newman, Simon P. *Parades and the Politics of the Street: Festive Culture in the Early American Republic*. Philadelphia: University of Pennsylvania Press, 1997.

———. "Principles or Men? George Washington and the Political Culture of National Leadership, 1776–1801." *Journal of the Early Republic* 12, no. 4 (Winter 1992): 477–507.

O'Neal, William B. *Jefferson's Fine Arts Library for the University of Virginia*. Charlottesville: University of Virginia Press, 1976.

Onuf, Peter S. *Jefferson's Empire: The Language of American Nationhood*. Charlottesville: University of Virginia Press, 2000.

———. *Mind of Thomas Jefferson*. Charlottesville: University of Virginia Press, 2007.

Onuf, Peter S., and Nicholas P. Cole, eds. *Thomas Jefferson, the Classical World, and Early America*. Charlottesville: University of Virginia Press, 2011.

O'Shaughnessy, Andrew Jackson. *The Men Who Lost America: British Leadership, the American Revolution, and the Fate of the Empire*. New Haven, CT: Yale University Press, 2013.

Pasley, Jeffrey L., Andrew W. Robertson, and David Waldstreicher. *Beyond the Founders: New Approaches to the Political History of the Early American Republic*. Chapel Hill: University of North Carolina Press, 2004.

Peden, William. "A Book Peddler Invades Monticello." *William and Mary Quarterly* 6 (1949): 631–36.

Peterson, Merrill D. *The Jefferson Image in the American Mind*. New York: Oxford University Press, 1960.

———. *Thomas Jefferson and the New Nation: A Biography.* Oxford, UK: Oxford University Press, 1970.

———. *Visitors to Monticello.* Charlottesville: University of Virginia Press, 1989.

Pierson, Hamilton W. "The Private Life of Thomas Jefferson." In *Jefferson at Monticello: Memoirs of a Monticello Slave,* edited by James A. Bear Jr. Charlottesville: University of Virginia Press, 1967.

Pointon, Marcia. *Hanging the Head: Portraiture and Social Formation in Eighteenth-Century England.* New Haven, CT: Yale University Press, 1993.

Poulet, Anne L. *Jean-Antoine Houdon: Sculptor of the Enlightenment.* Chicago: University of Chicago Press, 2003.

Prown, Jules David. *Art as Evidence: Writings on Art and Material Culture.* New Haven, CT: Yale University Press, 2001.

Quincy, Edmund. *Life of Josiah Quincy.* Boston, 1868.

Randall, Henry S. *The Life of Thomas Jefferson.* 3 vols. New York: Derby & Jackson, 1858.

Randolph, Edmund. *History of Virginia.* Edited by Arthur H. Shaffer. Charlottesville: University of Virginia Press, 1970.

Randolph, Sarah N. *The Domestic Life of Thomas Jefferson.* 1871; reprinted, Charlottesville: University of Virginia Press, 1978.

Read, James H. "Alexander Hamilton's View of Thomas Jefferson's Ideology and Character." In *Many Faces of Alexander Hamilton: The Life and Legacy of America's Most Elusive Founding Father,* edited by Douglas Ambrose and Robert W. T. Martin, 77–108. New York: New York University Press, 2006.

Ribeiro, Aileen. *The Art of Dress: Fashion in England and France, 1750–1820.* New Haven, CT: Yale University Press, 1995.

———. *Dress in Eighteenth-Century Europe, 1715–1789.* New Haven, CT: Yale University Press, 2002.

———. "Fashion in the Eighteenth Century: Some Anglo-French Comparisons." In *Fabrics and Fashions,* edited by N. B. Harte, 329–45. London: Pasold Research Fund, 1985.

———. *Fashion in the French Revolution.* London: B. T. Batsford, 1988.

Rice, Howard C., Jr. *Thomas Jefferson's Paris.* Princeton, NJ: Princeton University Press, 1976.

Richardson, Jonathan. *The Works of Jonathan Richardson.* London, 1792.

Roche, Daniel. *The Culture of Clothing: Dress and Fashion in the Ancien Regime.* Translated by Jean Birrell. Cambridge, UK: Cambridge University Press, 1994.

Roosen, William. "Modern Diplomatic Ceremonial: A Systems Approach." *Journal of Modern History* 52, no. 3 (September 1980): 452–76.

Rosenthal, Norman, and Mary Anne Stevens, eds. *Citizens and Kings: Portraits in the Age of Revolution, 1760–1830.* London: Royal Academy of Arts, 2007.

Rozbicki, Michal J. *The Complete Colonial Gentleman: Cultural Legitimacy in Plantation America.* Charlottesville: University of Virginia Press, 1998.

Rudolph, William Keyse, and Carol Eaton Soltis. *Thomas Sully: Painted Performance.* New Haven, CT: Yale University Press, 2013.

Ruppert, Jacques. *Le Costume Époques Louis XVI et Directoire.* Paris: Flammarion, 1990.

Sadik, Marvin S. *Colonial and Federal Portraits at Bowdoin College.* Brunswick, ME: Bowdoin College, 1966.

Saunders, Richard H., and Ellen G. Miles. *American Colonial Portraits, 1700–1776*. Washington, DC: Smithsonian Institution Press, 1987.

Schutz, John A., and Douglass Adair. *The Spur of Fame: Dialogues of John Adams and Benjamin Rush, 1805–1813*. San Marino, CA: Liberty Fund, 1966.

Scofield, Merry Ellen. "The Fatigues of His Table: The Politics of Presidential Dining during the Jefferson Administration." *Journal of the Early Republic* 26, no. 3 (Fall 2006): 449–69.

Seale, William. *The White House: The History of an American Idea*. Washington, DC: American Institute of Architects Press, 1992.

Sellers, Charles Coleman. *Benjamin Franklin in Portraiture*. New Haven, CT: Yale University Press, 1962.

———. *Charles Willson Peale*. New York: Scribner's, 1969.

Shawe-Taylor, Desmond. *Genial Company: The Theme of Genius in Eighteenth-Century British Portraiture*. Nottingham, UK: University Art Gallery, 1987.

———. *The Georgians: Eighteenth-Century Portraiture and Society*. London: Barrie & Jenkins, 1990.

Simon, Robin. *The Portrait in Britain and America: With a Biographical Dictionary of Portrait Painters, 1680–1915*. Oxford, UK: Phaidon, 1987.

Sizer, Theodore. *The Works of Colonel John Trumbull: Artist of the American Revolution*. Rev. ed. New Haven, CT: Yale University Press, 1967.

Sloan, Herbert E. *Principle and Interest: Thomas Jefferson and the Problem of Debt*. Charlottesville: University of Virginia Press, 1995.

Solkin, David H. *Painting for Money: The Visual Arts and the Public Sphere in Eighteenth-Century England*. New Haven, CT: Yale University Press, 1993.

Squire, Geoffrey. *Dress and Society, 1560–1970*. New York: Viking, 1974.

Stanton, Lucia. *"Those Who Labor for My Happiness": Slavery at Thomas Jefferson's Monticello*. Charlottesville: University of Virginia Press, 2012.

———. "'A Well-Ordered Household': Domestic Servants in Jefferson's White House." *White House History* 17 (Winter 2006): 5–23.

Steadman, William E. "Sully Portraits at West Point." *Portrait Painting in America: The Nineteenth Century*, edited by Ellen G. Miles. New York: Main Street/Universe Books, c. 1977.

Stein, Susan R. *Worlds of Thomas Jefferson at Monticello*. New York: Harry N. Abrams, 1993.

Sweet, Timothy. "Jefferson, Science, and the Enlightenment." In *The Cambridge Companion to Thomas Jefferson*, edited by Frank Shuffelton. Cambridge, UK: Cambridge University Press, 2009.

Taylor, Alan. *Civil War of 1812: American Citizens, British Subjects, Irish Rebels, and Indian Allies*. New York: Knopf, 2010.

———. *William Cooper's Town: Power and Persuasion on the Frontier of the Early American Republic*. New York: Knopf, 1995.

Thomson, Keith. *Jefferson's Shadow: The Story of His Science*. New Haven, CT: Yale University Press, 2012.

Tocqueville, Alexis de. *Democracy in America*. 1835, 1840. Translated and edited by Harvey C. Mansfield and Delba Winthrop. 2 vols. bound in 1. Chicago: University of Chicago Press, 2000.

Tucker, George. *The Life of Thomas Jefferson*. 2 vols. Philadelphia: Carey, Lea & Blanchard, 1837.

Turner, Lynn W. *William Plumer of New Hampshire.* Chapel Hill: University of North Carolina Press, 1962.

Verplanck, Gulian, William Cullen Bryant, and Robert Sands, eds. *The Talisman* 3 (1830): 338–41. New York.

Waldstreicher, David. *In the Midst of Perpetual Fetes: The Making of American Nationalism, 1776–1820.* Chapel Hill: University of North Carolina Press, 1997.

———. "Why Thomas Jefferson and African Americans Wore Their Politics on Their Sleeves." In *Beyond the Founders: New Approaches to the Political History of the Early American Republic,* edited by Jeffery L. Pasley, Andrew W. Robertson, and David Waldstreicher, 79–97. Chapel Hill: University of North Carolina Press, 2004.

Ward, David C. *Charles Willson Peale: Art and Selfhood in the Early Republic.* Berkeley: University of California Press, 2004.

Watston, Katherine, ed. *Legacy of James Bowdoin III.* Brunswick, ME: Bowdoin College 1994.

Watson, Samuel J. "Developing 'Republican Machines.'" In *Thomas Jefferson's Military Academy,* edited by Robert M. S. McDonald, 168–74. Charlottesville: University of Virginia Press, 2004.

Waugh, Norah. *Cut of Men's Clothes, 1600–1900.* London: Faber and Faber, 1964.

Wilcox, R. Turner. *Mode in Furs: A Historical Survey.* 1951; reprinted, Mineola, NY: Dover, 2010.

Wilentz, Sean. *The Rise of American Democracy: Jefferson to Lincoln.* New York: Norton, 2005.

Wills, Garry. *Cincinnatus, George Washington, and the Enlightenment.* Garden City, NY: Doubleday, 1984.

Wilson, G. S. "Recording History: The Thomas Sully Portrait of Thomas Jefferson." In *Light and Liberty: Thomas Jefferson and the Power of Knowledge,* edited by Robert M. S. McDonald, 187–206. Charlottesville: University of Virginia Press, 2012.

———. "Thomas Jefferson and Creating an American Image Abroad." In *Old World, New World: America and Europe in the Age of Jefferson,* edited by Leonard J. Sadosky et al., 155–78. Charlottesville: University of Virginia Press, 2010.

———. "Thomas Jefferson and Creating an Image for a New Nation." In *Cosmopolitanism and Nationhood in the Age of Jefferson,* edited by Peter Nicolaisen and Hannah Spahn, 138–67. Heidelberg: Universitätsverlag Winter, 2013.

———. "Thomas Jefferson's Portrait of Thomas Paine." In *Paine and Jefferson in the Age of Revolutions,* edited by Simon P. Newman and Peter Onuf, 229–51. Charlottesville: University of Virginia Press, 2013.

Wilson, Richard Guy. "Thomas Jefferson's Classical Architecture." In *Thomas Jefferson, the Classical World, and Early America,* edited by Peter S. Onuf and Nicholas P. Cole, 99–127. Charlottesville: University of Virginia Press, 2011.

Wilton, Andrew. *Swagger Portrait: Grand Manner Portraiture in Britain from Van Dyck to Augustus John, 1630–1930.* London: Tate Gallery, 1992.

Wood, Gordon. *The Americanization of Benjamin Franklin.* New York: Penguin, 2004.

———. *Empire of Liberty: A History of the Early Republic, 1789–1815.* Oxford, UK: Oxford University Press, 2009.

———. *Revolutionary Characters: What Made the Founders Different.* New York: Penguin, 2006.

Wrigley, Richard. *Politics of Appearances: Representations of Dress in Revolutionary France.* Oxford, UK: Berg, 2002.

Zakim, Michael. *Ready-Made Democracy: A History of Men's Dress in the American Republic, 1760–1860.* Chicago: University of Chicago Press, 2003.

Ziesche, Philipp. "American Exceptionalism: Cosmopolitanism by Another Name?" In *Cosmopolitanism and Nationhood in the Age of Jefferson,* edited by Peter Nicholaisen and Hannah Spahn, 225–34. Heidelberg: Universitätsverlag Winter, 2014.

ILLUSTRATION CREDITS

American Antiquarian Society, Worcester, MA: fig. 35

American Philosophical Society, Philadelphia: fig. 45 (gift of William Short, 1830)

Architect of the Capitol, Washington, DC: fig. 42

Boston Athenæum: fig. 9 (bequest of George Francis Parkman, 1908, UR72)

Bowdoin College Museum of Art: figs. 36–47 (bequest of the Honorable James Bowdoin III)

Bristol Museum and Art Gallery, UK/Bridgeman Images: fig. 26

British Museum: fig. 25

Harvard Art Museums/Fogg Museum: fig. 5 (gift of William Gray from the collection of Francis Calley Gray, G3526; photo: Imaging Department, President and Fellows of Harvard College); fig. 39 (gift of Mrs. T. Jefferson Newbold and family, in memory of Thomas Jefferson Newbold, Class of 1910, 1960.156)

Harvard University Portrait Collection: fig. 7 (bequest of Ward Nicholas Boylston to Harvard College, 1828, H74; photo: Imaging Department, President and Fellows of Harvard College)

Independence National Historical Park: figs. 18, 47

Kimball Art Museum, Fort Worth: fig. 2 (AP 1981.03)

Library Company of Philadelphia: fig. 21

Library of Congress: fig. 30 (Prints and Photographs Division); fig. 33 (James Papers, Manuscript Division); fig. 54

Massachusetts Historical Society/Bridgeman Images: fig. 10

Metropolitan Museum of Art/Art Resource, NY: fig. 16 (*top right*; bequest of Cornelia Cruger, 1923, 24.19.1); fig. 24 (purchase Mr. and Mrs. Charles Wrightsman; gift in honor of Everett Fahy, 1977, 1977.101)

Museum of Fine Arts, Boston: fig. 4 (Elizabeth Day McCormick Collection, 44.1516)

National Gallery of Art, Washington, DC: fig. 3 (given in memory of Gov. Alvan T. Fuller by the Fuller Foundation, Inc., 1961.2.2); fig. 52 (Corcoran Collection, museum purchase, gallery fund)

National Portrait Gallery, Smithsonian Institution: fig. 8 (bequest of Charles Francis Adams); figs. 23, 29 (acquired as a gift to the nation through the generosity of the Donald W. Reynolds Foundation)

New-York Historical Society: fig. 28 (object #1867.306)

Pennsylvania Academy of the Fine Arts: fig. 43 (Pennsylvania purchase from the estate of Paul Beck Jr.)

Tate, London 2017: fig. 1

Thomas Jefferson Foundation at Monticello: figs. 13 (gift of the Gilder-Lehrman Collection of New York, and its principals, Richard Gilder and Lewis E. Lehrman), 11, 12, 16 (*bottom*), 17, 19–20, 32, 34, 53 (photograph by J. Robertson)

University of Virginia: fig. 27

Virginia Museum of Fine Arts: fig. 6 (gift of Mrs. A. D. Williams 49.11.21)

West Point Museum Collection, United States Military Academy: figs. 46, 48–50

White House Collection/White House Historical Association: figs. 16 (*top left*), 22

Worchester Art Museum: fig. 41 (museum purchase, 1954.82)

Yale University Art Gallery: fig. 14 (Trumbull Collection, 1832.3); fig. 15 (Trumbull Collection, 1832.4); figs. 31, 38 (Mabel Brady Garvan Collection); fig. 40 (transfer from Yale University Library, Numismatic Collection, 2001, gift of Charles Wyllys Betts, B.A. 1867, M.A. 1871); fig. 44 (gift of Waleska Evans James); fig. 51 (Lelia A. and John Hill Morgan, B.A. 1893, LL.B. 1896, M.A. [Hon.] 1929, Collection)

INDEX

Italicized page numbers refer to illustrations.

Humphreys, David, 27, 30–31
Hunter, Will, 79–80

Independence Day, 119–20, 189, *195*

Jackson, Andrew, 256n29
Jaffe, Irma, 59
Jay, John, 30, 72, 101, 108
Jay Treaty, 106, 107, 120, 140
Jefferson, Jane Randolph, 7
Jefferson, Maria (Mary), 16, 65, 77, 105, 156, 166, 177
Jefferson, Martha (wife), 9–10, 11, 14–15, 16, 18
Jefferson, Martha (daughter), 16, 19, 26–27, 63–67, 72, 77, 79, 86, 151–52, 156, 163, 166, 177, 193, 200, 241n14
Jefferson, Peter, 7–8
Jefferson, Thomas: architectural designs, 1, 2, 55, 87, 202–3, 205–7, 215, 219, 223, 226; on the arts, 137, 205; *Autobiography*, 60, 207; aversion to monarchism, 4–5, 17, 73–74, 83–85, 95, 98, 100, 111, 118, 131, 137, 140, 186, 198, 199–200, 229; background and education, 1, 7–9; clothing choices, 1–2, 6, 9, 10–12, 81–83, 88–91, 98, 117, 128, 133–34, 140–44, 147–55, 157, 158–59, 160–61, 164, 180, 193–96, 259n19; death of, 226–29; death threats against, 165–66; on education, 16, 201–2, 225–26; entertainment style, 161–63, 180; equipage, 87–88, 105, 166–67; financial worries, 200–201; Francophilia, 16, 18, 21, 23, 73, 82, 100–102, 107, 115, 117–18, 156, 200, 225; fur cloaks, *132,* 149–53, 159, 174, 208, *209,* 211, 259n24; governorship of Virginia, 16, 18, 60–63, 79, 111, 196; hairstyles, 2, 10, 39, 41, *64,* 65–66, 88, 90, 124–25, 147, 159, 161, 177–78; horseback riding, 164–67; household arrangements, 88, 104–5, 163, 193; mannerisms, 81–83, 111, 116, 147; musical abilities, 8, 17; *Notes on the State of Virginia,* 41, 42–43, 69–70, 108–10, 136, 157; Paris years, 1, 2, 6, 14, 18–19, 23–38, 45–48, 53, 56–57, 59, 60, 62–63, 68–74, 86, 124, 154–55, 187–88, 227; philosopher

image, 6, 17, 53, 97, 102, 107–11, 115, 120, 136, 140–41, 155–57; portrait and sculpture collection, 44–50, 89, 95–97, 101, 169, 179; presidency, 9, 125, 129, 131–81, 199–200, 208, 210–11, 215; publicity aversion, 94–95, 100, 106–7, 114; religious views, 102, 107, 109–10, 115, 118; retirement years, 4, 6, 151–52, 179, 183, 185–229; Revolution years, 16, 228; secretary of state years, 6, 77–101, 103, 105–6, 108, 116, 136, 154, 165; slave ownership, 10, 11, 16, 77, 108–9, 194, 201; "A Summary View of the Rights of British America," 53–54, 159; University of Virginia, 16, 201–3, 206–7, 215, 225–26; vice presidency, 6, 101–28, 167. *See also* Declaration of Independence; Monticello
—, portraits and other depictions: Brown, 38–43, *39;* Ceracchi, 92–93; Houdon, 47–49, *48,* 177; C. W. Peal, 80, 89–92, *90,* 120; Rembrandt Peale, *121,* 121–22, 124, *132, 134, 135,* 136, 148–49, 152–53, 159; "A Philosophic Cock," 156; Polk, 125–26, *127;* "The Providential Detection," *112;* Reich, 176–78, *177;* Saint-Mémin, 178, *179;* Sharples, 125, *126;* Stuart, 167–72, *171, 174*–76, *175, 176,* 178; Sully, 204–22, *208, 209, 218,* 260n31; Trumbull, 59, 57–60, *58,* 63–67, *64,* 154–55, 188–92, *190, 191, 202*
Jones, John Paul, 47, 95, *96,* 116
Joseph (servant), 88, 105–6, 165, 243n51
Julien, Honoré, 160, 163

Kern, Susan, 232n12
King, Rufus, 141
"kit-kat" portraits, 67, 240n56
Knox, Henry, 81
Kosciuszko, Thaddeus, 139, *150,* 150–52, 159, 211–12, 259n24
Krimmel, John Lewis, 194–95, *195*

lace, 26–27, 33, 124, 134, 140, 172
Lafayette, marquis de (Gilbert du Motier), 16, 68, 69, 72–73, 95, 107; bust of, 46–47, *96,* 116; portrait of, *210*

Recent Books in the JEFFERSONIAN AMERICA SERIES

Maurizio Valsania
Nature's Man: Thomas Jefferson's Philosophical Anthropology

John Ragosta
Religious Freedom: Jefferson's Legacy, America's Creed

Robert M. S. McDonald, editor
Sons of the Father: George Washington and His Protégés

Simon P. Newman and Peter S. Onuf, editors
Paine and Jefferson in the Age of Revolutions

Daniel Peart
Era of Experimentation: American Political Practices in the Early Republic

Margaret Sumner
Collegiate Republic: Cultivating an Ideal Society in Early America

Christa Dierksheide
Amelioration and Empire: Progress and Slavery in the Plantation Americas

John A. Ruddiman
Becoming Men of Some Consequence: Youth and Military Service in the Revolutionary War

Jonathan J. Den Hartog
Patriotism and Piety: Federalist Politics and Religious Struggle in the New American Nation

Patrick Griffin, Robert G. Ingram, Peter S. Onuf, and Brian Schoen, editors
Between Sovereignty and Anarchy: The Politics of Violence in the American Revolutionary Era

Armin Mattes
Citizens of a Common Intellectual Homeland: The Transatlantic Origins of American Democracy and Nationhood

Julia Gaffield, editor
The Haitian Declaration of Independence: Creation, Context, and Legacy

Robert M. S. McDonald
Confounding Father: Thomas Jefferson's Image in His Own Time

Adam Jortner
Blood from the Sky: Miracles and Politics in the Early American Republic

Spencer W. McBride
Pulpit and Nation: Clergymen and the Politics of Revolutionary America

Maurizio Valsania
Jefferson's Body: A Corporeal Biography

G. S. Wilson
Jefferson on Display: Attire, Etiquette, and the Art of Presentation